American Denominational History

RELIGION AND AMERICAN CULTURE

American Denominational History

Perspectives on the Past, Prospects for the Future

EDITED BY KEITH HARPER

THE UNIVERSITY OF ALABAMA PRESS
Tuscaloosa

Copyright © 2008
The University of Alabama Press
Tuscaloosa, Alabama 35487-0380
All rights reserved
Manufactured in the United States of America

Typeface: Minion

∞
The paper on which this book is printed meets the minimum requirements of
American National Standard for Information Sciences-Permanence of Paper for
Printed Library Materials, ANSI Z39.48-1984.

Library of Congress Cataloging-in-Publication Data

American denominational history : perspectives on the past, prospects for the
future / edited by Keith Harper.
p.   cm. — (Religion and American culture)
Includes bibliographical references.
ISBN 978-0-8173-1632-7 (cloth : alk. paper) — ISBN 978-0-8173-5512-8 (pbk. :
alk. paper) — ISBN 978-0-8173-8108-0 (electronic) 1. Sects—United States—
History. 2. United States—Church history. 3. Christianity—United States.
I. Harper, Keith, 1957—
BR516.5.A425 2008
280.0973—dc22

2008018609

Dedicated to the memory of Lance Banning
Scholar, Teacher, Friend

Contents

Preface

This project began when I suggested that The University of Alabama Press consider republishing William Warren Sweet's four-volume *Religion on the American Frontier.* Published between 1931 and 1946, this series featured volumes devoted to America's Baptists, Presbyterians, Congregationalists, and Methodists. My proposal was that The University of Alabama Press secure authors to edit these volumes, update the sources, and write historiographical essays for each work. The press found merit in the proposal, especially the historiography component, and suggested a single volume of historiographical essays on American denominations. And thus was born *American Denominational History: Perspectives on the Past, Prospects for the Future.*

I owe many debts of gratitude to those who helped produce this volume. First, I must thank The University of Alabama Press for wanting to work on a project like this. What a joy to work with such a dedicated group of professionals! Also, each of the essayists in this work solicited advice and critical feedback for their essays from specialists in their respective fields. I cannot mention everyone by name, but on behalf of each contributor, thank you all for your input and suggestions. While I'm at it, I want to thank the essayists themselves for contributing to this volume. Each answered a phone call inviting him or her to write an essay with a gracious "Yes, thank you." Some of them had no idea who I was—still don't—but they liked what they heard about the project, and they have been an editor's dream. Thanks again to each of you.

In a slightly different vein, everyone needs friends like Hughie Lawson, Dan Smith, and Mike Travers. Each of them has helped me in ways too numerous to mention here, but their assistance is always welcome and greatly appreciated. And where would I be without Eliza Rutter, Nathan Finn, Sarah Hammond, and J. Wayne Ray? Eliza helped with proofreading and found numerous tidbits of information for me, while Nathan, Sarah, and J. R. have been sounding boards for this project and several others. I treasure my friends, and you guys are the very best!

Finally, on a personal note, I want to dedicate these essays to the late Lance Banning. His probing questions followed by those painfully long periods of silence intimidated even the most fearless history graduate students at the University of Kentucky. It took awhile for us to understand what he was up to, but we came to see that Lance weighed his words carefully. He worked hard and he set high standards for himself. He expected no less from fledgling historians. We also learned three things about Professor Banning. First, he was always willing to help students. Second, he had an unbelievably dry sense of humor. Third, he was apt to separate you from your lunch money if you shot pool with him. Lance died on January 31, 2006, after complications following lung surgery. Even though he was not a student of American religious history, I suspect that he would have welcomed this project. He was a world-class scholar and an excellent teacher. His colleagues and friends miss him.

Introduction

American denominational history. Some may wonder, why bother with the subject? Others may wonder if such a disciplinary creature still exists. Yet in the middle of the twentieth century, the study of denominational history enjoyed an enviable status. William Warren Sweet's *Religion on the American Frontier* featured volumes on Baptists, Presbyterians, Congregationalists, and Methodists. Sweet positioned denominational history near the forefront of historical inquiry by linking the "Big Four" with Frederick Jackson Turner's "Frontier Thesis," vis-à-vis westward expansion in the late eighteenth and early nineteenth centuries. These works remain valuable to scholars interested in early denominational life among America's frontier folk.[1]

It appeared that denominational history would always be a regular feature of the study of America's historical landscape until 1964, when Henry F. May wrote of American religious history's "recovery" and scarcely mentioned denominationalism. Since May's seminal essay, works on American religious history have appeared at a dizzying pace, yet denominational history barely warrants an "honorable mention" in most historiographical surveys. Did the academy take its cue from H. Richard Niebuhr's scathing critique of American denominations and relegate them to the dustbin of irrelevance? Did scholars come to see purely denominational history as a less attractive alternative to other, more nuanced aspects of American religious history? Or did historians simply distance themselves from often racially and economically segregated denominations as the nation embraced multiculturalism and postmodernism? At the end of the twentieth century Anne Loveland wrote a follow-up essay to May's work in which she noted that the study of American religious history was alive and well. But, like May, she said nothing about denominational history.[2]

Recent trends in American religious historiography represent more an eclipse of denominational history than its abandonment. Henry Warner Bowden's *Church History in the Age of Science: Historiographical Patterns in the United States, 1876–1918* and *Church History in an Age of Uncertainty: Historiographical Patterns in the United States, 1906–1990,* along with the multivolume series on American denominations that he edited, have kept denominational history studies from slipping into complete obsolescence.[3] Likewise, Robert Bruce Mullin's and Russell E. Richey's edited work, *Reimagining Denominationalism: Interpretive Essays,* suggested new directions for those interested in denominational history. This work featured essays by prominent scholars who collaborated under the sponsorship of the Lilly Endowment. They explored various aspects of denominationalism grouped under three headings: "Overviews," "Models," and "Case Studies."[4]

Overall, the introductory essay by Mullin and Richey represents one of *Reimagining Denominationalism*'s strongest features. They argue that denominational history has long been an important feature of American religion. But, if denominational history as a discipline has fallen on hard times, at least part of the blame lies with denominational historians. Mullin and Richey note that denominational histories are notorious for two tendencies that distance them from the scholarly mainstream. On the one hand, they tend to be written *by* denominational "insiders" *for* denominational insiders. Celebratory and triumphal, this literature recounts how great men in bygone eras vanquished heresy hip and thigh to preserve "pure" Christianity—in a Baptist, Methodist (insert the denomination of choice here) form, of course. On the other hand, even when denominational historians tried to write for "outsiders," they tended to produce uneven works that lacked depth and contextualization.[5]

Another collaborative effort, *New Directions in American Religious History,* edited by Harry S. Stout and Daryl G. Hart, suggests that a seismic shift rocked the profession in the latter third of the twentieth century. They note that "Church History," which in generations past had been the realm of white Protestants and rooted largely in intellectual history (or historical theology), has been supplanted by "religious history," which is "non-mainline-centered" and open to a variety of perspectives, ranging from social and cultural history to sociology and anthropology. As far as religious history is concerned, Stout and Hart see a field that is "exploding." Interest in American religious life may be at an all-time high, and serious inquiry is no longer the exclusive domain of either history departments or divinity schools. The current scholarship is impressive, but Stout and Hart caution, "Like virtually all fields of American history, religious history is simultaneously rich in its diversity of interests and methods, and rudderless in its overall direction or sense of professional priorities."[6]

In light of the numerous inquiries into American religious thought and practice over the past several decades, now is an opportune time to assess the historiography of denominational history and offer suggestions for future inquiry. The essays in this volume seek to bring a modicum of structure to a burgeoning field of inquiry. Each essay is framed around an intentionally broad understanding of denominationalism. The *Westminster Dictionary of Church History* defines denominationalism as "[t]he system and ideology founded in the division of the religious population into numerous ecclesiastical bodies, each stressing particular values and traditions and each competing with the other in the same community under substantial conditions of freedom."[7] This definition implies that denominations emphasize elements of commonality, both doctrinal and functional, within a distinct structure. It also implies that American denominations have a legacy of open competition with one another for converts in America's religious free market.

Additionally, the essays in this volume explore changes in mainline denominations as well as the increasing importance of "non-mainline-centered" religious groups. American Catholicism and Mormonism merit consideration because they have played crucial roles in American religious development, even though they were never part of the nation's Protestant hegemony. Moreover, Catholic and Mormon scholars have generated a remarkably rich literature not always understood or appreciated by nonspecialists. In a similar vein, Pentecostalism, African American Protestantism, and evangelicalism are obviously not denominations.[8] However, Pentecostalism and black Protestantism represent some of the nation's most dramatic growth at various denominational sublevels, and they cannot be ignored. Finally, one can scarcely think of American religious history without some consideration of evangelicalism. Certainly, evangelicalism may not *be* a separate denomination, but professing evangelicals form groups and coalitions that often *act* like denominations, especially in the political and social arenas. Besides, evangelicalism offers scholars a common framework to explore various points of convergence and divergence among competing religious groups.[9]

Taken together, these essays suggest that American denominations and their histories have experienced dramatic upheaval over the past half century.[10] Rapidly changing social, political, and cultural contexts, not to mention shifting theological trends, have led to fragmentation in the older, mainline denominations. Likewise, students of American religion benefited from changing perspectives in the academy. For instance, the scholarship of the latter twentieth century led to numerous studies of important issues like race and gender as they relate to American denominations, while not focusing on the denominations as a whole. As a result, scholars have gained remarkable insight into aspects of denominational life that had been neglected far too long.

One sees two prominent themes emerging from these essays. Each denomination or religious group has a tenuous relationship with American culture. At one time or another each group has enjoyed "insider" status. At other times they have been "outsiders."[11] Yet, how does one influence American culture without becoming tainted by the culture? What becomes of a denomination or religious tradition that loses its prophetic voice against evil and injustice? Beyond this uneasy relationship with culture, each group faces a strong challenge to retain its own distinct identity. For instance, what is the difference between Methodists and Congregationalists? What does it mean to be a Catholic? What does it mean to be a Mormon? The answers to these questions reflect the diversity and vitality of the American religious experience.

Denominational history may never again be what it once was—namely, white, male, intellectual history that drearily recounted which preacher served where. Even so, anyone who suggests that denominational history is either dead or dying has surely overstated the case.[12] As Wayne Flynt observes, millions of Americans still order their religious lives around some sort of "ecclesiastical structure," even though experts continue to prophesy doom for the nation's denominations. As long as there are denominations, denominational history will matter.[13]

Is there a new denominational synthesis in the offing? Perhaps. After all, inquiry into nearly all aspects of the denominational experience remains a vibrant aspect of American religious history. And, if such a synthesis is forthcoming, it will likely examine religious authority as it relates to denominational structure and community; it may examine the role that women and persons of color have played in shaping those structures; it will take theology and spiritual formation seriously. In short, it will rely on scholars who are mining some of the richest source material imaginable.[14]

Notes

1. See William Warren Sweet, *Religion on the American Frontier: The Baptists, 1783–1830* (New York: Harper and Bros, 1931); *The Presbyterians, 1783–1832* (New York: Harper and Bros, 1936); *The Congregationalists, 1783–1850* (Chicago: University of Chicago Press, 1939); *The Methodists, 1783–1840* (Chicago: University of Chicago Press, 1946). These volumes were reprinted: New York: Cooper Square, 1964.

2. Compare Henry F. May, "The Recovery of American Religious History," *American Historical Review* 70, no. 1 (1964): 79–92, and Anne C. Loveland, "Later Stages of the Recovery of American Religious History," in *New Directions in American Religious History,* ed. Harry S. Stout and Daryl G. Hart (Oxford and New York: Oxford University Press, 1997), 487–502. See also H. Richard Niebuhr, *The Social Sources of Denominationalism* (New York: Henry Holt, 1929).

3. Henry Warner Bowden, *Church History in the Age of Science: Historiographical Patterns in the United States, 1876–1918* (Chapel Hill: University of North Carolina Press, 1971) and *Church History in an Age of Uncertainty: Historiographical Patterns in the United States, 1906–1990* (Carbondale and Edwardsville: Southern Illinois University Press, 1991). Bowden's series (1985–2004) is published by the Greenwood Publishing Group and is comprised at present of *The Universalists and the Unitarians,* by David Robinson; *The Baptists,* by William Henry Brackney; *The Quakers,* by Hugh Barbour and J. William Frost; *The Congregationalists,* by J. William T. Youngs; *The Presbyterians,* by Randall Balmer and John R. Fitzmier; *The Roman Catholics,* by Patrick W. Carey; *The Orthodox Church,* by Thomas E FitzGerald; *The Methodists,* by James S. Kirby, Russell E. Richey, and Kenneth E. Rowe; *The Lutherans,* by L. DeAne Lagerquist; *The Churches of Christ,* by Richard T. Hughes and R. L. Roberts; and *The Episcopalians,* by David Hein and Gardiner H. Shattuck. See also Russell Richey, ed., *Denominationalism* (Nashville: Abingdon, 1977).

4. Robert Bruce Mullin and Russell E. Richey, eds., *Reimagining Denominationalism: Interpretive Essays* (New York: Oxford University Press, 1994).

5. Ibid., 3–4. See also *The Encyclopedia of the American Religious Experience,* vol. 1, s.v. "The Historiography of American Religion," by Henry Warner Bowden.

6. Stout and Hart, *New Directions,* 5.

7. *Westminster Dictionary of Church History,* s.v. "Denominationalism."

8. See Stout and Hart, *New Directions,* 4, for a similar listing of "outsider" groups that merit scholarly inquiry.

9. Evangelicalism may work best as a unifying theme in older, mainline denominations but not among other groups not usually associated with the movement. For a carefully crafted use of evangelicalism as a transdenominational theme, see George Marsden, *Religion and American Culture* (Boston: Wadsworth, 2000) and *Understanding Fundamentalism and Evangelicalism* (Grand Rapids, MI: Eerdmans, 1991).

10. See, for example, Robert Wuthnow, *The Restructuring of American Religion: Society and Faith since World War II* (Princeton: Princeton University Press, 1988).

11. See especially R. Laurence Moore, *Religious Outsiders and the Making of Americans* (Oxford and New York: Oxford University Press, 1986). Here I am using "insider" to denote social acceptance in the broadest sense.

12. Compare Henry Warner Bowden, "The Death and Rebirth of Denominational History," in Mullin and Richey, *Reimagining Denominationalism,* 17–30; and Robert

Bacher and Kenneth Inskeep, *Chasing Down a Rumor: The Death of Mainline Denominations* (Minneapolis: Augsburg, 2005).

13. Wayne Flynt, "The Persistence of Evangelical Denominationalism in the South and the Case for Denominational History: Alabama Baptists," in *Religion in the Contemporary South: Changes, Continuities, and Contexts,* ed. Corrie E. Norman and Don S. Armentrout (Knoxville: University of Tennessee Press, 2005).

14. For an example of recent denominational history at its best, see Wayne Flynt, *Alabama Baptists: Southern Baptists in the Heart of Dixie* (Tuscaloosa and London: University of Alabama Press, 1998).

1
Catholic Distinctiveness and the Challenge of American Denominationalism

Amy Koehlinger

The task of contemplating the past, present, and future of denominational scholarship is uniquely challenging for historians of American Catholicism because this approach raises the uncomfortable question of whether Catholicism is properly considered a denomination at all. Of course, upon reflection, this is not such a stretch—Catholicism is one among many varieties of Christianity practiced in the United States, and the suggestion that Catholicism can be defined and studied as a denomination should not raise scholarly eyebrows. And yet, including Catholicism under the rubric of denominationalism is somewhat novel for scholars of U.S. Catholic history. Until recently historians of American religion and American Catholicism—not to mention American Catholics themselves—have not interpreted the Catholic tradition in a denominational idiom, and the reasons why illuminate important and at times overlooked dimensions of Catholic historiography.

The origins of the term *denomination* among seventeenth-century English Puritans, and its subsequent popularization by eighteenth-century evangelical preachers in the American colonies, reflected Protestant desires for mutual respect and cooperation among diverse sects of Protestantism. Though the central concept behind denominationalism was religious tolerance, it was a tolerance limited by the foundational desires of reforming and dissenting Brethren to rid both church and society of papist influence, a tolerance thus confined to those who experienced the "new birth" of Protestant salvation. When George Whitefield interjected the question "Father Abraham, whom have you in heaven?" before a Philadelphia crowd in the 1740s, the answer he provided—"Any Episcopalians? No! Any Presbyterians? No! Any Independents or Methodists? No, no, no! All who are here are Christians!"— was inclusive only to a point. Catholics were not numbered among those undenominationalized Christians inhabiting the paradise Whitefield imag-

ined.[1] The term *denomination* was later expanded to include Catholics and
non-Christians, most notably by Will Herberg in his seminal 1955 study, *Protestant, Catholic, Jew,* but in the interim Catholics were considered by religious
historians and the general population alike to be a people apart, distinct
from the Protestant majority.[2] Whereas Protestants could be broken down
into different denominations, this perspective held, Catholics were a different category altogether. For much of the nation's history Catholicism existed
in popular culture not as one facet of Christian pluralism in the United States
but rather as the necessary foil against which the differences between Protestant sects seemed less central than the theologies and ideologies that united
them against their common enemy.

It should be noted that animosity toward Catholics also colored the early
scholarship on the history of religion in the United States. To the extent that
foundational paradigms of American religious history—and the mythologies
of American civil religion—equated Protestantism with democracy, meritoc-
racy, rationalism, and progress, Catholicism, as historiographical foil, by in-
ference took on such unsavory characteristics as authoritarianism, coercion,
superstition, and regression. More often, Catholicism was simply ignored
by the early generations of historians writing about religion in the United
States. As late as 1968 David J. O'Brien wrote, "Outside of a few universities
where the field is taken seriously, neither American Catholicism nor its history is in very high repute."[3] As evidence of the low status of Catholic history, O'Brien cited an article by Henry F. May on the resurgence of religion
in American history in which May stated that Catholics and atheists "have
contributed least" to the revival of religious scholarship in the United States.[4]
As a result of this early elision of Catholicism from American religious history, until recently a historian who approached Catholicism as a denomination faced the interesting challenge of representing and analyzing the tradition using a problematic paradigm, one that carried within it anti-Catholic
residue in the American context.

Equally important, Catholics themselves historically have not interpreted
their identity in a denominational idiom. Common use of the term *denominationalism* carries connotations of pluralism and voluntarism that exist in
some degree of tension with the orthodox Catholic views of their Church.
Most Catholics in the United States, particularly before the Second Vatican
Council (1962–65), understood their tradition not as a version of Christian
faith chosen from among the other varieties of Christianity but rather as the
one true Church—a sacred inheritance, instituted by Christ, entrusted to
Peter and the apostles, and continued in unbroken succession to the present
moment through the institutions and structures of the worldwide Catholic

Church. Historians rightly take issue with this characterization, pointing to the historical ruptures and internal pluralism of the tradition, but the point remains that American Catholics by and large have not in the past, nor would they now, recognize their tradition as a denomination. After all, the Catholic Church historically did not characterize deviations from its doctrine as simply benign alternatives to Catholicism; from the Desert Fathers to the Inquisition to the current Pope Benedict XVI's former curial role as "God's rottweiler," the Catholic Church consistently described deviations from its teachings with the dismissive "heresy." Thus a historian who attempts to interpret Catholic history as denominational history faces the challenging commission of representing the tradition's past in a way that fundamentally contradicts the central model of identity used by its leaders and a significant number of its adherents.

There are good reasons, then, to pause before adding Catholics to the list of American denominations and consider how the complicated relationship between Catholicism and denominationalism has affected the historiography on the American Catholic experience. Both the Protestant origins of the term *denominationalism* and Catholic resistance to inclusion under its umbrella— anti-Catholicism and Catholic exceptionalism, in other words—shaped the experience of Catholics as well as historical scholarship about them. From the 1940s through the 1980s scholarship on American Catholicism was structured by a dialectic in which the history of Catholic institutions and Catholic experience in the United States was alternately framed by two apparently conflicting interpretive paradigms: Catholic exceptionalism and Americanist assimilation. Some scholars emphasized the uniqueness or superiority of American Catholicism on the American religious landscape. Other historians—often in indirect response to anti-Catholic depictions of Catholicism as incompatible with American political values—suggested that Catholics fit with and even best exemplified certain characteristics of American religion and culture. Scholars whose work navigated a degree of compromise between these perspectives were forced to address the inherent tension between these two dominant interpretive frameworks.

The dialectic was not simply an intellectual phantom, conjured by insular scholarly debate. Rather, to a significant extent, the historiographical dualism of scholarship on American Catholicism reflected the actual historical experience of Catholics for much of U.S. history, caught as they were between religious exhortations that they remain distinctively Catholic and concrete social, political, and economic pressures to adapt to American culture. And while both scholarly perspectives produced important monographs documenting central facets of Catholic experience, the contrasting portraits of

American Catholicism that often resulted from these two competing foci of historical analysis proved confusing to students of Catholic history. Ultimately, this dialectic within Catholic historiography was often more successful at documenting the poles that shaped Catholic experience than it was at representing the complex ways that American Catholics inhabited, resisted, and creatively managed the tension inherent in their in-between location.

Catholic Uniqueness, Catholic Exceptionalism

Following the trend within the larger field of American religious history of placing Catholicism outside the mainstream, the earliest scholars of American Catholicism in the nineteenth century focused on Catholic institutions as entities unto themselves. Their works explored the internal dynamics and contours of American Catholicism employing analytical models that emphasized Catholicism's "differentness" from Protestantism, underscoring the separateness of Catholics from an American culture assumed to be molded according to Protestant perspectives and priorities. The first historical monographs about American Catholicism were internalist documents commissioned by and written for the use of Catholic diocese and religious congregations. Such works proliferated through the nineteenth century as American bishops and religious superiors progressively acquired financial and personnel resources that could be invested in documenting the development of dioceses and congregations, or commemorating anniversaries of their founding. Similarly, the journal *American Catholic Quarterly Review,* published in Philadelphia beginning in 1876, featured substantial essays on theology, history, and philosophy by prominent American Catholic bishops and intellectuals. Though the editorial policy of the review permitted freedom of expression and contributors included a wide range of Catholic perspectives, the journal was written for a Catholic audience and so was primarily oriented toward apologetics.[5] By contrast, the work of John Gilmary Shea stands as a strong exception to the generalization that early American Catholic history was primarily written by and for Catholic religious institutions. Often referred to as "the father of American Catholic history," Shea was a professional historian who wrote about both U.S. and American Catholic history at the turn of the century.[6]

In the 1940s and 1950s a new generation of Catholic historians, building on this considerable existing literature about individual dioceses and religious communities, began to write monographs that were independent of official sponsorship.[7] One outstanding example of this new autonomy in American Catholic historiography is Sister Maria Kostka Logue's congregational study

The Sisters of Saint Joseph of Philadelphia, 1847–1947.[8] This new historical literature retained the source-based attention to detail and the documentary quality of early diocesan and congregational histories and episcopal biographies but toned down the hagiographical elements in portraits of Catholic bishops, religious founders, and superiors—a change one observer described as a "decrease in Catholic historical writing produced for the conscious purpose of edification."[9] Instead, the new monographs painted a broader and more inclusive portrait of the history of Catholic institutions as historians grounded themselves more firmly in the interpretive norms of the historical profession.

The surge in historical scholarship on American Catholicism following the 1950s was partly the result of Catholic separatism. By the 1940s the expansive network of Catholic colleges and universities had grown sufficiently robust to train, house, and support the work of a cadre of Catholic professional historians who devoted themselves to documenting the history of the Church in the Americas. By the mid-1950s a few universities (Catholic University of America, the University of Notre Dame, Marquette University, Xavier University) had begun to offer graduate study in U.S. Catholic history, further nurturing future scholarship in this area. Catholic dioceses and religious congregations were beginning to train and employ archivists to facilitate the work of outside researchers. Catholic and independent presses emerged to publish and distribute monographs on Catholic history. And the American Catholic Historical Association developed an outward-looking sense of professional mission, one that included "the bridging of a scholarly gap . . . between the Catholic Church and the secular historian in this country."[10] In the mid-1950s historian and monsignor John Tracy Ellis provided the final catalyst to mobilize Catholic scholars toward academic engagement with the history of their religious tradition. Ellis's 1955 essay "American Catholics and the Intellectual Life" sharply criticized the intellectual timidity of American Catholics, arguing that the meagerness of their contributions to academic debate betrayed the Roman Catholic tradition of scholarly rigor. Ellis's essay provoked both controversy and self-criticism in Catholic circles, but it also bolstered the enthusiasm and confidence of a generation of subsequent Catholic scholars who would turn Ellis's critique into a mandate to apply the historian's tools to understanding Catholicism's place in American life.[11] The resulting scholarship documented the richness and internal complexity of the distinct culture that characterized Catholic life in the United States before the 1960s, when postwar economic changes in American society and internal changes in the Church removed many of the barriers that had isolated U.S. Catholics from American society and culture.

The subsequent emergence and prominence of concepts like "Catholic subculture" and "Catholic ghetto" in Catholic scholarship after the 1960s reflect the extent to which some historians imagined Catholic experience in ways that assumed the essential separateness of Catholics from other Christians in the United States. Father Thomas T. McAvoy, CSC, laid the foundation for this historical approach in 1959 in a series of articles in which he developed what later came to be known as the "minority thesis," an argument that the central component of Catholic self-understanding in the United States was an awareness among U.S. Catholics that they were a numerical minority who were fundamentally different from their Protestant neighbors.[12] Historians in the 1980s would eventually complicate McAvoy's concept of Catholic identity as fundamentally, self-consciously distinct from that of the Protestant majority, but influential works in the field would continue to be at least partially influenced by McAvoy's assumption that American Catholic culture was primarily separate and largely sui generis.

Works in the tradition of Catholic uniqueness generally focused on a specific facet of Catholicism that was exclusive to the tradition or closely associated with it. Both Leslie Tentler's *Seasons of Grace: A History of the Archdiocese of Detroit* and Paula Kane's *Separatism and Subculture: Boston Catholicism, 1900–1920*, for example, explore the unit of the diocese as a determinative force in local Catholic culture. Taken together, the studies provide a detailed portrait of ways Catholic dioceses—as discrete, bounded worlds governed by a particular bishop—functioned as the primary point of orientation for Catholics formed within their auspices.[13] Philip Gleason's *Contending with Modernity: Catholic Higher Education in the Twentieth Century* documents the development of separate Catholic colleges and universities in the twentieth century. Gleason argues that while Catholic institutions of higher education adopted many of the modern bureaucratic forms of their non-Catholic or secular competitors, Catholic colleges vigorously resisted the ideological and philosophical components of modernism taught in other institutions of higher education at the time. Gleason points to the singular influence exercised by the pope and the magisterium in American Catholicism; by mandating neo-Thomistic philosophy and promoting Catholic Action, religious leaders were able to create a coherent and increasingly self-confident culture of Catholic triumphalism in American Catholic colleges and universities.[14] Christopher Kauffman's *Faith and Fraternalism: A History of the Knights of Columbus, 1882–1982* examines the unique role played by the Knights of Columbus in defining manhood for American Catholic men. As a fraternity and a secret society, the Knights offered Catholic men a religiously acceptable Catholic alternative to Masonry and other popular forms of fraternalism.

Kauffman documents the Knights' efforts to counter anti-Catholic perceptions of Catholic men through public support for war efforts and through the renarration of American history to emphasize the contributions of Catholic men like their namesake, Christopher Columbus.[15]

Catholicism stands as most clearly differentiated from other forms of American Christianity in works that explore the history of Catholic devotional practices in the United States. Preconcilar Latin liturgy, the sacraments, Mariology, and the cult of the saints shaped and reinforced Catholic worldviews even while they elicited derision from Protestant quarters. From Paul Marx's treatment of Benedictine liturgical reformer Virgil Michel to Robert A. Orsi's influential study of an Italian *feste* honoring Mary, the historiography of Catholic devotional worlds often places readers squarely within the "Catholic ghetto" to observe the meaning and effect of distinctively Catholic rituals in the lives of the devout.[16] Catholics, so these works suggest, were most distinctively Catholic (and most isolated from other Christians) when in prayer—whether in sanctuaries, gathered around home altars, or crowded into the streets of Italian Harlem. In *Living Stones: The History and Structure of Catholic Spiritual Life in the United States,* Rev. Joseph Chinnici, OFM, takes a longer view of U.S. Catholic devotionalism, tracing the evolution and transformation of Catholic orientations toward worship through the lens of prescriptive devotional literature.[17]

By the mid-1980s, some scholars documenting uniquely Catholic facets of American religious experience began framing their studies within analytical structures that moderated the tendency of Catholic historians to equate Catholic uniqueness with Catholic separatism or Catholic exceptionalism. Several important monographs produced in this period explored how devotional traditions as distinctive to Catholicism as scapulars, rosaries, and the enthronement of the Sacred Heart were shaped by American cultural, political, and economic developments. Colleen McDannell's *The Christian Home in Victorian America, 1840–1900* offers a fascinating comparative analysis of Catholic and Protestant forms of "domestic religion" in the late nineteenth century, locating Catholic devotional practices within a larger context of Victorian efforts to transform the home into a religious sanctuary.[18] Ann Taves's *The Household of Faith: Roman Catholic Devotions in Mid-Nineteenth-Century America* concludes that Catholics consciously chose to privatize certain distinctively Catholic religious practices in order to participate more freely in a Protestant-dominated public sphere that was increasingly hostile to Catholicism in the 1830s and 1840s.[19] Robert Orsi's *Thank You, Saint Jude: Women's Devotion to the Patron Saint of Hopeless Causes* documents how in the twentieth century Catholic women turned to Saint Jude for assistance with problems that emerged as Catholic families moved from ethnic and religious ghettos to religiously diverse suburbs.[20]

Other works from the late 1980s and early 1990s examined connections between Catholic intellectual and social movements and their non-Catholic counterparts. By documenting a uniquely American incarnation of European Catholic modernism, R. Scott Appleby's *Church and Age Unite! The Modernist Impulse in American Catholicism* offers one clear example of how Catholicism in the United States was affected by its American context.[21] In *The Catholic Counterculture in America, 1933–1962* James T. Fisher traces the common Catholic roots of the "alternative American ethos" exemplified by midcentury Catholic literary and social pioneers like Dorothy Day and Jack Kerouac. Fisher portrays Catholic communitarian and literary experiments between the 1930s and 1950s (like Day's Catholic Worker Movement) as efforts to provide authentically Catholic alternatives to what some perceived as the materialism and superficiality of Protestant-dominated American culture. Though Fisher stresses the European roots of the Catholic personalism and Catholic romanticism he describes, his subtle analysis also suggests that by the late 1950s some of these uniquely Catholic forms of self-expression were able to find resonances within the larger American culture.[22] Similarly, in *Breaking Bread: The Catholic Worker Movement and the Origin of Catholic Radicalism in the U.S.* Mel Piehl stresses the links between Dorothy Day and other, non-Catholic proponents of pacifism at midcentury.[23]

The methodological sophistication of these groundbreaking monographs documenting unique facets of Catholic culture helped to integrate the historiography of American Catholicism into the wider field of North American religious history. At the same time, by identifying Catholicism with its unique practices—practices that may have seemed particularly exotic to non-Catholic scholars and students of American religion—these works also, perhaps unwittingly, reinforced the marginalization of Catholicism from dominant narratives about the history of American religious life, unintentionally blunting the challenge that scholarship on Catholic presence in the United States raised against paradigms that placed Protestants (particularly Puritans) at the center of American religious history. As a result, well into the 1990s some textbooks on religion in America continued to begin the story of American religion with the arrival of English Puritans in New England in the 1630s rather than with the encounter between Native Americans and French and Spanish Catholics a century before. And in the present moment, Catholics still appear in survey courses on American religious history during "others week," when Catholics, Jews, Muslims, and other religious groups are combined in a single category of traditions whose experience is considered too peculiar or exotic to illuminate larger trends in the American religious past.

Americanism and Assimilation

In contrast to the historiography emphasizing Catholic uniqueness, other historians minimized Catholic difference and Catholic isolation, arguing that American Catholicism either existed in innate harmony with American political and cultural norms or, at the very least, that it quickly and fully assimilated to them. This Americanist historiography (not to be confused with the nineteenth-century intra-Catholic Americanist controversy) maintained that the Catholic Church in the United States was fundamentally different than the Church in Europe, a difference often summarized in the contrasting labels "Roman Catholicism" and "American Catholicism." Furthermore, this perspective held, the American Catholic "ghetto" of inward-facing isolation, to the extent that it existed at all, was porous enough that the Church in the United States absorbed values and practices from its American context.

Two developments outside academia gave strength and support to Americanist interpretations of the American Catholic experience. First, the continued presence of anti-Catholicism in American culture influenced historians of the 1940s and 1950s to downplay components of the Catholic tradition that reinforced stereotypes of Catholics as a subversive presence in the national body politic. Thus, in his ambitious history of colonial Catholicism, *The Life and Times of John Carroll,* Peter Guilday, an early precursor of Americanist historiography, argued that "to understand the Catholic Church in America, one must see how naturally and integrally the spiritual allegiance of its members knit into the national allegiance so as to round each other out."[24] For such historians, there was no essential incompatibility between American Catholicism and American political culture. In the narratives produced under this rubric, eighteenth-century Catholicism in the United States was far more democratic and egalitarian than its monarchist European incarnations, American Catholics in the nineteenth century largely ignored Vatican complaints about the deleterious effect of the American secular political environment on the social order, and in the twentieth century a healthy dose of American pragmatism and patriotic anti-Communism moderated the extremes of Catholic neo-Thomistic thought. In his grand narrative, *American Catholicism,* published in 1956, John Tracy Ellis repudiated long-standing anti-Catholic perceptions that Catholics in the United States were primarily loyal to Rome, that they were prone to authoritarian impulses, or that they feigned American patriotism but secretly waited for the day when the pope's legions would conquer the United States. In place of—indeed, in conscious repudiation of—these conspiracy theories, Ellis presented an American Catholicism that was deeply loyal to American political and social institutions, a steadfast contributor to the national good rather than a seditious religious minority. His rendering of U.S. Catholic history distanced American Catholics from Rome, highlighted and perhaps exaggerated tensions between Roman authorities and American bishops, and emphasized the civility and loyalty of Catholic citizens to American traditions.[25]

The Second Vatican Council strengthened Americanist interpretations, directing them away from Catholic patriotism toward an effort to recover examples of democracy in American Catholicism. The significance of the Council as a watershed in U.S. Catholic historiography cannot be overstated. It bifurcated Catholic history into a periodization of pre- and postconciliar eras. The rupture it introduced into Catholic experience of the Church left many scholars searching for historical explanations for the cause of the stagnation that had presumably given rise to the need for dramatic reform in the 1960s. More important, in place of previous ecclesial models of the Church as the static repository of divine revelation, Vatican II affirmed a vision of the Catholic tradition as a dynamic, ongoing creation. This liberated Catholic historians from the analytical limitations imposed by the paradigm of Catholicism as a collection of unchanging truths, allowing and even encouraging scholars to consider development and discontinuity as essential parts of Catholic history. The modern historian of Catholicism would no longer bear the burden of serving as "the historical spokesman for a self-conscious and defensive Church," David O'Brien enthused in a historiographical essay penned at the peak of the Council's reception in 1968. "Rather with John XXIII he will look forward with hope, anxious to learn from history and to teach others that all things human are transient, that change is inevitable but that men can, within limits, make their own future."[26] The optimism and openness of this period captured the imagination of a generation of young American historians like O'Brien, shaping their subsequent work. Finally, the Council's endorsement of collegiality and its experiments with inclusive participation as legitimate forms of decision making within Church structures diffused some of the lingering tension between Catholic models of hierarchical authority and American ideals of democratic governance. This in turn allowed Catholic historians to reevaluate the diverse forms of governance that had existed in different moments of the American Catholic past.

Beginning in the late 1960s, the dissatisfaction of progressive Catholics with the outcome of the Council—particularly their feelings of dismay and betrayal at the resurgence of hierarchical and monarchical models of authority in the Roman curia in the 1970s and later under the papacy of John Paul II in the 1980s and 1990s—led some historians to retrospectively highlight elements of American Catholic experience that seemed to affirm the legitimacy of democratic forms of Church governance. Though Andrew Greeley is best known for his incisive sociological analysis of American Catholic life in the postwar period, his *The Catholic Experience: An Interpretation of the History of American Catholicism* stands as a clear example of Americanist history written in response to the tumult of the conciliar years. In a not-too-subtle jab at contemporary curial authorities, Greeley extolled Americanizing bishops like John England as "heroes" who fought against the "suspicious, defensive, and reactionary mentality" of the Counter-Reformation European Church. Highlighting examples like the colonial trustee system of parish governance or John Carroll's call for direct election of bishops in his initial plan for the U.S. Church, Greeley and other historians implied that democracy had a long pedigree in the American Church, and that deep within the U.S. Church's history and traditions lay antiauthoritarian resources that could be marshaled against the hierarchical authority exercised by Rome in the present moment. "We can well imagine the shock to European Catholicism when John Ireland with his fiery rhetoric and imperious manner appeared on the scene announcing that the rest of the Catholic world ought to look to America for guidance in solving its problems," Greeley mused. Lest his readers miss the contemporary implications of this historical example, Greeley added, "John Ireland would have enjoyed Vatican II immensely."[27]

The new social history in the 1970s added another layer of complexity and a new momentum to Americanist historiography. The new appreciation for the pluralistic character of American society, the quest to recover and include previously ignored historical voices, and the attentiveness to anthropological ideas about the nature and operation of "culture" that were the central hallmarks of social history during its last resurgence manifested themselves in Catholic historiography in works that shifted the focus away from Catholic ecclesiology and institutions toward sustained consideration of the perspective and experiences of Catholic immigrants in the nineteenth and early twentieth centuries.[28] Though David O'Brien's foundational *Public Catholicism* and James Hennesey's *American Catholics* both took seriously the difficult charge of writing a "people's history" of American Catholicism, the "immigrant thesis" that emerged to dominate Catholic historiography through the 1980s and 1990s is most closely associated with the work of Jay P. Dolan.[29] From his early study *The Immigrant Church* to his later, definitive work, *The American Catholic Experience: A History from Colonial Times to the Present,*

Jay Dolan translated the new social history's emphasis on history written "from the bottom up" into a compelling and inclusive master narrative about the struggle of the American Catholic Church to realize its potential to be a dynamic and prophetic contributor to American society. While Dolan researched, documented, and analyzed (as none had before) the intricacies of ethnic, immigrant Catholic culture, the trajectory of his narrative displays a clear preference for the independent, pragmatic, democratic American Catholic Church that emerged in (as he names it in a chapter title) the "Republican Interlude, 1780–1820" in the immediate aftermath of the American Revolution under the leadership of John Carroll over the insular and authoritarian Catholicism he identified with the ethnic Catholic ghetto of the "Immigrant Church, 1820–1920."[30]

In the last decade, Americanist historiography has gradually but decisively moderated its characterization of American Catholicism as synonymous with American culture. There are two reasons for this shift. First, as anti-Catholicism waned from the 1960s on, Catholic scholars were freed of the burden of arguing that Catholics could be loyal, patriotic members of American society. "The assumption of Protestant hostility made by Catholic historians no longer seems viable in an age of self-criticism and ecumenical understanding," David O'Brien noted in the late 1960s.[31] Catholic historians since have been progressively liberated to explore distinctive elements of Catholicism without fear that their work might exacerbate animus toward Catholics in society or confirm anti-Catholic tropes. In addition, the emergence of a generation of historians who either are not Catholic or who have no direct memory of the Second Vatican Council (and so lack strong feelings about its outcome) has made it possible for the field of Catholic history to consider anew the complex bonds that linked American Catholics with Rome and the monarchical authority structures housed there. Thus, recent works of American Catholic history have moved steadily away from Americanism, with its emphasis on Catholic assimilation to American Protestant religious norms and democratic authority.

Catholic Distinctiveness and Future Inquiry

The softening of Americanist interpretations of Catholic history occurred at roughly the same time that exceptionalist interpretations were moving toward a more nuanced understanding of the intricate ties between American society and Catholic experience. As both partners in the exceptionalist-Americanist dialectic moved toward the other in the 1990s, the dialectic gradually resolved into a model of *Catholic distinctiveness,* an interpretive paradigm that emphasizes unique elements of Catholicism distinguishing the tradition from other forms of Christianity while framing those distinctions not as exceptionalism, but rather as the grounds for Catholic engagement with larger American culture. Drawing methodologically from identity theory, ethnography, and cultural studies, the emerging trend toward Catholic distinctiveness explores cultural ground where Catholic selves were constituted in order to better understand the ways in which those Catholic selves encountered and interacted with American society. The historiographical move toward Catholic distinctiveness does not necessarily repudiate either Americanist or exceptionalist scholarship, both of which documented important facets of Catholic experience in the United States. Rather, emerging scholarship in U.S. Catholic history and Catholic Studies resolves the contrary portraits of American Catholicism that each school presented by highlighting ways in which American Catholics lived in a dynamic and at times difficult relationship with the dictates of Catholic faith and the norms of American national identity.

Two important book series have directly or indirectly contributed to the proliferation of scholarship on Catholic distinctiveness. Orbis Books' nine-volume series American Catholic Identities: A Documentary History, edited by Christopher Kauffman, brings primary sources in U.S. Catholicism into the historiographical present by focusing on areas of Catholic social history and experience that were largely ignored in John Tracy Ellis's foundational 1954 collection, *Documents of American Catholic History*.[32] Offering documents on such topics as gender, prayer, intellectual life, public activism, as well as the unique experience of female, African American, Latino, and Native American Catholics, the Orbis collection provides future scholars with a solid foundation of primary sources selected by knowledgeable scholars with an appreciation for the "protean" character of "what constitutes being American and Catholic in relation to the formation of religious identities."[33] The Cushwa Center Studies of Catholicism in Twentieth-Century America series from Cornell University Press, edited by R. Scott Appleby, brings together scholarly monographs that resulted from the three-year research initiative Catholicism in Twentieth-Century America Project, funded by the Lilly Endowment at the Cushwa Center for the Study of American Catholicism at Notre Dame. The research initiative's focus on documenting links between the Catholic community and American society in the twentieth century has resulted in a collection of historical monographs on the Catholic engagement with modern American culture and politics, particularly how "Catholics and their church have responded to, shaped, and been influenced by developments in American society, culture, politics, and religion."[34]

Several forms of Catholic distinctiveness have taken center stage in the recent works on the history of American Catholicism. Space limitations do not allow for a listing of all the forms this new emphasis has taken in recent historiography, but what follows is a listing of seven areas where emphasis on Catholic distinctiveness has been fully realized, four where this focus is emergent, and four understudied forms of distinctiveness that merit further scholarly attention.

Transnational Catholic identity. Peter D'Agostino's *Rome in America* explores the singular place that the Vatican occupied in the Catholic imagination in the twentieth century. Purposely provocative, D'Agostino's book argues that American Catholics, like all Catholics, were primarily oriented toward Rome as a metropole of Catholic identity and ideology. As a result, D'Agostino argues, Italian Catholics in the United States in the early twentieth century mourned the demise of the papal states, opposed the Risorgimento, and supported a fascist Italian government that promised to restore a sphere of autonomous territory to the pope, drawing back from support for Mussolini only under pressure when the United States entered the Second World War.[35] D'Agostino's work highlights the transnational nature of Catholic identity—a direct challenge to Americanist portrayals of Catholicism grounded in and closely identified with the United States. Among other works in this vein is John McGreevy's *Catholicism and American Freedom: A History,* which contends that both ultramontane and liberal strands of American Catholic thought—particularly different notions about the essential meaning of "freedom"—developed as a trans-Atlantic conversation between the Roman Church, European liberals, American Catholics, and American society.[36] Such works by McGreevy, D'Agostino, and others reveal the extent to which, even in periods characterized in terms of an insular "Catholic ghetto," the lived identity of Catholics in the United States was a fluid, dynamic, notoriously unstable compromise between American nationalism and Catholic transnational universalism.

The parish as a central institution of Catholic experience. Though the very good histories of Catholic dioceses published by Leslie Tentler and Paula Kane in the 1990s have been joined by more recent works like Mary Lethert Wingerd's *Claiming the City: Politics, Faith, and the Power of Place in St. Paul,* several newer studies move the primary focus of Catholic geography away from the diocese toward the smaller unit of the parish.[37] To the extent that the parish functioned as the primary place where Catholics encountered the universal Church—it was the central location where Catholics experienced the liturgy, the sacraments, the teachings, and the authority of the Church—the parish also stood as the central site where Catholic identities were formed, articulated, sustained, and displayed. John McGreevy's *Par-*

ish Boundaries: The Catholic Encounter with Race in the Twentieth-Century Urban North looks at northern parishes during the social and racial transformations of the 1950s and 1960s. McGreevy contends that the religiously determined dedication of northern ethnic Catholics to their urban parishes prevented them from participating in "white flight" suburbanization. This parish orientation also allowed white Catholics to oppose racial integration on the grounds that it posed a threat to the integrity of their spiritual home in the parish, in spite of and at times in direct conflict with emerging movements for racial justice within the Catholic Church.[38] In a similar vein, a collection of very strong essays by R. Scott Appleby, Pat Byrne, Debra Campbell, and Jay Dolan titled *Transforming Parish Ministry: The Changing Roles of Catholic Clergy, Laity, and Women Religious* divides the composition of the parish into the categories of persons present there (priests, women religious, laity), asking how the role of each group changed through the transitions of the twentieth century.[39]

Celibacy and monasticism in congregations of vowed religious. The conventions and tropes of sustained religious sexual celibacy remains one of the most pronounced forms of Catholic distinctiveness because it facilitates the existence of the sacramental priesthood as well as congregations of monks and nuns. A recent blossoming of works on sisters and priests sheds new light on the experience of individuals living under vows or in consecrated celibacy. Leslie Tentler's *Catholics and Contraception: An American History* reveals the ways that the Church's ban on contraception weighed heavily on priests who, in their role as confessors, became both de facto sex educators and unwilling apologists for the doctrine to their increasingly resistant parishioners.[40] Other recent works, such as Martha Smith and Carol Coburn's *Spirited Lives: How Nuns Shaped Catholic Culture and American Life*, Maureen Fitzgerald's *Habits of Compassion: Irish Catholic Nuns and the Origins of New York's Welfare System, 1830–1920*, Rebecca Sullivan's *Visual Habits: Nuns, Feminism, and American Postwar Popular Culture*, Amy Koehlinger's *The New Nuns: Racial Justice and Religious Reform in the 1960s*, and Suellen Hoy's *Good Hearts: Catholic Sisters in Chicago's Past*, explore the public roles that women religious have played in the development of charitable organizations and justice movements in American society.[41] Fitzgerald, for example, argues that the public welfare system in New York was produced not by nineteenth-century Protestant female reformers but rather by congregations of sisters who vigorously resisted Protestant models of relief that equated poverty with moral failing.

Catholic sexuality, particularly the prohibition against contraception. The Catholic prohibition on artificial contraception marks a significant difference between Catholic and non-Catholic approaches to sexuality. As mentioned before, Leslie Tentler's *Catholics and Contraception* documents the development of the doctrine over the last century while also tracing the varied experiences of American Catholic encounters with the teaching in various moments. Tentler traces the historical development of Catholic teaching about contraception from delicately worded late nineteenth-century sermons about the "sin of Onanism" through the 1968 promulgation of *Humanae Vitae,* the papal encyclical that affirmed the Catholic ban on birth control in the wake of the emergence of the anovular pill. Placing the evolution of Catholic teaching on contraception alongside developments within Catholic popular and clerical culture throughout the twentieth century, Tentler effectively documents diverse ways that contraception intersected with and affected practices, institutions, and relationships within American Catholicism. By focusing on the nexus of religious authority and lay response, Tentler offers a subtle case study of the ways Catholics negotiated national, religious, and class identities through sexual practices.

Sacramentalism and Catholic devotional practices. Much of Catholic religious practice centers on the seven sacraments, but a sacramental imagination—one that acknowledges the possibility for the radical presence of the divine in mundane or material facets of human life—infuses significant aspects of Catholic culture, becoming manifest in diverse facets of Catholic religious life.[42] Sacramentalism contributes to incarnational theologies like the Mystical Body of Christ, the personalism advocated by Catholic social reform groups like Dorothy Day's Catholic Worker Movement, and the meeting of spiritual and material in nonsacramental devotions like scapulars, rosaries, and appeals to the healing powers of Lourdes water or dirt from Chimayo. Though Joseph Chinnici's work has long probed the subtle currents of religious imagination that lay underneath American Catholic devotional practices, a recent collection of essays by Chinnici, Paula Kane, James O'Toole, and Margaret McGuinness published under the title *Habits of Devotion* adds a tightly structured historical approach to understanding continuities and changes within four American Catholic sacramental and devotional practices in the twentieth century: the Eucharist, confession, prayer, and devotions to Mary.[43] Robert Orsi begins his most recent book, *Between Heaven and Earth: The Religious Worlds People Make and the Scholars Who Study Them,* with a personal anecdote about the saints who "crowded in with the humans" around his late mother's hospital bed in the form of stories, statues, and holy cards. The essays collected in this provocative volume explore these "relationships that form between humans and holy figures," particularly the complex interaction of American Catholics with Mary and various saints in the twentieth century through nonsacramental devotional practices. Orsi continues to develop new methodological approaches to the field of religious history in *Between Heaven and Earth,* advocating for an intersubjective approach to sources, informants, and cultural idioms, but also—and of particular importance for historians of American Catholicism—by replacing linear interpretations of modern Catholic history (such as exceptionalism or Americanism) with "braided" narratives that allow for scholarly appreciation of the devotions as "engagements with the complexities and ambiguities of the times, not adaptations to a normative trajectory toward the modern."[44]

Anti-Catholicism. As anti-Catholicism continues to wane in American culture, Catholic scholars are gaining new distance from which to reevaluate the sources of American anti-Catholicism, the forms it took in different places and times, and its effect on Catholic institutions and Catholic identities in the United States. Over a decade ago, literary scholar Jenny Franchot depicted antebellum anti-Catholicism as largely the product of Protestant imaginations, Protestant fears, and Protestant desires in her provocative *Roads to Rome.* "Anti-Catholicism operated as an imaginative category of discourse through which antebellum American writers of elite and popular fictional and historical texts indirectly voiced the tensions and limitations of mainstream Protestant culture," she explained.[45] Though Franchot's model revealed the extent to which anti-Catholic tropes hinged on anxieties about the vulnerability of democratic political institutions and the patriarchal family, it also effectively reduced Catholics to figments of particular Protestant fantasies. More recent works within Catholic Studies have explored anti-Catholicism as a broad field of cultural discourse wherein Catholic and non-Catholics argued about the nature of Roman Catholicism, the character of American society, and the proper relationship between the two. Following on the heels of a major conference on this topic in 2002 at Fordham's Curran Center, Mark Massa's book *Anti-Catholicism in America* explores the contributions of the Ku Klux Klan, Know-Nothingism, and even Chick track comics to animus against Catholics. But Massa also acknowledges the role Catholics themselves voluntarily played in constructing cultural maxims of "Catholic otherness," replacing simplistic models of Catholic victimhood in the face of anti-Catholic animus with a more subtle model of a distinctive Catholic imagination that shaped the negotiation, resistance, and accommodation by Catholics to negative perceptions of them.[46] John McGreevy's *Catholicism and American Freedom,* already mentioned, documents several important episodes in the long history of political and intellectual anti-Catholicism in the United States. McGreevy's narrative offers an especially fascinating portrait of resurgent anti-Catholicism in mid-twentieth-century liberalism and the self-criticism it generated among American Catholic intellectuals.

Latino presence, perspectives, and traditions. The "immigrant Church" remains an influential trope for presenting American Catholic ethnic diversity and explaining the power of immigrant "ghetto" enclaves and ethnic parishes. Spanish-speaking Catholics (from Mexico, Puerto Rico, Cuba, and Central America) now constitute the single largest group of Catholics in the United States. They also, as a group and as individual national groups, contradict many of the central assimilationist narratives that pervaded earlier scholarship on the immigrant Church. The growing prominence of Latino Catholics challenges Catholic historians to develop interpretive models that accommodate the *mestizaje* culture and religious practices of Latino Catholics, and that acknowledge the unique effect of religious competition with Pentecostalism on the Church's efforts to minister to Spanish-speaking Catholics.[47] The past decade has seen a proliferation of literature on Hispanic Catholicism in the United States, including such works as Thomas A. Tweed's *Our Lady of the Exile: Diasporic Religion at a Cuban Catholic Shrine in Miami,* Eileen Oktavec's *Answered Prayers: Miracles and Milagros along the Border,* Luis D. Leon's *La Llorona's Children: Religion, Life, and Death in the U.S.-Mexican Borderlands,* and Timothy Matovina's *Guadalupe and Her Faithful: Latino Catholics in San Antonio, from Colonial Origins to the Present.*[48] Characteristic of these works is a recognition of the complex social processes and fluid identities Latino/a Catholics inhabit in the American religious landscape. Roberto Trevino's *The Church in the Barrio* brings a borderlands sensibility to a microstudy of several Hispanic parishes in Houston, producing a textured portrait of how Tejano Catholics have inhabited the Catholic tradition and used it to pursue change in the Church and in society beyond.[49] Similarly, Kristy Nabhan-Warren's *The Virgin of El Barrio: Marian Apparitions, Catholic Evangelism, and Mexican American Activism* explores the intersections of Mexican popular, charismatic, and Roman strands of Catholicism in Mary's Ministries, a Catholic evangelization and social outreach group that grew from one family's devotion to the apparition of the Virgin of the Americas (a mestiza madonna) in South Phoenix in the 1980s.[50]

There are four additional fruitful areas of Catholic distinctiveness for which scholarly literature is just beginning to emerge.

Children and childhood in Catholicism. The history of the unique role played by children (and the trope of childhood) in Catholic institutions and experiences was first introduced by Robert Orsi in his essay "Material Children: Making God's Presence Real for Catholic Boys and Girls and for Adults in Relation to Them" in *Between Heaven and Earth.* Susan Ridgely offers a contemporary portrait of Catholic "children's religion" in her ethnographic study of first communion classes, *When I Was a Child: Children's Interpretations of First Communion.*[51]

Catholic bodies. Julie Byrne's *O God of the Players: The Story of the Immaculata Mighty Macs* offers a nuanced interpretation of the bodily experience—

particularly the sheer physical pleasure—of female Catholic basketball players from the 1940s through the 1970s.[52] Byrne's attentiveness to the body as an especially intense site for the creation and contestation of religious meaning and identity stands as a model for understanding the embodied experience of Catholics in other areas, such as religious rituals and sexual mores.

Catholic arts and literature. Building on the foundation of Ross Labrie's *The Catholic Imagination in American Literature* and Andrew Greeley's *The Catholic Imagination,* Paul Elie's 2003 exhaustive comparative study of Catholic authors Dorothy Day, Thomas Merton, Walker Percy, and Flannery O'Connor, *The Life You Save May Be Your Own: An American Pilgrimage,* explores the surprisingly diverse forms of Catholicism that emerged within the creative worlds of American Catholic contemporaries at midcentury.[53] These works suggest the rich insights into Catholic experience to be gained through close attention to the work of Catholic writers, artists, and musicians.

African American Catholic experience. Though Cyprian Davis and Albert Raboteau both have made important scholarly contributions to historical knowledge about the unique (and often painful) experience of African American Catholics in the American Church, Diane Batts Morrow's study *Persons of Color and Religious at the Same Time: The Oblate Sisters of Providence, 1828–1860* provides a detailed account of the ways in which African American women employed their status as celibate vowed religious to challenge both white supremacist characterizations of black women as sexually immoral and the indifference of the Catholic Church to the plight of its African American members. Her work stands as a model for future studies of the ways that African American Catholics navigated the tension between Catholic rhetoric of universalism and American norms of white supremacy, both within and beyond the Church.[54]

Finally, a few areas of Catholic distinctiveness remain largely untouched by recent scholarship. Hopefully future students in Catholic Studies will turn their attention to the following: (1) issues of religious power in the authority wielded by the Roman magisterium and its effect on American structures and practices; (2) the pervasive violence in American Catholicism, from the legendary ruler-wielding nun to the Irish and Italian mobs to the affinity of Catholics for the sport of boxing; (3) the singular and unprecedented transformation caused by the Second Vatican Council, particularly how the Council was interpreted, received, and implemented in the American context; and (4) the experience of African American Catholics, particularly how they navigated the tension between Catholic notions of human solidarity and the racial specificity and white supremacy that pervaded American culture and, more important, the American Catholic Church.

In a lecture at Notre Dame in 2005 on future directions in American

Catholic Studies, Jim Fisher described the project of Catholic studies in the twenty-first century as drawing a "cognitive map" of U.S. Catholic experience and Catholic sensibilities.[55] Fisher urged Catholic historians to re-imagine American Catholicism as a diverse field of phenomenology in which the work of the historian is not to form broad generalizations about Catholics as a group, but rather to become experts at documenting Catholicism as a changeable human experience—recovering Catholicism "where you are" (or were, rather), in Fisher's words. As the dialectic of Catholic exceptionalism and Americanist assimilation in the historiography of American Catholicism continues to resolve itself into renewed consideration of those elements of religious experience that are distinctive to Catholics, religious historians in this field enter new terrain of history that is more self-consciously attentive to the ways that religious traditions function not just as denominations, but more so as the ground of human experience, cultural meaning, and social engagement.

Notes

1. Amanda Porterfield offers a thoughtful analysis of the origins and expansion of the term *denomination* in *The Protestant Experience in America* (Westport, CT: Greenwood, 2006), xvi–xvii.

2. Will Herberg, *Protestant, Catholic, Jew: An Essay in American Religious Sociology* (New York: Doubleday, 1955).

3. David J. O'Brien, "American Catholic Historiography: A Post-Conciliar Evaluation," *Church History* 37, no. 1 (1968): 81.

4. Henry F. May, "The Recovery of American Religious History," *American Historical Review* 70, no. 1 (1964): 90.

5. *American Catholic Quarterly Review* (Philadelphia: Hardy and Mahony, 1876–1924).

6. John Gilmary Shea, *Our Church and Country: The Catholic Pages of American History* (New York: Catholic Historical League of America, 1905). See also his *Discovery and Exploration of the Mississippi Valley* (New York: E. Maynard, 1890) and *History of the Catholic Missions among the Indian Tribes of the United States, 1529–1854* (New York: P. J. Kennedy, 1896).

7. Thomas F. O'Connor, then "historiographer of the Archdiocese of New York," organized major books and articles of American Catholic history under the central headings documents, general, regional, biography, religious orders and congregations, and education. The majority of books and articles cited fell under the categories biography and religious orders and congregations. "Writings on United States Catholic History, 1947: A Selective Bibliography," *Americas* 4, no. 4 (1948).

8. Maria Kostka Logue, *The Sisters of Saint Joseph of Philadelphia, 1847–1947* (Westminster, MD: Newman, 1950).

9. Henry J. Browne, "American Catholic History: A Progress Report on Research and Study," *Church History* 26, no. 4 (1957): 375.

10. Ibid.

11. John Tracy Ellis, "American Catholics and the Intellectual Life," *Thought* 30 (Autumn 1955): 351–88. For further discussion of the effect of Ellis's essay, see Philip Gleason, *Contending with Modernity: Catholic Higher Education in the Twentieth Century* (New York: Oxford University Press, 1995), 278–92.

12. Thomas T. McAvoy, "The American Catholic Dilemma," *Review of Politics* 20 (April 1959): 456–60, and "American Catholics: Tradition and Controversy," *Thought* 36 (Winter 1960): 583–600.

13. Leslie Tentler, *Seasons of Grace: A History of the Archdiocese of Detroit* (Detroit: Wayne State University Press, 1990); Paula M. Kane, *Separatism and Subculture: Boston Catholicism, 1900–1920* (Chapel Hill: University of North Carolina Press, 1994).

14. Gleason, *Contending with Modernity.*

15. Christopher Kauffman, *Faith and Fraternalism: A History of the Knights of Columbus, 1882–1982* (New York: Simon and Schuster, 1992).

16. Paul Marx, *Virgil Michel and the Liturgical Movement* (Collegeville, MN: Liturgical, 1957); Robert Orsi, *The Madonna of 115th Street* (New Haven: Yale University Press, 1985).

17. Joseph Chinnici, *Living Stones: The History and Structure of Catholic Spiritual Life in the United States* (New York: Macmillan, 1989).

18. Colleen McDannell, *The Christian Home in Victorian America, 1840–1900* (Bloomington: Indiana University Press, 1986).

19. Ann Taves, *The Household of Faith: Roman Catholic Devotions in Mid-Nineteenth-Century America* (Notre Dame: University of Notre Dame Press, 1986).

20. Robert Orsi, *Thank You, St. Jude: Women's Devotion to the Patron Saint of Hopeless Causes* (New Haven: Yale University Press, 1996).

21. R. Scott Appleby, *Church and Age Unite! The Modernist Impulse in American Catholicism* (Notre Dame: University of Notre Dame Press, 1992).

22. James T. Fisher, *The Catholic Counterculture in America, 1933–1962* (Chapel Hill: University of North Carolina Press, 1989).

23. Mel Piehl, *Breaking Bread: The Catholic Worker Movement and the Origin of Catholic Radicalism in the U.S.* (Philadelphia: Temple University Press, 1984).

24. Peter Guilday, *The Life and Times of John Carroll* (New York: Encyclopedia, 1922), 773.

25. John Tracy Ellis, *American Catholicism* (Chicago: University of Chicago Press, 1956).

26. O'Brien, "American Catholic Historiography," 94.

27. Andrew Greeley, *The Catholic Experience: An Interpretation of the History of American Catholicism* (New York: Doubleday, 1967), 22, 23.

28. For further reading on the new social history, see Alice Kessler-Harris, "Social History," in *The New American History*, ed. Eric Foner (Philadelphia: Temple University Press, 1990), 164.

29. David J. O'Brien, *Public Catholicism* (New York: Macmillan, 1989); James Hennesey, *American Catholics: A History of the Roman Catholic Community in the United States* (New York: Oxford University Press, 1981).

30. Jay Dolan, *The Immigrant Church: New York's Irish and German Catholics, 1815–1865* (Baltimore: Johns Hopkins University Press, 1975); Jay Dolan, *The American Catholic Experience: A History from Colonial Times to the Present* (Notre Dame: University of Notre Dame Press, 1992). Peter D'Agostino offers an incisive, if perhaps unnecessarily dismissive, evaluation of Americanist historiography, particularly Dolan's contribution to it, in the epilogue of his *Rome in America: Transnational Catholic Ideology from the Risorgimento to Fascism* (Chapel Hill: University of North Carolina Press, 2003), 309–15.

31. O'Brien, "American Catholic Historiography," 90.

32. John Tracy Ellis, *Documents of American Catholic History* (Milwaukee: Bruce, 1956).

33. Christopher Kauffman, series introduction, "American Catholic Identities: A Documentary History," in *Gender Identities in American Catholicism*, ed. Paula Kane, James Kenneally, and Karen Kennelly (New York: Orbis, 2001).

34. R. Scott Appleby, series introduction, "Cushwa Center Studies of Catholicism in Twentieth-Century America," http://www.cornellpress.cornell.edu/cup8_series-cushwa.html.

35. D'Agostino, *Rome in America.*

36. John T. McGreevy, *Catholicism and American Freedom: A History* (New York: W. W. Norton, 2004).

37. Tentler, *Seasons of Grace;* Kane, *Separatism and Subculture;* Mary Lethert Wingerd, *Claiming the City: Politics, Faith, and the Power of Place in St. Paul* (Ithaca: Cornell University Press, 2003).

38. John T. McGreevy, *Parish Boundaries: The Catholic Encounter with Race in the Twentieth-Century Urban North* (Chicago: University of Chicago Press, 1996).

39. Jay P. Dolan, R. Scott Appleby, Patricia Byrne, and Debra Campbell, *Transforming Parish Ministry: The Changing Roles of Catholic Clergy, Laity, and Women Religious* (New York: Crossroad, 1990).

40. Leslie Tentler, *Catholics and Contraception: An American History* (Ithaca: Cornell University Press, 2004).

41. Carol Coburn and Martha Smith, *Spirited Lives: How Nuns Shaped Catho-*

lic Culture and American Life, 1836–1920 (Chapel Hill: University of North Carolina Press, 1999); Maureen Fitzgerald, *Habits of Compassion: Irish Catholic Nuns and the Origins of New York's Welfare System, 1830–1920* (Urbana: University of Illinois Press, 2006); Rebecca Sullivan, *Visual Habits: Nuns, Feminism, and American Postwar Popular Culture* (Toronto: University of Toronto Press, 2005); Amy L. Koehlinger, *The New Nuns: Racial Justice and Religious Reform in the 1960s* (Cambridge: Harvard University Press, 2007); Suellen Hoy, *Good Hearts: Catholic Sisters in Chicago's Past* (Urbana: University of Illinois Press, 2006).

42. Ross Labrie explores the effect of sacramentalism—particularly incarnation—on Catholic creativity in *The Catholic Imagination in American Literature* (Columbia: University of Missouri Press, 1997).

43. James O'Toole, ed., *Habits of Devotion: Catholic Religious Practices in Twentieth-Century America* (Ithaca: Cornell University Press, 2004).

44. Robert A. Orsi, *Between Heaven and Earth: The Religious Worlds People Make and the Scholars Who Study Them* (Princeton: Princeton University Press, 2005), 9.

45. Jenny Franchot, *Roads to Rome: The Antebellum Protestant Encounter with Catholicism* (Berkeley: University of California Press, 1994), xvii.

46. Mark Massa, *Anti-Catholicism in America: The Last Acceptable Prejudice* (New York: Crossroad, 2003).

47. On mestizaje culture, see Virgilio Eliozondo, *Galilean Journey: The Mexican American Promise* (Maryknoll, NY: Orbis, 1983) and *The Future Is Mestizo: Life Where Cultures Meet* (Bloomington, IL: Meyer-Stone, 1988).

48. Thomas A. Tweed, *Our Lady of the Exile: Diasporic Religion at a Cuban Catholic Shrine in Miami* (New York: Oxford University Press, 1997); Eileen Oktavec, *Answered Prayers: Miracles and Milagros along the Border* (Tucson: University of Arizona Press, 1998); Luis D. Leon, *La Llorona's Children: Religion, Life, and Death in the U.S.-Mexican Borderlands* (Berkeley: University of California Press, 2004); Timothy Matovina, *Guadalupe and Her Faithful: Latino Catholics in San Antonio, from Colonial Origins to the Present* (Baltimore: Johns Hopkins University Press, 2005).

49. Roberto Trevino, *The Church in the Barrio: Mexican-American Ethno-Catholicism in Houston* (Chapel Hill: University of North Carolina Press, 2006).

50. Kristy Nabhan-Warren, *The Virgin of El Barrio: Marian Apparitions, Catholic Evangelism, and Mexican American Activism* (New York: New York University Press, 2005).

51. Susan Ridgely Bales, *When I Was a Child: Children's Interpretations of First Communion* (Chapel Hill: University of North Carolina Press, 2005).

52. Julie Byrne, *O God of the Players: The Story of the Immaculata Mighty Macs* (New York: Columbia University Press, 2003).

53. Labrie, *The Catholic Imagination in American Literature*; Andrew Greeley, *The*

Catholic Imagination (Berkeley: University of California Press, 2000); Paul Elie, *The Life You Save May Be Your Own: An American Pilgrimage* (New York: Farrar, Straus, Giroux, 2003).

54. Cyprian Davis, *A History of Black Catholics in the United States* (New York: Herder and Herder, 1995); Albert J. Raboteau, *A Fire in the Bones: Reflections on African-American Religious History* (Boston: Beacon, 1995); Diane Batts Morrow, *Persons of Color and Religious at the Same Time: The Oblate Sisters of Providence, 1828–1860* (Chapel Hill: University of North Carolina Press, 2002).

55. The Future of American Catholic History: A Conference in Honor of Christopher Kauffman, University of Notre Dame, April 8, 2005.

2

New Directions on the Congregational Way

Margaret Bendroth

Whatever happened to the Congregational Way? Just a scant half century ago, the editor of the Religions in America series declared it "fitting" that the heirs of the Puritans should lead the way for the rest. "They were the first in order, and at times you would think that they were the first in color," he declared with a wry chuckle. Indeed, despite its dwindling numbers, the denomination deserved its primary position because it was, put simply, a core narrative, "an enactment and a preview of the drama and the tumult of the American religious story."[1]

That traditional understanding of Congregationalism has deep roots. When the first American Church History series appeared in the 1890s, the denomination held a pivotal position, boasting a single volume of the total thirteen. An eminent Congregational scholar, Leonard Woolsey Bacon, even wrote the series' capstone volume, a magisterial meditation on the workings of divine providence. One hundred years later, a much smaller and more diverse collection omitted Calvinist musings, but still included Congregationalists in the top tier because, as the series editor wrote, they represented the "solid core" of the old roster.[2]

But such survivals are not the rule: in the general run of recent religious scholarship, Congregationalists are fast disappearing.[3] Though the production of studies on standard topics like the New England Puritans and the theology of Jonathan Edwards continues unabated, the specifics of Congregational history play a smaller and smaller role in the larger story of American religion. The downward trend is easy to document through a quick perusal of indexes in popular textbooks on American religion. John Winthrop, Anne Hutchinson, and Unitarians still carry a considerable amount of plot development in the opening chapters, but Congregationalists become scarce after the Civil War. By the mid-nineteenth century, they have generally outlived their narrative purpose; after a parting mention of the disastrous Plan of Union with the Presbyterians, Congregationalists vanish under an energetic wave of Methodists, Baptists, and immigrant Catholics, to surface again only in footnotes.

Certainly the change is understandable. In a modern scholarly world properly attentive to the full diversity of religion in the United States, white New Englanders with three last names are less important and perhaps less interesting subjects for study than groups out on the creative margins of American religious culture. The well-chronicled story of Congregationalism does not, for example, explain nearly enough about the vast array of spiritual practices that have made religion so durable within American society. As Jon Butler observed in his influential recasting of the religious history narrative, the traditional focus on New England simply cannot "explain Christianity's extraordinary power and its highly variable expressions in nineteenth- and twentieth-century America—a society where, by the traditional formulation, religion should have been weak, rather homogenously evangelical, thoroughly uncoercive, and dominated by the direct descendents of Puritans."[4]

As Butler's statement suggests, not just Congregationalism but denominational history in general is losing its old preeminence. In comparison with, say, Hispanic Catholics or Chinese Buddhists, the differences separating Baptists, Presbyterians, and Congregationalists seem fairly minimal, suggesting a long-dead family quarrel more than a promising line of academic inquiry. And to be sure, denominationally based narratives do tend to demand a traditional, nuts-and-bolts approach to scholarship, inevitably focusing attention on men and institutions and their predictable concerns with budgets and programs. In contrast to the new scholarship on the "lived religion" of American believers, with its broad theological, ethnic, and racial sweep, denominational history can have a quaint, almost old-fashioned feel.[5]

But a shifting scholarly agenda is not the only reason why Congregationalists have become relatively invisible, at least in the world of printed books. There are also deeper causes, embedded further within the interpretive canons of American religious history and in the internal dynamics of the tradition itself. For one thing, Congregationalists are difficult to study: people who have long taken pride in their lack of an ideological or institutional core are not likely to produce a compact narrative, nor an easily accessible trail of documents. Students of this intensely local tradition must be prepared to travel.[6]

Moreover, Congregationalists have also suffered, as they once benefited, from the persistent scholarly fascination with denominational rank and influence. It is true perhaps that in terms of absolute cash value the tradition no longer merits the prestige it once received as a matter of course; there is no denying that in the great demographic rush for members and money, Congregationalists were also-rans. Their numbers dwindled throughout the nineteenth century and today, strictly speaking, most no longer travel under the name "Congregationalist," having been absorbed by denominational merger. But, setting aside for a moment the pragmatic assumptions underlying so much religious scholarship today, the diminishing heirs of the Puritans do have a few remaining stories to tell. Indeed, sometimes unsuccessful contestants have as much to say about the race as those who make it first across the finish line.

As all the essays in this volume would argue, denominational history is still a useful tool for understanding the past, especially when its mythic assumptions are systematically unpacked. It is tempting, for example, to think of "Congregationalism" or even "Protestantism" as fixed and stable entities, self-evident labels that evolved little over time. But the historical record suggests that proper nouns like these were the objects of long and often subtle debate. While the details of those discussions may no longer be interesting to any but a select few, their overall shape and purpose speak directly to the evolution of American religious patterns. Specifically, they witness to the never-ending need within a religious "free market" to establish and police institutional boundaries. In some traditions, especially those with visible hierarchies, questions about who belongs and who does not travel through set institutional channels. Thus, for example, the line separating Catholics from non-Catholics is rarely an object of dispute—although internal debates about what constitutes a "good Catholic" might well persist. But when hierarchy is weak, continuing and often irresolvable debate is almost compulsory; boundaries stay strong only under regular scrutiny. In recent years, this theoretical understanding has proved very important in analysis of modern evangelicalism, a diverse movement that has generally lacked a central institutional or ideological core.[7] Congregationalism, a tradition with its own strongly centrifugal tendencies, provides another good example of this process at work.

A more nuanced understanding of Congregationalism's role thus begins not with the issues of primacy—who ranks first—but with the ongoing question of identity. As might be expected in a decentralized, lay-oriented tradition, that issue has no single answer. Moreover, given the denomination's high visibility among past generations of historians, the conversation has been wide-ranging, involving both scholars and "insiders," those people who for all kinds of different reasons thought of themselves as Congregationalists. At times sharply self-aware and at other times amazingly shortsighted, those latter do not fit easily within a simple explanation of religious success or failure. The Congregational Way, as this essay suggests, leads down other paths, sharper and more winding.

The Burden of Congregational History

Congregational history has been particularly vulnerable to changing interpretive paradigms. The burden and privilege of its association with New England origins have added an air of importance not just to scholarly debates but to internal denominational ones. From the mid-nineteenth century onward, while other Protestants tangled over wordings of creeds or modes of baptism, the descendents of the Pilgrims sat somewhat apart—their identity issues stretched into much farther reaches of religious as well as secular American history, to the origins of democracy itself.

Largely because of its proximity to Puritanism, Congregationalism almost effortlessly assumed a prestigious academic track record. As many scholars have by now made clear, the old consensus model of the 1940s and 1950s, which rooted American democracy in seventeenth-century New England, simply afforded the region and its religious inhabitants too much explanatory power. Scholarly writing of the mid-twentieth century elevated Calvinism as the core problem of American culture and measured the secularization of Puritan ideals by the erosion of doctrines like predestination and infant damnation.[8] Indeed, Congregational history provided a variety of object lessons for students of secularization, a concept that, at midcentury, few scholars openly questioned. Events in New England far too easily flowed (at least in the minds of many Boston-based scholars) into national trends, as the ebb and flow of religious zeal among Puritanism's Congregational heirs merged into a cosmic tale of declension and revival.[9]

Of course, among Congregationalists themselves, the flattering portrait drawn by academics had long been gospel. The earliest denominational histories tended to focus on Calvinism as its ideological core, reflecting the intellectual power of the so-called New England Theology at Yale and Andover seminaries.[10] But during the 1840s and 1850s, a time of rising denominational consciousness and secular political tensions, the idea that Congregationalism represented the perfection of American democracy found a ready audience among churches still smarting from losses to their Unitarian competitors. "Where is education the most generally diffused and religious principle the most firmly rooted?" a popular pamphlet queried in 1843. The confident answer: "In Congregational New England." "Where do objects of benevolence most frequently find an origin, and where are they the most liberally supported? In Congregational New England. . . . Where do liberty and equality breathe their purest air, untainted by oppression on the one hand and licentiousness on the other? In Congregational New England."[11] A few years later another enthusiast similarly declared that the "full and powerful development" of Congregational principles was "essential to the perpetuation, defense, and perfection" of American civil institutions.[12]

After the Civil War, denominational pride "reached an orgy of self-congratulation," as many of the New England churches began to observe bicentennial celebrations, and many in the Midwest reached the hundred-year mark.[13] In the 1870s, as Congregationalists began their nervous movement from a collection of independent churches into a national denomination, the rhetoric of freedom and democracy grew even more insistent.[14] A spate of historical volumes appearing in the post–Civil War decades routinely claimed that the tradition was "germane to the liberal, practical, and truth-trusting spirit of the American people."[15] Henry Martyn Dexter's wondrously entitled volume, *Congregationalism: What It Is; Whence It Is; How It Works: Why It Is Better Than Any Other Form of Church Government and Its Consequent Demands,* argued that nearly half of all American Christians, some 31,446 out of 72,459, were strictly speaking Congregationalists—that is, if the total included all of the Unitarians, Universalists, Baptists, and even Methodist offshoots who practiced a democratic polity.[16]

By the early twentieth century, Congregationalists had all but forgotten their past association with Puritan witch hunting or their erstwhile status as state churches in New England. With little sense of historical irony, in 1931 the denomination pursued and consummated a merger with the Christian Connection, one of the small dissenting sects that had proved such a headache for the clerical establishment in the early nineteenth century. On paper at least, the two believed they had more in common than otherwise: "the freedom of the individual soul and the right of private judgment," the "autonomy of the local church," and the "fellowship of churches" united together for "counsel and cooperation."[17]

By the mid-twentieth century, Congregationalists had thoroughly accepted their preeminent position in the formation of American democratic institutions. During the late 1940s, Gaius Glenn Atkins's popular booklet, *An Adventure in Liberty,* became the standard historical account, read in churches and Sunday school classes across the country. The table of contents included the expected chapters on "The New England Way," the "Unitarian Departure," and "Westward Ho!" But woven throughout is an assumption that, at heart, all American traditions were really Congregational—or at least wished they could be. Behind all of the "massive and entangled action of Protestantism," Atkins declared, was a desire for the "independence of the spirit-guided Christian life, both in theory and in practice," though of course only American Congregationalists had ever known its true fullness.[18]

In the mid-twentieth century, when the Congregational Christian churches discussed merger with the Evangelical and Reformed, denominational historiography took a sharply political turn. Those who opposed the formation of a single "United Church of Christ" argued that Congregationalism's central—and in fact defining—principle was the freedom of the individual church. Thus, by definition, any form of association more binding than a loose federation would mean the end of the historic tradition. To argue their point, merger opponents tracked all the way back to the early seventeenth century, centering their narrative on Robert Browne, William Bradford, and that famous ocean voyage to Plymouth Rock. Very deliberately they identified the Plymouth Pilgrims as the true originators of the Congregational Way, contrasting their simple communitarianism with the Quaker-baiting practices of their presumably more authoritarian neighbors up in Boston.[19]

For their part, merger supporters argued that the true essence of Congregationalism was not freedom but, as ecumenical statesman Douglas Horton stated, "freedom with fellowship." Their historiography centered not on the Pilgrims but on the connectional polity laid out by William Ames and in the 1648 Cambridge Platform, which encouraged individual congregations to come together for mutual oversight and care.[20] The original Congregationalists, said Horton, "abhorred the separateness of Separatism as cordially as they did the authoritarian penchant of Presbyterianism and Episcopacy."[21] Merger supporters also drew an alternative lesson from their New England past, arguing that the denomination's open-ended polity made it uniquely suited for ecumenical ventures. The 1957 United Church of Christ merger was, in their view, a fulfillment rather than a betrayal of their historic past. Far from giving up the mythic association with American civil institutions, they insisted that Congregationalism's long history of nonsectarian tolerance embedded it even more deeply in the canons of liberal democracy.

But as Congregational polemicists fought each other for ideological high ground, the scholarly foundations beneath them were shifting decisively. Led by Perry Miller's pioneering work on the English and American Puritans, a new generation of scholars began to observe the old institutions of New England democracy with deeper scrutiny, subjecting even the hallowed town meeting tradition to academic skepticism. By the 1960s, a growing number of scholars had concluded that though the Puritans may well have prized religious liberty, they never intended it to apply to anyone but themselves.[22] According to this new narrative, the real birthplace of American freedom was considerably south of the present-day Massachusetts Turnpike, in colonies like Pennsylvania, New York, and New Jersey, where Anglicans, Quakers, Lutherans, Presbyterians, and an astonishing array of Anabaptist and Pietist sects—Dunkers, Mennonites, Moravians, Winebrennarians, to name only a few—lived peacefully side by side.[23]

The result was a growing gap between academic conversations about the Puritan legacy and the self-image of Congregational insiders. All religious groups smart a bit under academic scrutiny, but this parting of the ways proved unusually painful, effectively disenfranchising a generation of denominational scholars with considerable stake in the outcome of their own story.

Winners or Losers?

Recent developments in American religious historiography have challenged Congregational hegemony even more directly. New models based on the competitive dynamics of the economic marketplace have thoroughly reversed the old denominational pecking order: no longer the core tradition of American democracy, Congregationalists have become its primary negative example. As the genteel heirs of the old New England cartel, so the argument goes, early nineteenth-century churchmen seemed consistently unaware of the raging battle for souls that Methodists, Baptists, and many other smaller sects were waging around them. Thus, the "winners" in the religious marketplace—Methodists and Baptists by far—were the most entrepreneurial, consistently focused on growth and expansion, planting new churches with circuit riders and stump preachers. "Losers" insisted on Christopher Wren church spires and the spit and polish of a Harvard-educated minister.[24]

So, within this new formulation, Congregationalists had almost nothing to do with the rise of democracy except as a negative foil. In their influential book, *The Churching of America,* Roger Finke and Rodney Stark contrast the "genteel origin" of "highly trained and well educated" established clergy with early nineteenth-century Baptists and Methodists, who were simply "of the people." Congregational clergy emerge as effeminate "snobs" who willingly walked down the path of New England–style secularization rather than contend for souls in the hinterlands. Too busy "flirting with Unitarianism," Congregational clergy would have "been of little worth out where the great harvest of souls was under way, even had they been willing to venture forth." And in fact, the news is even worse than that: Finke and Stark also report that Congregationalists did well only in more "civilized" geographic areas where the sex ratio was skewed more heavily female.[25]

Numbers, of course, do not lie. By any statistical standard, Congregation-alists were inept competitors in the religious marketplace. Though the single largest church body in 1776, with about 20 percent of all individual congre-gations, they accounted for only 4 percent of that total in 1850. Between 1890 and 1926, Congregationalists lost about eight hundred churches, a decline of about 14 percent, and they had fallen to seventh in rank. By the mid-1950s, Congregationalist Christians reported around 1.3 million members, which placed them far behind Southern Baptists (8.2 million), Methodists (9.2 mil-lion), and even northern Presbyterians (2.5 million).[26]

But whether they willed their own decline is far from clear.[27] According to Finke and Stark, nineteenth-century Congregational leaders expressed "sur-prisingly little concern" about their declining numbers. They were, so the ar-gument goes, either unable or unwilling to admit their slow but steady de-cline in comparison to the dramatic rise in the American population; thus, they lived in a kind of statistical limbo for much of the nineteenth and early twentieth centuries. "It was not until the 1960s," Finke and Stark contend, "when the failures of the Congregationalists first turned into losses in actual numbers rather than just in market share, that serious expressions of alarm were heard."[28]

But in fact, many nineteenth-century Congregationalists were sharply aware of their demographic problem and, if the documents they left behind are any indication, rarely tired of analyzing it. From the 1840s onward church leaders tracked their statistical growth almost obsessively, reporting and ana-lyzing trends with anxious, critical eyes.[29] During the 1870s and 1880s, a time of intense self-scrutiny, contributors to the denominational press offered a variety of diagnoses for a range of different organizational ailments. Many of them worried, for example, that their decentralized polity would not produce a stable supply of clergy, and they decried the tendency, especially in more sparsely settled territories, for ministers to be ordained but not installed (in other words, to forego official inspection by a local ecclesiastical council or as-sociation).[30] The question of ministerial credentialing was another huge bug-bear, especially in the shadow of the Henry Ward Beecher scandal. Congrega-tional leaders no doubt endured many sleepless nights wondering how they could ever guarantee qualified pastoral candidates to large urban churches like Beecher's, and even more problematically, to isolated rural ones.[31] The issue of financial support was equally troubling. In 1877, a lengthy report to the National Council blamed the vestiges of the old parish system for drain-ing local church resources.[32] Supporters of a movement toward "free seats" in churches, who wanted to do away with pew rents, worried that sole reliance on voluntary contributions would decimate local church budgets.[33] In retrospect, of course, these Congregational growing pains look fairly emblematic of larger structural changes within American society—indeed, the historical shift from local "island communities" to the bureaucratic and professionalized institutions associated with modernity reverberated deeply in the denominational deliberations of the late nineteenth century.[34]

And in fact, for all their fascination with mythic American themes, late nineteenth-century Congregationalists also understood their own history in very pragmatic terms. In 1876, W. W. Patton, president of Howard University, offered a lengthy list of reasons why his denomination was visibly falling behind the rest. He readily admitted that Congregationalists had a reputation for class snobbery, exacerbated by long years as a legally established religion in much of New England. They had endured a debilitating schism with their Unitarian cousins as well as a disastrous Plan of Union with some less than forthright Presbyterians. But Congregationalists also faced geographic and political challenges. Their leading role in the abolitionist cause had prevented their expansion into the South, though, as Patton sniffed, "we have no regrets to express over our failure."[35]

Hardly the slumbering elitists they are sometimes depicted, Congregational thinkers were in a sense almost too pragmatic. They focused so closely on matters of polity that ideological clarity often suffered in comparison; Congregationalists grew accustomed to identifying themselves in the negative. As retiring moderator Alonzo Quint declared at the National Council of 1895, "We are not separated from the great Church of Christ by any distinctive doctrines. We affirm no provincial theologies. We hold the historic faith in common with all christendom."[36] To many of his fellow churchmen, this level of generalization was an advantage, especially alongside the excesses of their heresy-hunting Presbyterian cousins. As Brooklyn pastor James G. Roberts exulted, "A Congregationalist is not bound by these trammels. He may think north and south, east and west, and up to the zenith. His thinking and teaching may be as wide as the truth itself." Anticipating his critics, Roberts merely pointed out that those religious bodies most bound by top-down doctrinal orthodoxy—Roman Catholics and European Lutheran and Reformed churches—were the most riddled with heresies or plagued by cold rationalism.[37] Years later, in 1924, a *Christian Century* editorial still wondered "What is meant by Congregational 'faith and order?' Is there a single doctrine that can be pointed out as peculiarly Congregational?"[38] Such questions raised a defensive reaction, but not a counterargument. Praising the denomination's long-standing commitment to "liberty of thought," one respondent offered the conclusion that "Congregationalism is for most of us nothing more than a gateway to Christian liberty and service. It is not a substitute for Christianity or a barrier between the soul and Christ. Its only value is in the extent to which it is, or can be made Christian."[39]

Almost proudly, Congregationalists pointed to the rough treatment they had endured from denominational competitors. In a speech to the Andover Seminary alumni in 1876, Christopher Cushing admitted that the numerical losses of the nineteenth century were "so vast as to be embarrassing," especially in comparison to the rapid growth of the American population. But the reasons for failure were altogether commendable: "in our extreme catholicity and excessive generosity, we have spent our strength in building up other denominations." Thus the high intentions behind Plan of Union with the Presbyterians brought the loss of hundreds of churches and leading clergy, many of them educated at Congregational expense. But if the Presbyterians had won, at least Congregationalists had emerged with their ethics intact: "We do not care to be responsible for all their faults," Cushing harrumphed about his Calvinist cousins, "but we do think we can claim no small measure of credit for their true progress and enlightenment."[40]

What nineteenth- and early twentieth-century Congregationalists feared most was irrelevance. As preacher Joel Hawes reminded those present at the Albany Convention in 1852, Congregationalists should have "nothing to do with the spirit of sect which would separate us from other branches of the Church of Christ, and draw us off to work *within ourselves and for ourselves,* regardless of the general good." Some level of "denominational zeal" was probably unavoidable, he readily admitted, but it would be definitely out of character. "Congregationalists, properly speaking, never were a sect," Hawes insisted, "and never can be, till they renounce the true spirit of their order."[41]

At its first meeting in 1865 the National Council encoded these broad ideals in a published statement, *Ecclesiastical Polity.* As Congregationalists began to recognize their own particularities, they took special pains to acknowledge the basic integrity of other Christian church traditions, even promising to "pray for their peace and prosperity." Thus what looks like an internal statement about polity included an express invitation, directed at members of other denominations, to "occasional communion with us in worship and in sacramental ordinances" and proclaimed a readiness to be "edified by their ministers" and to "consult and co-operate with them for the advancement of the gospel."[42] The scholarly Henry Martyn Dexter also waded into the fray with a series of densely woven historical lectures, arguing that Congregationalists should not feel intimidated by the theological heavyweights they encountered in the denominational ring. A few flaws were inevitable: the fundamental feature of their distinctive polity was its freedom from spiritual limitations. "What the hierarchical organizations seek through their hierarchy, and presbyterial congregations look for through their graded courts, Congregational believers seek—and rightly seeking find—at first hand, directly from the inspiration of God within their own souls." Dexter defined Congregationalism as "that polity which puts least in the way of machinery—of symbols, rites, functionaries,—between the individual soul, and that God in whom it lives and moves and has its being."[43]

The formation of the United Church of Christ in 1957 only deepened Congregational reticence about distinctiveness. By then, the old tradition had splintered into three separate bodies, divided along liberal/conservative lines as well as by opposition or support for the merger.[44] The smaller groups ran constant risk of falling into the sectarian rhetoric that earlier generations of Congregationalists had so assiduously avoided; insisting that the essence of their polity was local church independence, they steered perilously close to complete decentralization. The majority group within the United Church of Christ, now bound to a new ecumenical partner, necessarily edged away from talk about the Congregationalist "good old days." Too much open nostalgia for a past single life suggested disloyalty, and even hinted at unfaithfulness.

With Congregationalists increasingly unable or unwilling to define themselves, their history, as we have seen, easily lent itself to academic morality tales. Certainly in its broad outline, it contained all of the basic dramatic ingredients for a narrative of secularization and decline: the erstwhile heirs of the Puritans frittering away their theological inheritance for the sake of easy popularity, and then losing the family name to an unfortunate dalliance with an opportunistic suitor.

Perhaps a far more compelling human tale lies beneath that simple story. If one takes seriously the concerns of Congregational thinkers over the past century or more, it is clear that church growth was not always the core Protestant agenda; rational self-interest is not the only model for understanding American religion. There is no doubt that, according to the rules of the market, nineteenth-century Congregationalists followed a dysfunctional course. They failed to define a brand, recruit new clientele, and protect their copyright—and in the end their customer base moved on.

The interesting question is why the Congregationalists of the late nineteenth and early twentieth centuries followed this course. What does the apparent failure, or perhaps one might say the modest success, of a major religious body like Congregationalists say about the tradition itself, and about the conditions for spiritual survival in American society? What kinds of choices were available to them? In recent years, scholarly focus on the so-called winners in the American denominational game has tempered discussion of secularization theory, especially as model of a grand and inexorable change. The statistics are clear: dramatically rising numbers of worldwide Pentecostal and evangelical churches suggest that the backwards spiritual drift of modern society has enlivened religious belief, not lessened it. But, as the Congregational case suggests, there is still no denying that "something" clearly happened, even among the well intentioned; for all its deliberation and worry, the denomination did not prosper in the twentieth century. Secularization is no simple myth. Beneath that simple fact of decline and the many moralistic conclusions that immediately spring to mind are likely a host of good analytical questions awaiting further exploration.

Why Study Congregationalists?

Though the New England Puritans are well-traveled scholarly territory, the lives of nineteenth- and twentieth-century Congregationalists are still an open field for investigation. True, there is no lack of creative study on traditional topics in denominational history: theology, foreign and home missions, westward expansion, and social reform.[45] A few treatments also tend to race and gender.[46] In general, however, these topical approaches explain relatively little about the growth and development of the tradition itself; we still lack a critical, fully contextualized narrative of Congregationalism in American culture, one that covers its transformation from a Puritan experiment to a leading voice of twentieth-century liberal ecumenism.

That story would be useful for a number of reasons. Historians, for example, know relatively little about the meaning of liberalism among turn-of-the-century Protestant laypeople. The debates of seminary professors and denominational officials are well known; but what of its appeal, or lack of appeal, on Sunday morning? To be sure, American liberal Protestantism was in many ways a "product of the pulpit," "imagined and defended," as Gary Dorrien writes, by preachers who knew something of the restlessness in church pews.[47] But it was also talked about, pondered, and debated in horse sheds and church parking lots and around the Sunday dinner table. Those conversations, many of them encoded in stacks of church records and committee minutes, might reveal a far more complex story than the common stereotypes about liberal Protestants currently held.

The scholarly history of fundamentalism offers an instructive parallel. The past two decades have seen an energetic spate of new books variously explaining the movement's origins and growth. And certainly that story, with its colorful personalities, powerful appeal to ordinary people, and endlessly quotable sermons and tracts, is a relevant and fascinating one, especially with the influential role of religious conservatives today. But serious scholarly attention has also yielded significant benefits, reversing harmful stereotypes and sharpening angles of critique: in recent years the old view of fundamentalists as rural, southern, and uneducated has given way to a much more theorized and useful understanding of religious antimodernism's social and intellectual roots.

Might not the same be true for the study of "grassroots liberalism"? It seems likely that a more nuanced reading of the late nineteenth and early twentieth centuries would reveal not a rigid divide between Protestant liberals and conservatives, but a series of shifting alliances, as ordinary people wrestled with questions of enormous consequence. A closer reading of Congregational history, especially as it played out in local churches, might shed some important light on the reasons why, during a time of spiritual "crisis," some Protestants turned to fundamentalism and others chose more tolerant approaches to faith. No doubt, during our own time of deepening religious conflict, that story could hold significant explanatory power.

Within a more clearly defined and fully imagined framework, Congregational history still has much to contribute, especially in regard to the religious underpinnings of American liberal democracy.[48] The years of mythic interpretations are certainly long since past, and the old Congregational Way can no longer be a source of automatic sectarian pride. But within the largely unexplored practices and ideals of nineteenth- and twentieth-century Congregationalism there is a terribly significant story about civic engagement, one that transcends the current preoccupations with "right-wing" and "left-wing" religion. In the present age, polarized between extremes of "faith-based boosterism" and dogmatic secularism, the efforts of Congregationalists to chart a middle path are well worth careful exploration—and perhaps, as well, worth painstaking recovery.[49]

As modern-day Congregationalists, under all of their various denominational labels, contemplate their shift toward the demographic margins of American religion, their common history may well take on new meaning and importance. To be sure, their old unwillingness to identify boundary lines was a function of social privilege; the predominantly white, middle-class denomination's open-ended sense of itself was a luxury that hard-pressed sectarian groups could simply not afford. But the institutional shift of the past several decades, a realignment that has thrust conservative evangelical denominations into a culturally defining role while sidelining the old "mainline," lends new urgency to the historical work of the older Protestant traditions. It may well be that "Congregationalism" still awaits further definition. This time around, however, the discussion should acknowledge the tradition's broad historic foundation without becoming trapped by undue nostalgia; it should also deal with the sharp realities of religious life in an increasingly diverse, post-Christian society.

This is an interesting time to study Congregational history. The dusty old books lying fallow in many small libraries, almost begging to be read, have some new stories to tell. They offer an opportunity for one more long look back into the past, and for the rediscovery of some old but compelling ideas that sent an earlier generation of Congregationalists out into unknown waters, into ships bound for the New England shore.

Notes

1. Charles Ferguson, "A Statement by the Editor," in Marion L. Starkey, *The Congregational Way: The Role of the Pilgrims and Their Heirs in Shaping America* (New York: Doubleday, 1966), vii.

2. The Congregationalists were not first, however, as the books were presented alphabetically. See Williston Walker, *A History of the Congregational Churches in the United States* (New York: Christian Literature, 1894); Leonard Woolsey Bacon, *History of American Christianity* (New York: Christian Literature, 1897); "Series Foreword," in J. William Youngs, *The Congregationalists* (Westport, CT: Greenwood, 1990), xi. Bacon also wrote his own single-volume history, *The Congregationalists* (New York: Baker and Taylor, 1904).

3. The most recent single-volume history was published by a denominational press primarily for a church audience: John Von Rohr, *The Shaping of American Congregationalism, 1620–1957* (Cleveland: Pilgrim, 1992). The other main source for Congregational history was likewise reprinted for denominational use: Williston Walker, *The Creeds and Platforms of Congregationalism* (1893; repr., Cleveland: Pilgrim, 1991).

4. Jon Butler, *Awash in a Sea of Faith: Christianizing the American People* (Cambridge: Harvard University Press, 1990), 2.

5. See, for example, David D. Hall, *Lived Religion in America: Toward a History of Practice* (Princeton: Princeton University Press, 1997); Laurie Maffly-Kipp, Leigh Schmidt, and Mark Valeri, eds., *Practicing Protestants: Histories of Christian Life in America, 1630–1965* (Baltimore: Johns Hopkins University Press, 2006).

6. Significant reference tools include Harold Field Worthley, *An Inventory of the Records of the Particular (Congregational) Churches of Massachusetts, Gathered 1620–1805* (Cambridge: Harvard University Press, 1970); and a series of historical inventories by Richard H. Taylor: *The Churches of Christ of the Congregational Way in New England* (Benton Harbor, MI: Richard H. Taylor, 1989); *Congregational Churches of the West* (Benton Harbor, MI: Richard H. Taylor, 1992); *Plan of Union and Congre-*

gational Churches of Christ in the Middle Atlantic States (Providence, RI: Richard H. Taylor, 2005).

7. A good theoretical statement is found in Christian Smith, *American Evangelicalism: Embattled and Thriving* (Chicago: University of Chicago Press, 1998).

8. See, for example, Ralph Henry Gabriel, *The Course of American Democratic Thought* (New York: John Wiley and Sons, 1956); Sacvan Berkovitch, *The Puritan Origins of the American Self* (New Haven: Yale University Press, 1975).

9. Jon Butler argues, for example, that the idea of an eighteenth-century "Great Awakening" was an "interpretive fiction" first given historical credence by Congregational minister Joseph Tracy in his 1841 volume, *The Great Awakening*. See Butler, *Awash in a Sea of Faith*, 164–65.

10. See, for example, Joseph S. Clark, *A Historical Sketch of the Congregational Churches in Massachusetts, from 1620 to 1858* (Boston: Congregational Board of Publication, 1858).

11. *Reasons Why I Am a Congregationalist* (Hartford, CT: D. B. Moseley, 1843), 20–21.

12. "The Convention at Albany," *Congregationalist*, October 1, 1852, 157, quoted in Elizabeth C. Nordbeck, "Introduction to the 1991 Edition," in *Creeds and Platforms of Congregationalism,* ed. Williston Walker (1893; repr., New York: Pilgrim, 1991), xiii.

13. Dewey D. Wallace Jr., "Charles Oliver Brown of Dubuque: A Study in the Ideals of Midwestern Congregationalists in the Late Nineteenth Century," *Church History* 53 (1984): 57.

14. For an overview of this process, see Samuel C. Pearson Jr., "From Church to Denomination: American Congregationalism in the Nineteenth Century," *Church History* 38 (1969): 67–87.

15. Richard S. Storrs, introduction to Albert E. Dunning, *Congregationalists in America: A Popular History of Their Origin, Belief, Polity, Growth, and Work* (Boston: Pilgrim, 1894), xiv.

16. Henry Martyn Dexter, *Congregationalism: What It Is; Whence It Is; How It Works: Why It Is Better Than Any Other Form of Church Government and Its Consequent Demands* (Boston: Congregational Publishing Society, 1878), 5–7.

17. "Plan of Union of the Congregational and Christian Churches," *Herald of Gospel Liberty,* November 14, 1929, 890–92; "The Preamble and Basis," *Congregationalist and Herald of Gospel Liberty,* July 9, 1931, 923. See also "Union Accomplished," in *The Living Theological Heritage of the United Church of Christ,* vol. 6, *Growing toward Unity,* ed. Elsabeth Slaughter Hilke (Cleveland: Pilgrim, 2001), 249–59.

18. Gaius Glenn Atkins, *An Adventure in Liberty: A Short History of the Congregational Christian Churches* (New York: Missionary Herald, 1947), 48.

19. The antimerger history of the period was Gaius Glenn Atkins and Frederick

Fagley, *History of American Congregationalism* (Boston: Pilgrim, 1942); a typical po-
lemic is Malcolm K. Burton, *Destiny for Congregationalism* (Oklahoma City, OK:
Modern, 1953). The literature on both sides is simply too voluminous to cite; however,
for helpful overviews, see Charles Harvey, "Individualism and Ecumenical Thought:
The Merger Controversy in Congregationalism, 1937–1961" (Ph.D. diss., University
of California, Riverside, 1968), chap. 1; Theodore Trost, *Douglas Horton and the Ecumenical Impulse in American Religion* (Cambridge: Harvard Theological Studies and
Harvard University Press, 2002), 82–103; Verne D. Morey, "American Congregationalism: A Critical Bibliography, 1900–1952," *Church History* 21 (1952): 336–39. One side-
piece of this larger debate was over the role of Plymouth doctor Samuel Fuller, who,
it was said, taught Congregational polity to the Puritan immigrants in Salem while
"on loan" from the original colony during an epidemic. The account is described in
William Warren Sweet, *Religion in Colonial America* (New York: Charles Scribner's
Sons, 1992), 83.

20. Douglas Horton, "Let Us Not Forget the Mighty William Ames," *Religion in
Life* 29 (Summer 1960): 434–42; Henry Wilder Foote, *The Cambridge Platform of 1648*
(Boston: Pilgrim and Beacon, 1949). For his part, eminent church historian Roland
Bainton, who was involved in merger politics, thought both sides were overreaching,
and that at best Congregationalism was only moderately connectional. See Harvey,
"Individualism and Ecumenical Thought," 242.

21. Douglas Horton, *Congregationalism: A Study in Church Polity* (London: Independent, 1952), 11.

22. See, for example, Perry Miller, "Thomas Hooker and Connecticut Democracy,"
in *Errand into the Wilderness* (Cambridge: Harvard University Press, 1956). During
the 1970s, some important studies also critiqued the democratic process in town
meetings. See, e.g., Kenneth A. Lockridge, *A New England Town: The First Hundred
Years* (New York: Norton, 1970); Michael Zuckerman, *Peaceable Kingdoms: New England Towns in the Eighteenth Century* (New York: Alfred A. Knopf, 1970).

23. See, for example, F. Ernest Stoeffler, ed. *Continental Pietism and Early American
Christianity* (Grand Rapids, MI: Eerdmans, 1976); Randall Balmer, *A Perfect Babel of
Confusion: Dutch Religion and English Culture in the Middle Colonies* (New York: Ox-
ford University Press, 1989); Butler, *Awash in a Sea of Faith.*

24. The most graphic (and controversial) version of the argument is found in
Roger Finke and Rodney Stark, *The Churching of America, 1776–1990: Winners and
Losers in Our Religious Economy* (New Brunswick: Rutgers University Press, 1992).
One of the most eloquent historical statements of a related thesis is Nathan Hatch,
The Democratization of American Christianity (New Haven: Yale University Press,
1989).

25. Finke and Stark, *The Churching of America,* 76, 86, 103–4, 71. See also, for example, Peter S. Field, *The Crisis of the Standing Order: Clerical Intellectuals and Cul-*

tural Authority in Massachusetts, 1780–1833 (Amherst: University of Massachusetts Press, 1998).

26. Finke and Stark, *The Churching of America,* 25, 55; U.S. Department of Commerce, Bureau of the Census, *Religious Bodies: 1926,* vol. 2, *Separate Denominations* (Washington, DC: U.S. Government Printing Office, 1929), 447; Benson Y. Landis, ed., *Yearbook of American Churches, Edition for 1956* (New York: National Council of the Churches of Christ in the U.S.A., 1955), 238–44.

27. Finke and Stark, for example, fault Congregationalists for being too "Congregational," that is, too decentralized to match the organizational feats of methodically inclined Methodists (*The Churching of America,* 74). Then, on the other hand, they are criticized for being overinstitutionalized, too much in the thrall of educated clergy and top-down pressures, and thus no match for the free and easy expansionist policies of Methodists and Baptists (73). Congregationalists are depicted as generally indifferent to the call of western expansion, and then disparaged for having to support their home missionary churches with institutional subsidies (65–66).

28. Ibid., 55–56.

29. The first "official" statement was a reprint of an 1847 analysis: Joseph Clark, "Progress and Prospects for Congregationalism," in *Year-Book of the American Congregational Union, for the Year 1854* (New York and Boston: American Congregational Union and Congregational Library Association, 1854), 305–13. Others followed regularly in published yearbooks and at national gatherings, e.g., Isaac P. Langworthy, "Lessons from Statistics," *Congregational Quarterly* 4 (July 1862): 293–96; George F. Pentecost, "The Relation of the Congregational Churches to the Work of Evangelization," in *Minutes of the National Council of the Congregational Churches of the United States, at the Sixth Session Held in Chicago, Ill., October 13–20, 1886* (Boston: Congregational Publishing Society, 1887), 209–10.

30. "Do We Need a Ministerial Bureau?" *Congregationalist,* April 24, 1873, 130; "New-Fangled Congregationalism," *New Englander,* January 1878; Hugh M. Scott, "The Need and Importance of an Increase in the Supply of Ministers," in *Minutes of the National Council of the Congregational Churches of the United States, at the Seventh Session Held in Worcester, Mass., October 9–14, 1889* (Boston: Congregational Sunday School and Publishing Society, 1889), 204–5.

31. "Ministerial Credentials," *Congregationalist,* May 1, 1873, 140; "Christian-Service Reform," *Advance,* January 12, 1883, 24.

32. "Report upon the Parish System," in *Minutes of the National Council of the Congregational Churches of the United States, at the Third Session Held in Detroit, Michigan, October 17–21, 1877* (Boston: Congregational Publishing Society, 1877).

33. George B. Leavitt, "Beware of Free Seats," *Congregationalist,* May 1, 1873, 138.

34. The image of the "island community" comes from Robert Wiebe, *The Search for Order, 1877–1920* (New York: Hill and Wang, 1966).

35. W. W. Patton, *The Last Century of Congregationalism* (Washington, DC: W. M. Stuart, 1878), 3.

36. "Address by Rev. A. H. Quint," in *Minutes of the National Council of the Congregational Churches of the United States, at the Ninth Session Held in Syracuse, N.Y., October 9–14, 1895* (Boston: Congregational Sunday School and Publishing Society, 1896), 73, 74.

37. James G. Roberts, *What Is Congregationalism? Paper Read by Rev. James G. Roberts before the New York and Brooklyn Association of Congregational Churches, Patchogue, Long Island, October 5, 1885* (New York: New York and Brooklyn Association of Congregational Churches, 1886), 5, 7.

38. "Denominational Loyalty," *Christian Century,* January 10, 1924, 35–36. See also reply, "Our Denominational Paradox," *Congregationalist,* January 31, 1924, 133.

39. "Making Congregationalism Christian," *Congregationalist,* April 17, 1924, 486.

40. Christopher Cushing, *What Congregationalism Has Accomplished during the Past Century* (Boston: Alfred Mudge and Son, 1876), 7, 8.

41. *Proceedings of the General Convention of Congregational Ministers and Delegates in the United States, Held at Albany, N.Y. on the 5th, 6th, 7th, and 8th of October, 1852: Together with the Sermon Preached on the Occasion by Rev. Joel Hawes, D.D.* (New York: S. W. Benedict, 1852), 45, 46.

42. *Ecclesiastical Polity: The Government and Communion Practised by the Congregational Churches in the United States of America, Which Were Represented by Elders and Messengers in a National Council at Boston, A.D. 1865* (Boston: Congregational Publishing Society, 1872), 43–44.

43. Henry Martyn Dexter, *The Congregationalism of the Last Three Hundred Years, as Seen in Its Literature: With Special Reference to Certain Recondite, Neglected, or Disputed Passages. In Twelve Lectures, Delivered on the Southworth Foundation in the Theological Seminary at Andover, Mass., 1876–1879* (New York: Harper and Brothers, 1880), 712, 706–7, 714.

44. As of 2006, the National Association of Congregational Christian Churches reported a membership 65,392 and the Conservative Congregational Christian Conference reported 42,725. See Eileen W. Lindner, ed., *Yearbook of American and Canadian Churches, 2006* (Nashville: Abingdon, 2006), 377, 381.

45. For foreign and home missions, see William R. Hutchison, *Errand to the World: American Protestant Thought and Foreign Missions* (Chicago: University of Chicago Press, 1987); John A. Andrew, *Rebuilding the Christian Commonwealth: New England Congregationalists and Foreign Missions, 1800–1830* (Lexington: University Press of Kentucky, 1976); Amy DeRogatis, *Moral Geography: Maps, Missionaries, and the American Frontier* (New York: Columbia University Press, 2003); Clara DeBoer, *His Truth Is Marching On: African Americans Who Taught the Freedmen for the American Missionary Association, 1861–1877* (New York: Garland, 1995); Joe Martin Richardson,

Christian Reconstruction: The American Missionary Association and Southern Blacks, 1861–1890 (Athens: University of Georgia Press, 1986). For westward expansion, see James Rohrer, *Keepers of the Covenant: Frontier Missions and the Decline of Congregationalism, 1774–1818* (New York: Oxford University Press, 1995). For social reform, see William F. and Jane Ann Moore, *Owen Lovejoy: His Brother's Blood; Speeches and Writings, 1838–64* (Champaign: University of Illinois Press, 2004); Clara DeBoer, *Be Jubilant My Feet: African American Abolitionists in the American Missionary Association, 1839–1861* (New York: Garland, 1994).

46. For race, see John Saillant, *Black Puritan, Black Republican: The Life and Thought of Lemuel Haynes, 1753–1833* (New York: Oxford University Press, 2003); J. Taylor Stanley, *A History of Black Congregational Christian Churches of the South* (New York: United Church, 1978); A. Knighton Stanley, *The Children Is Crying: Congregationalism among Black People* (New York: Pilgrim, 1979). For gender, see Elizabeth Cazden, *Antoinette Brown Blackwell: A Biography* (Old Westbury, NY: Feminist, 1983); Richard Shiels, "The Feminization of American Congregationalism, 1730–1835," *American Quarterly* 33 (1981): 46–62; Randi Walker, *Emma Newman: A Frontier Woman Minister* (Syracuse: Syracuse University Press, 2000).

47. Gary Dorrien, *The Making of American Liberal Theology: Imagining Progressive Religion, 1805–1900* (Louisville: Westminster John Knox, 2001), xxii.

48. See, for example, Peter Dobkin Hall, "The Rise of the Civic Engagement Tradition," in *Taking Faith Seriously,* ed. Mary Jo Bane, Brent Coffin, and Richard Higgins (Cambridge: Harvard University Press, 2005), 21–59.

49. See introduction to Bane, Coffin, and Higgins, *Taking Faith Seriously,* 2–6.

3

Presbyterians in America

Denominational History and the Quest for Identity

Sean Michael Lucas

If there is a Protestant denomination that typifies the apparent death of denominational history, it has to be the Presbyterians. Even though the various Presbyterian branches recently noted the three-hundredth anniversary of the first American presbytery, there were no major conferences, commemorative books, or retrospective assessments aside from a single issue of the *Journal of Presbyterian History*. That journal, sponsored by the Department of History of Presbyterian Church (USA), continues to limp along with barely a large enough subscription list to justify its existence. Likewise, the PC (USA) Department of History made news over the past several years with its decision to consolidate its archives into one central location, citing declining denominational funding for two locations. Increasingly, in denominational seminaries, Presbyterian history is subsumed under larger historical categories, and the idea of having a dedicated "Presbyterian historian" on a faculty is often viewed as strange. No doubt about it, writing history about Presbyterians has fallen on tough times.[1]

Part of the difficulty has been the loss of a coherent denominational identity in which to center the Presbyterian story.[2] And perhaps this confusion over identity has resulted from Presbyterianism's too-cozy relationship with American culture. As historian James Moorhead has noted, Presbyterians have long seen themselves "as close to the center of their culture." During the Eisenhower age, Presbyterian historians generally made the case that Presbyterians were quintessentially American—as founders and custodians of American civilization, Presbyterians presented themselves as the bulwark of American liberties, institutions, and good manners. If Presbyterians were anything, these historians claimed, they were *mainline*. The historiography during this era supported Presbyterian self-identification by showing that they exercised their responsibilities carefully, seeking justice for blacks and women in measured ways, forging new possibilities of cooperation within ecumenical American Protestantism, and making sure that America remained one nation under God.[3]

When American culture experienced the challenge of pluralism and the resultant religious restructuring during the 1960s and 1970s, Presbyterians were at a loss to identify themselves in meaningful ways. Also during this period, the southern Presbyterian Church in the United States experienced a painful rupture in 1973, with over forty thousand communicants departing to form the conservative Presbyterian Church in America. While they continued to focus their historiography on issues related to institutional self-preservation, especially the role of women and missions, Presbyterian historians also began to look seriously at what American pluralism meant for their denominations. The most extensive historical assessment was the Presbyterian Presence, a major Lilly Endowment–funded study that produced seven volumes in the early 1990s. And though the authors and editors of the Presbyterian Presence celebrated the diversity and pluralism of the church, there was also a strong sense that the church had become decidedly *oldline,* when compared to resurgent conservative Christianity.[4]

As a result of this loss of a centering identity, the desire to tell Presbyterian stories by engaging in Presbyterian historiography is at an all-time low. Ironically, the most creative vein for this work has come from historians associated with historically *sideline* Presbyterian denominations. As these sideline Presbyterians mine their tradition's history for a meaningful and workable religious identity, they have posed important questions, both about Presbyterianism's relationship to American culture and about the increasingly apparent failure of mainline Presbyterianism. This is not to say that these historians are the only ones doing this kind of work; however, it is to say that the historical stance, and the religious identity on which it is based, offers the way forward for a new generation of Presbyterian historians and believers.

Mainline

Presbyterian historiography in the post–World War II era sought to reinforce the denomination's self-image as a centrist, "mainline" force upholding the best American values, especially moderation, cooperation, and religious liberty. Also key was the way Presbyterian historians reflected the changing ways Americans thought about cultural and ethnic assimilation. Drawing upon sociological analyses that were beginning to question assumptions of Anglo conformity, Presbyterian historians would shift how they talked about assimilation into the church and American culture. In place of older stories of a Presbyterian-Puritan inheritance that gave the Presbyterian church a decidedly Anglo hue, Presbyterian historians groped toward stories that would emphasize the differences in the way minorities of race, class, and gender experienced the Presbyterian way of faith. The struggle for Presbyterian historiography was to honor the developing pluralistic model for understanding modern American life while still holding onto a center for religious identity and demonstrating Presbyterianism's value and relevance for Americans.[5]

Perhaps the best example of how Presbyterian historians adopted assumptions of Anglo conformity was Leonard J. Trinterud's magisterial *The Forming of an American Tradition* (1949). Trinterud argued that American Presbyterianism came into existence through the combination of ethnically diverse elements: namely, Scots-Irish Presbyterianism and English Congregationalism. As the church experienced the trauma of forging these elements together, American Presbyterianism came to stand for the supremacy of the Bible and religious liberty, seasoned by an appropriate dose of evangelistic piety and interest in education. But above all, for Trinterud, "to be the Body of Christ in history meant to be an American Church, within a divinely directed mission in American history, and not a mere colonial offshoot of some foreign Church which had neither part nor lot in American life." As disparate "foreign" elements came to embrace the Anglo-American identity of the Presbyterian Church, they would enter into God's divine mission for both church and country. Yet Trinterud, with other Presbyterian historians, further suggested that to be an American church also meant to champion theological moderation. After all, the apparent heroes of Trinterud's book were the New Side Presbyterians, who affirmed the supremacy of scripture over all "man-made" creeds and who fought any sense of "strict" subscription to the Westminster Standards.[6]

This sense that mainline Presbyterian identity should stress theological moderation and broadness, while inculcating others into an American faith, received historical reinforcement in Lefferts Loetscher's *The Broadening Church* (1954). Loetscher traced the history of the northern Presbyterian Church from the Old School–New School reunion in 1869 to the end of the fundamentalist-modernist controversy in 1929. Suggesting that the conflict of the 1920s was one between "extreme conservatives" and "extreme liberals," Loetscher held that the end result demonstrated that the Presbyterian Church stood for theological moderation over opposing poles. In the short term, the controversy allowed "moderate liberals" to gain a voice in the church. However, the long-term consequence was that "the frank and realistic discussion of theological questions which the times and present opportunity call for" were inhibited; " 'the less theology the better' seems to be the lurking implication." By broadening the church theologically, attempting to encompass more theological pluralism, the church was unable to have constructive conversations about Presbyterian identity and mission in the world.[7]

There was a growing sense that the way of continuing to provide intellectual and spiritual direction in an increasingly pluralistic America with theologically diverse denominations was to develop Christian unity across denominational lines. Not surprisingly, Presbyterian historiography also moved to support and engage this line of thinking. Loetscher, for example, used his 1962 presidential address for the American Society of Church History to focus on the early nineteenth century as a period of unprecedented denominational unity among mainstream Protestants.[8] Others joined Loetscher in making similar arguments, particularly in the pages of the *Journal of Presbyterian History* (*JPH*).[9] For example, *JPH* ran essays to further ecumenical relationships among Presbyterian and Reformed denominations, both to motivate northern and southern Presbyterians to reunite and to provide context for a proposed union between the northern Presbyterian Church in the United States of America and the Reformed Church in America. In these ways, Presbyterian historiography supported the denomination's sense of being an ecumenical leader in an increasingly diverse America.[10]

By the early 1960s, there was a growing sense that all was not well, either within mainline Protestantism or in America itself. Minority voices, especially women and African Americans, demanded to be heard. Presbyterian historians took up their cause in a continuing attempt to relate the Presbyterian faith to the issues of American society. Andrew Murray's *Presbyterians and the Negro* (1966) described how northern Presbyterians attempted to evangelize black Americans while southern Presbyterians rationalized enslaving them. In addition, he noted that in the postbellum period, black Presbyterians went from "equal status" in white churches into separate denominations outside white control. While twentieth-century white Presbyterians made strides toward new relationships with their black brothers and sisters, Murray observed that "it is evident that in the foreseeable future most American Negro Protestants will continue to be members of Negro denominations, rather than becoming a part of white denominations like the Presbyterian Church." Though he did not believe that the 1960s black power movement would ultimately prove attractive, Murray suggested that "the role of white denominations, like the Presbyterians, will probably be to identify themselves with the Negro's struggle for full equality and help him secure full participation in housing, jobs, and education."[11]

Southern Presbyterian historians, such as E. T. Thompson, tried to use their historiography to force their branch of the church to confront its poor

record on social issues. In particular, Thompson believed that southern Presbyterian commitments to the doctrine of the "spirituality of the church"—
the ideas that the church's mission is spiritual; that it should be restricted
to preaching the Bible and administering the sacraments; and, as a result,
that it should avoid proclamations on public matters, especially those dealing
with racial justice—were restricting the church from speaking prophetically
to contemporary culture in the American South. As a result, Thompson's historical work consistently highlighted the negative aspects of the spirituality
doctrine. In his little booklet *The Spirituality of the Church* (1961), Thompson
traced the antebellum debates over slavery and suggested that the spirituality
of the church doctrine was forged in that controversy; further, this doctrine
was preventing reunion with the northern church and cooperation with the
National Council of Churches, he held.[12]

Thompson expanded this argument in a massive, multivolume work, *Presbyterians in the South* (1963–1973). In his telling, southern Presbyterians' involvement in the national church prior to the Civil War helped shape the
way they viewed their calling and task after the war. In particular, the development of a defensive posture over slavery, the increasing attention to "divine right" Presbyterianism, and the preservation of Old School Calvinism
shaped southern Presbyterianism in ways that placed it in an intellectual
and cultural "backwater" by the start of the twentieth century. The catalyst
for change, for entering into the "mainstream," was a generation of young,
moderately liberal scholars like Thompson who were determined to open the
church to contemporary theological scholarship, move toward greater theological latitude, and engage in a prophetic call for social change. Thompson's
telling of southern Presbyterian progressivism matched the tone of Presbyterian historiography in the 1950s and early 1960s: as long as progressive change
was regulated by benevolent, moderate leadership, the identity of the church
as a mainline, moderating force and upholder of key American values would
continue to be preserved.[13]

Oldline

During the 1960s, as Presbyterian historians began to work toward models
that emphasized theological and cultural pluralism within the church, sociologists and historians were developing evidence that brought the value of
theological and cultural pluralism into question. In fact, the data seemed to
suggest that "fundamentalist" churches that pursued theological and ethical
particularity were growing, while the mainline churches experienced numerical decline. The most celebrated of these studies, Dean Kelley's *Why*

Conservative Churches Are Growing (1972), suggested that mainline churches were declining because they had capitulated to the standards of the American culture they were attempting to reach. Mainstream Presbyterians promoted a rational, democratic, ecumenical, and doctrinally tolerant faith, American values all; and yet, these values "are a recipe for the failure of the religious enterprise," Kelley concluded. Growing conservative churches, Kelley pointed out, stressed definitive belief systems, distinctive behavioral patterns with institutional discipline for transgressors, and demands for time commitments to local and international evangelism and missions.[14]

Several mainline Presbyterian defenders as well as other sociologists agreed with Kelley's diagnosis. One example came from John R. Fry, author of *The Trivialization of the United Presbyterian Church* (1975). Fry argued that the reason for the decline in the mainline Presbyterian Church was theological—it had failed to "attend to the requirements of faithfulness placed on a modern, complex, national ecclesiastical institution." Instead, it had focused its attention on denominational reorganization, ecumenical activity, and ecclesiastical merger with the southern Presbyterian Church in the United States (PCUS). Like Kelley, Fry approached these issues as a Presbyterian insider and challenged the church to take stronger theological stances to meet the challenge of the emerging culture instead of focusing on bureaucratic solutions. Another sociological analysis that drew attention to the growing division in northern Presbyterianism was Dean R. Hoge's *Division in the Protestant House* (1976). Perhaps the best exponent of the "two-party" approach to intrachurch conflict, Hoge recognized that there were theological as well as broader cultural and economic issues in the Presbyterian difficulties of the 1960s and 1970s.[15]

This type of sociological analysis reached its high point in Robert Wuthnow's *The Restructuring of American Religion* (1988). Profoundly influential both within the historical profession and among sociologists of religion, Wuthnow suggested that the period after the 1960s was one of "religious realignment," in which religious conservatives and liberals found greater commonalty with fellow believers across denominational lines than with each other inside the same denomination. For Presbyterians, as this conflict between conservatives and liberals played out within their denominational borders, there was a concurrent loss of denominational identity that produced the statistical decline upon which earlier sociologists had commented. This evidence, building from the early 1970s, that the loss of denominational identity and decline were related, continued to be affirmed by Dean Hoge's team of researchers in *Vanishing Boundaries* (1994). Studying baby boomers who grew up within mainline Presbyterianism, these researchers confirmed Kelley's description of "mainline Protestant denominations as weak" and supported his emphasis upon "the critical importance of *belief*—or 'meaning,' as he puts it—in creating and sustaining strong religious bodies." Because of its willingness to accommodate ranges of theological belief and religious practices, which in turn led to a decline in denominational identity, mainline Presbyterianism was becoming "oldline."[16]

The reaction of mainstream Presbyterian historians, theologians, and sociologists to this apparently incontrovertible evidence was to forge a historiography that embraced this pluralism as central for denominational identity. The seven volumes produced by the Lilly Endowment–funded Presbyterian Presence project made this case in great detail. Theologians Jack Rogers and Don McKim celebrated the fact that "when functioning in day-to-day policy making on matters where scripture might be invoked [twentieth-century] Presbyterians behaved pragmatically and appealed to pluralism." Likewise, historian James Moorhead observed that during the twentieth century, "Presbyterians were on the verge of redefining the nature of what it meant to be a confessional church." This redefinition centered on the fact that doctrinal statements "have functioned as general guidelines for religious discourse rather than as specific prescriptions for belief; and theology has assumed an increasingly ad hoc character." Theologian Edward Farley agreed, describing the Presbyterian approach to theology in terms of "critical modernism," which willingly modified the Westminster Confession's seventeenth-century Calvinism and incorporated a diversity of belief. Finally, historian Rick Nutt positioned the conservative secession from the PCUS that led to the founding of the Presbyterian Church in America as a reaction against the broadening, pluralistic approach of the denominational leadership.[17]

This pluralism was affirmed not only in the theological heritage of the church but also in its educational and organizational structures. Historians John Mulder and Lee Wyatt welcomed the moves in theological education away from "the theological scholasticism and doctrinal rigidity of the Presbyterian theology and subscription to the Westminster Standards alone." At the same time, they questioned whether the Presbyterian embrace of pluralism allowed creative options only on the theological left while avoiding positions on the theological right that would inform denominational life. While theological pluralism was affirmed, organizational unity may have been a higher value: in fact, as David McCarthy recognized, in times of theological crisis, the Presbyterian Church most often made recourse to an organizational solution. "If polity constitutes the means whereby Presbyterians adjudicate their theological differences, it is appropriate that polity should become more important in the face of increasing theological pluralism,"

McCarthy suggested. And while this is certainly the case, McCarthy's observation also confirmed what John Fry had argued two decades before—that modern-day Presbyterian identity was centered less on common belief than on organizational loyalty. Yet what remained unclear in the Presbyterian Presence series as a whole was whether "pluralism" could provide an adequate sense of identity that would in turn produce either Presbyterian faithfulness or historiography over the long haul.[18]

Two studies produced near the same time as the Presbyterian Presence series shed historical light on the issue of pluralism while providing insight into contemporary Presbyterianism. Importantly, both looked at the key moment in twentieth-century northern Presbyterianism, the 1920s fundamentalist-modernist controversy, and both suggested that the church opted for a centrist, moderate solution that affirmed a "competitive pluralism" while denying the extremes of either liberal or conservative dissent. While Bradley J. Longfield's *The Presbyterian Controversy* (1991) pointed up the problems that both J. Gresham Machen's Old School Presbyterianism and William Sloane Coffin's radical liberalism presented to the church, he also recognized that the willingness of the church's theological moderates to allow mission to trump theology unwittingly "contributed to the current identity crisis of the church and helped to undermine the foundation of the church's mission to the world." William J. Weston argued along similar lines in his *Presbyterian Pluralism: Competition in a Protestant House* (1997). According to Weston, the theological moderates of the 1920s successfully argued that the church's mission would be harmed by theological particularity. By demonstrating their loyalty to the church's organization and constitution, these moderates sanctified "competitive pluralism" in the church's life. However, in his epilogue, Weston also noted that though this was the result of the immediate conflict of the 1920s, the church since has avoided theological conversation in meaningful ways and so has experienced a loss of denominational identity and numerical decline.[19]

The Presbyterian Presence series was not the only attempt to place pluralism at the center of Presbyterian identity and, concomitantly, Presbyterian historiography. The historiography produced within the denomination's *Journal of Presbyterian History* also reflected this desire to reorient Presbyterian identity around a pluralist paradigm. While the journal demonstrated a remarkable breadth of historiography under the editorial leadership of James Smylie and now James Moorhead and Frederick J. Heuser Jr., it seems that a basic historiographical pattern emerged: as they looked to the past, Presbyterians found an essential pluralism that provided the basis for redefined confessionalism, denominational extension, and social justice. And so, throughout the period, Presbyterian historians studied events related to doctrinal rigidity or confessional openness. The historical moment that received the greatest study was the 1920s fundamentalist-modernist controversy.[20] Other essays focused on Presbyterians and biblical authority generally, the revolutionary theological effect of the northern Presbyterians' Confession of 1967, battles over scientific evolution and its relation to the biblical materials of Genesis, and recent appeals to confessional and biblical authority in the controversy over homosexuality.[21] The net effect of these essays was to chart the continued and increased theological "broadening" of the church and movement away from doctrinal particularity.

In addition, a number of essays in *JPH* outlined the ways Presbyterians expanded the denomination's influence across cultures and around the world in missionary activity. Sometimes these missions occurred in North America, as Presbyterian women and men ministered to Native Americans.[22] Other times Presbyterian historians focused on missions far from home—in Africa, Burma, China, Korea, India, Egypt, and Brazil.[23] This historical work tended to highlight little-known contributors and to recognize the Presbyterian faith's movement throughout the world. And yet, this extension of Presbyterianism to the majority of the world came with a price, both for the denomination itself and for historians: how does one reconcile the exclusivist Presbyterian faith with the enterprise of missions in a postcolonial world? An entire issue of the journal wrestled with this question from the perspective of historians and practitioners; and yet, it still was unclear how the pluralist paradigm could provide a satisfactory rationale for either the task of missions or history.[24]

Finally, historical studies published in *JPH* supported the denomination's twentieth-century emphasis upon social justice in the public sphere. Nowhere was this the case more obviously than in essays focused on race, gender, and class. Historiography studying issues related to racial justice tended to look more to the nineteenth than the twentieth century, and more at the problems for biblical conservatives than the work of social reformers; yet all got their due representation in the pages of *JPH*.[25] Gender issues most often were treated in historical essays that stressed the little-recognized and yet large role for women in the life of the church and, as a result, often implicitly or explicitly dealt with women's ordination.[26] Matters related to class were far less frequent, although essays could be found on capitalism's uneasy relationship to the church's teaching on universal depravity and redemptive justice.[27] And while there was a note of the old mainline confidence in American political liberalism, especially in the admiration of progressive heroes Woodrow

Wilson, John Foster Dulles, and Eugene Carson Blake, it was muted compared to past postwar triumphalism.[28]

While this survey of twenty-five years of *JPH* reveals an amazing diversity of scholarship, it also suggests that increasingly Presbyterians were having difficulty telling their own stories. As former editor Smylie noted, during his tenure, he sought to broaden the ecumenical focus of the journal, including articles on various Presbyterian and Reformed denominations as well as widening its inclusiveness to cover women and ethnic and racial minorities. And yet, the unintended consequence of this approach may well have been the loss of interest in Presbyterian history itself among mainline Presbyterians. While the diversity of scholarship in *JPH* and the Presbyterian Presence project has produced reams of paper, this work has not produced Presbyterian historiography that inculcates a coherent understanding of the church and its place in the world because it is rooted in a faulty paradigm. The upshot is a general loss of interest in doing Presbyterian historiography itself from within oldline Presbyterianism.[29]

It should become clear that the main theme of Presbyterian historiography since the disruption of the 1960s has focused explicitly and implicitly on the issue of denominational identity. Study after study focused on the church's increasing diversity of belief, which it attempted to paper over by stressing loyalty to institutional organizations. And yet, the repeated conclusion of both sociological and historical studies from the period was that the Presbyterian Church had entered a period of deep decline, moving from the center of American culture to a position of being "oldline." Not coincidentally, this decentering of religious identity also has led to the increasing evaporation of Presbyterian historiography.

Sideline

The one bright spot for the entire enterprise of Presbyterian historiography can be found in the renewal of American religious history and in the increasing dominance in that literature of the theme of "evangelicalism."[30] Associated especially with the work of the Institute for the Study of American Evangelicals at Wheaton College, this scholarship has returned the focus in American religious historiography to "mainline" Protestant denominations that were historically "evangelical" in orientation; as a result, some of the best work on Presbyterianism has come out of this movement. Oddly enough, in this renewed evangelical historiography, the contribution of three historians who have been or currently are affiliated with "sideline" Presbyterian churches was especially important. In the early 1970s, the work of George Marsden, who grew up in the Orthodox Presbyterian Church (OPC), an offshoot from the main northern Presbyterian body, helped set the course for future American religious historians. Marsden's *The Evangelical Mind and the New School Presbyterian Experience* (1970) not only suggested that New School Presbyterians were far more important to understanding twentieth-century American Protestant fundamentalism than commonly believed, but also outlined how Presbyterian theology operated within American culture. By allowing their faith to merge so closely with America, nineteenth-century Presbyterians became "firmly institutionalized . . . fast becoming synonymous with the middle class *status quo.*" In other words, while the traditional coziness between Presbyterianism and American culture may have granted the church a sense of cultural custodianship, Marsden's study raised the question of how high the cost was for Presbyterian faithfulness.[31]

Likewise, Mark Noll, a ruling elder in the Evangelical Presbyterian Church, another offshoot from the main northern Presbyterian body, has focused attention on distinctively Presbyterian topics. Of these, perhaps the most important was his *Princeton and the Republic, 1768–1822* (1989). Focusing on a transitional moment in the history of Presbyterianism, Princeton College, and the United States, Noll directed attention to the ways that the Scottish Enlightenment, mediated to America by John Witherspoon and his disciple Samuel Stanhope Smith, shaped and transformed both Presbyterian theology and American political ideology. Once again, the interchange between Presbyterianism and America was not at all positive for Presbyterian faithfulness: toward the end of his work, Noll asked "if the science of the Enlightenment, with its large claims for the human autonomy of perception and action, could ever rest comfortably with traditional Reformed Protestantism, given the Calvinistic vision of both divine mystery and intractable human sinfulness." And though he decided not to give an answer to his "material question," it seemed from the preceding study that the answer had to be negative.[32]

A third historian working within the broader theme of American evangelicalism who has contributed a great deal to Presbyterian historiography was D. G. Hart. Currently a ruling elder in the OPC, Hart first received notice for his *Defending the Faith* (1994), an intellectual biography of J. Gresham Machen, one of the protagonists in the fundamentalist controversy. Hart turned the relationship between doctrinal particularity and religious pluralism on its head, suggesting that while Machen desired the Presbyterian Church to be a doctrinally particular church, adhering closely to the Westminster Standards, he also defended religious freedom and cultural pluralism in American society. As a result, the relationship between Presbyterianism and American culture was far less continuous than Machen's contemporaries on the theological right or left understood. Hart pursued this theme further in his denominational history of the OPC, arguing that the identity of that church was shaped by its uneasy relationship with American culture: "it is more accurate to say that the OPC is committed to the 'irrelevance' of the world to the church." In his recent writing, including a new history of Presbyterianism in America, Hart continued to press the issue of Presbyterian identity in relationship to American culture, asking "whether being a religion of the affluent, successful, and powerful was supposed to be the point of being Presbyterian in America." How the American context affected that debate shows up in nearly every historical project Hart undertakes.[33]

Each of these historians raised the same question as their counterparts from within the mainline—namely, the relationship between Presbyterian identity and American culture—but answered in tones that were markedly different from the historians on either side of the 1960s divide. Instead of trumpeting mainline Presbyterians' contribution to American culture or questioning or justifying oldline Presbyterians' relevance to an increasingly pluralistic culture, Marsden, Noll, and Hart all wondered about the effects of American culture upon Presbyterian identity. And not coincidentally, all three have been motivated by this question to produce a large amount of historical writing and reflection upon that topic. Or, to put it in a different and more historical way, I think these historians' contribution can be found in their production of historical accounts that recognize both the contribution of and the potential difficulties for religious commitments as they operate within cultural systems.[34]

By developing a thick description of how religion—in this case, Presbyterianism—interacts with other beliefs and practices, symbols, and stories to forge a conception of religious identity, religious historians can recognize and describe sensitively how religion sanctifies beliefs and practices seemingly at odds with its best insights even as it offers real contributions in other ways. And strikingly, some of the best contemporary "Presbyterian historiography" was produced when the Presbyterian faith was viewed as part of a larger, more complex, cultural system. For example, historian Erskine Clarke offered an example of the way forward in *Wrestlin' Jacob* (1979) and *Dwelling Place* (2005). In the earlier book, Clarke described the intersections between black and white religion in the country and city through the ministries of Charles Colcock Jones and his fellow Presbyterian minister John L. Girardeau; as both tried to win black slaves to Christianity, these Presbyterians found their faith transmuted in ways that they neither recognized nor endorsed. In the later book, Clarke traced four generations of the Jones family, both white and black, in order to understand the ways that race, region, and the Presbyterian religion formed master and slave alike. Both books demonstrate that historical writing that situates Presbyterianism within the complex cultural exchanges that characterize life in this world actually moves both Presbyterianism and our understanding of it forward in significant ways.[35]

And so, the worldview of controversial figures, such as the redoubtable and angry southern Presbyterian theologian Robert Lewis Dabney, can be meaningfully explored even when historians are repulsed by their rank racism and harsh commitment to gender hierarchy. Likewise, the interrelationship between twentieth-century religion, politics, and race in the PCUS could serve as a worthwhile topic because it raises questions about what constitutes faithful Presbyterian identity within the particular context of the American South. In other words, what is needed for the renewal of Presbyterian historiography is a commitment to both the belief and a method that stresses that these denominations, which represent Presbyterianism, really are "the Presbyterian Church *in* America." Only as historians pay attention to the positive *and* negative aspects of the interchange between Presbyterian identity and a particular American cultural context will we find new stories that will grant wisdom and insight for Presbyterian believers in our postmodern age. Only as historians model a certain embodiment, an entanglement in these larger, messy cultural systems, will we be used to motivate others to tell these stories well.[36]

Notes

1. On the three-hundredth anniversary of the first American presbytery, see *Journal of Presbyterian History* 84, no. 1 (2006). After the initial draft of this essay was completed, one collection of essays to commemorate the anniversary was produced: S. Donald Fortson III, ed., *Colonial Presbyterianism: Old Faith in a New Land* (Eugene, OR: Pickwick, 2007). On the closing of Montreat as a branch of the PC (USA) Department of History, see http://www.pcusa.org/ga217/newsandphotos/ga06127.htm. My assertion about "Presbyterian historians" on PC (USA) seminary faculties is based on a survey of Web sites done in fall 2006: of the twenty-seven identifiable church history professors at the eleven PC (USA) seminaries, only seven (counted generously) have written books on some aspect of American Presbyterian history (considered generously). It should also be noted that the *Journal of Presbyterian History* devoted an entire issue to the difficulties of Presbyterian denominational historiography in a "post-denominational age": see *Journal of Presbyterian History* 79 (2001): 181–238.

2. See Sean Michael Lucas, *On Being Presbyterian: Our Beliefs, Practices, and Stories* (Phillipsburg, NJ: P&R, 2006).

3. James H. Moorhead, "Redefining Confessionalism: American Presbyterians in the Twentieth Century," in *The Confessional Mosaic: Presbyterians and Twentieth-Century Theology,* ed. Milton J. Coalter, John M. Mulder, and Louis B. Weeks (Louisville: Westminster John Knox, 1990), 83; Martin Marty, *Modern American Religion,* vol. 3, *Under God, Indivisible, 1941–1960* (Chicago: University of Chicago Press, 1996).

4. Rick Nutt, "The Tie That No Longer Binds: The Origins of the Presbyterian Church in America," in Coalter, Mulder, and Weeks, *Confessional Mosaic,* 236–56; Bryan V. Hillis, *Can Two Walk Together Unless They Be Agreed? American Religious Schisms in the 1970s* (Brooklyn: Carlson, 1991); Robert Wuthnow, *The Restructuring of American Religion* (Princeton: Princeton University Press, 1988). There are several insider accounts of the PCUS division that are of limited value; the best may be Frank J. Smith, *The History of the Presbyterian Church in America: Silver Anniversary Edition* (Lawrenceville, GA: Presbyterian Scholars, 1999).

The volumes produced in the Presbyterian Presence series, edited by Milton J. Coalter, John M. Mulder, and Louis B. Weeks (and all published in Louisville, Kentucky, by Westminster John Knox Press), are: *Confessional Mosaic; The Presbyterian Predicament: Six Perspectives* (1990); *The Mainstream Protestant "Decline": The Presbyterian Pattern* (1990); *The Diversity of Discipleship: The Presbyterians and Twentieth-Century Witness* (1991); *The Pluralistic Vision: Presbyterians and Mainstream Protestant Education and Leadership* (1992); *The Organizational Revolution: Presbyterians and American Denominationalism* (1992); *The Re-forming Tradition: Presbyterians and Mainstream Protestantism* (1992).

5. One of the classic books for describing the various theories of assimilation is Milton M. Gordon, *Assimilation in American Life: The Role of Race, Religion, and National Origins* (New York: Oxford University Press, 1964). On this paragraph, see also, e.g., William B. Miller, "Presbyterian Signers of the Declaration of Independence," *Journal of the Presbyterian Historical Society* 36 (1958): 139–80; Ralph L. Ketcham, "James Madison and Religion—A New Hypothesis," *Journal of the Presbyterian Historical Society* 38 (1960): 65–90; Paul F. Boller Jr., "George Washington and the Presbyterians," *Journal of Presbyterian History* 39 (1961): 129–46; Richard M. Gummere, "Samuel Davies: Classical Champion of Religious Freedom," *Journal of Presbyterian History* 40 (1962): 67–74.

6. Leonard J. Trinterud, *The Forming of an American Tradition: A Re-examination of Colonial Presbyterianism* (Philadelphia: Westminster, 1949), 308. Trinterud's stance on how creeds should function was fitting since he was one of the main writers of the United Presbyterian Church's Confession of 1967; see John Wilkinson, "Edward A. Dowey, Jr., and the Making of the Confession of 1967," *Journal of Presbyterian History* 82 (2004): 5–22.

7. Lefferts A. Loetscher, *The Broadening Church: A Study of Theological Issues in the Presbyterian Church since 1869* (Philadelphia: University of Pennsylvania Press, 1954), 155–56. A similar point was made in Dallas M. Roark, "J. Gresham Machen: The Doctrinally True Presbyterian Church," *Journal of Presbyterian History* 43 (1965): 124–38, 174–81.

8. Lefferts A. Loetscher, "The Problem of Christian Unity in Early Nineteenth Century America," *Church History* 32 (1963): 3–16.

9. The *Journal of Presbyterian History* has operated under different names during its existence. Until 1961, it was called the *Journal of the Presbyterian Historical Society*. From 1961 to 1985, it was known as the *Journal of Presbyterian History;* for eleven years (1985–96), it operated under the title *American Presbyterians: Journal of Presbyterian History*. When new editors came on board in 1997, they changed the title back to its present *Journal of Presbyterian History* (hereafter *JPH* in the notes).

10. E. T. Thompson, "Presbyterians North and South—Efforts toward Reunion," *JPH* 43 (1965): 1–15; Herman Harmelink III, "The Ecumenical Relations of the Reformed Church in America," *JPH* 45 (1967): 71–94.

11. Andrew E. Murray, *Presbyterians and the Negro—A History* (Philadelphia: Presbyterian Historical Society, 1966), 240.

12. E. T. Thompson, *The Spirituality of the Church: A Distinctive Doctrine of the Presbyterian Church in the United States* (Richmond: John Knox, 1961). As noted, Thompson was a key protagonist in the shaping of southern Presbyterian liberalism; for the definitive study of his life, see Peter H. Hobbie, "Ernest Trice Thompson: Prophet for a Changing South" (Ph.D. diss., Union Theological Seminary and Presbyterian School of Christian Education, 1987). For a southern Presbyterian teaching as important as "the spirituality of the church," surprisingly little has been written about it: see Jack P. Maddex, "From Theocracy to Spirituality: The Southern Presbyterian Reversal on Church and State," *JPH* 54 (1976): 438–57; Preston D. Graham Jr., *A Kingdom Not of This World: Stuart Robinson's Struggle to Distinguish the Sacred from the Secular during the Civil War* (Macon: Mercer University Press, 2002); and D. G. Hart, *Recovering Mother Kirk: The Case for Liturgy in the Reformed Tradition* (Grand Rapids, MI: Baker, 2003), 51–65.

13. E. T. Thompson, *Presbyterians in the South*, 3 vols. (Richmond: John Knox, 1963–73). While Thompson's work is undeniably magisterial, it has not been beyond criticism: see John W. Kuykendall, "*Presbyterians in the South*, Revisited—A Critique," *JPH* 61 (1983): 445–60.

14. Dean Kelley, *Why Conservative Churches Are Growing: A Study in the Sociology of Religion* (New York: Harper, 1972), vii–viii.

15. John R. Fry, *The Trivialization of the United Presbyterian Church* (New York: Harper, 1975), viii; Dean R. Hoge, *Division in the Protestant House: The Basic Reasons Behind Intra-Church Conflicts* (Philadelphia: Westminster, 1976). In research commis-

sioned by the United Presbyterian Church focusing on a six-year period between 1968 and 1974, Wade Clark Roof and his researchers suggested that "among Presbyterians, at least, theologically conservative congregations are not growing appreciably more than are liberal congregations"; however, the hypotheses never adequately defined "conservative" or "liberal" in ways that could challenge or confirm Kelley's work (see Wade Clark Roof, Dean R. Hoge, John E. Dyble, and C. Kirk Hardaway, "Factors Producing Growth or Decline in United Presbyterian Congregations," in *Understanding Church Growth and Decline, 1950–1978*, ed. Dean R. Hoge and David A. Roozen [New York: Pilgrim, 1979], 198–223).

16. Wuthnow, *Restructuring of American Religion*, 132–72; Robert Wuthnow, "The Restructuring of American Presbyterianism: Turmoil in One Denomination," in *Presbyterian Predicament*, 27–48; Dean R. Hoge, Benton Johnson, and Donald A. Luidens, *Vanishing Boundaries: The Religion of Mainline Protestant Baby Boomers* (Louisville: Westminster John Knox, 1994), 181.

17. Jack B. Rogers and Donald K. McKim, "Pluralism and Policy in Presbyterian Views of Scripture," in *Confessional Mosaic*, 58; Moorhead, "Redefining Confessionalism," 60; Edward Farley, "The Presbyterian Heritage as Modernism: Reaffirming a Forgotten Past in Hard Times," in *Presbyterian Predicament*, 54–61; Nutt, "The Tie That No Longer Binds," 254.

18. John M. Mulder and Lee A. Wyatt, "The Predicament of Pluralism: The Study of Theology in Presbyterian Seminaries since the 1920s," in *Pluralistic Vision*, 67; David B. McCarthy, "The Emerging Importance of Presbyterian Polity," in *Organizational Revolution*, 302–3. Religious pluralism as a historiographical theme (and value) also received important treatment in William R. Hutchison, *Religious Pluralism in America: The Contentious History of a Founding Ideal* (New Haven: Yale University Press, 2003).

19. Bradley J. Longfield, *The Presbyterian Controversy: Fundamentalists, Modernists, and Moderates* (New York: Oxford University Press, 1991), 234–35; William J. Weston, *Presbyterian Pluralism: Competition in a Protestant House* (Knoxville: University of Tennessee Press, 1997), esp. 123–39. Weston himself has been an advocate for a particular approach to Presbyterian identity; see William J. Weston, *Leading from the Center: Strengthening the Pillars of the Church* (Louisville: Geneva, 2003). Historian D. G. Hart criticized both Longfield's and Weston's work in separate review essays: see Hart, "Presbyterians and Fundamentalism," *Westminster Theological Journal* 55 (1993): 331–42, and "Somewhere between Denial and Conspiracy: Explaining What Happened to the PCUSA," *Westminster Theological Journal* 61 (1999): 247–68.

20. John W. Hart, "Princeton Theological Seminary: The Reorganization of 1929," *JPH* 58 (1980): 124–41; James A. Patterson, "Robert E. Speer, J. Gresham Machen, and the Presbyterian Board of Foreign Missions," *JPH* 64 (1986): 58–68; Paul C. Kemeny, "Princeton and the Premillennialists: The Roots of the *mariage de covenance*," *JPH*

71 (1993): 17–30; D. G. Hart, "Fundamentalism, Inerrancy, and the Biblical Scholarship of J. Gresham Machen," *JPH* 75 (1997): 13–28; Bradley J. Longfield, "For Church and Country: The Fundamentalist-Modernist Conflict in the Presbyterian Church," *JPH* 78 (2000): 35–50. Perhaps the best series of articles, which focused on key fundamentalist players from this era, was produced by C. Allyn Russell, who would later collect them in his *Voices of American Fundamentalism: Seven Biographical Studies* (Philadelphia: Westminster, 1976).

21. Jack B. Rogers, "Biblical Authority and Confessional Change," *JPH* 59 (1981): 131–60; Randall H. Balmer, "The Princetonians, Scripture, and Recent Scholarship," *JPH* 60 (1982): 267–71; the Confession of 1967 is treated in *JPH* 61 (1983): 1–196; Win Winship, "Oren Root, Darwinism, and Biblical Criticism," *JPH* 62 (1984): 111–24; L. Gordon Tait, "Evolution: Wishart, Wooster, and William Jennings Bryan," *JPH* 62 (1984): 306–21; Jonathan Wells, "Charles Hodge on the Bible and Science," *JPH* 66 (1988): 157–66; Bradley J. Gundlach, "McCosh and Hodge on Evolution: A Combined Legacy," *JPH* 75 (1997): 85–102; Fred W. Beuttler, "Making Theology Matter: Power, Polity, and the Theological Debate over Homosexual Ordination in the Presbyterian Church (USA)," *JPH* 79 (2001): 5–22; Paul E. Capetz, "Defending the Reformed Tradition? Problematic Aspects of the Appeal to Biblical and Confessional Authority in the Present Theological Crisis Confronting the Presbyterian Church (USA)," *JPH* 79 (2001): 23–39; David N. Livingstone and Mark A. Noll, "B. B. Warfield (1851–1921): A Biblical Inerrantist as Evolutionist," *JPH* 80 (2002): 153–71.

22. Sister Claire Lynch, "William Thurston Boutwell and the Chippewas," *JPH* 58 (1980): 239–54; Mark T. Banker, "Presbyterians and Pueblos: A Protestant Response to the Indian Question, 1872–1892," *JPH* 60 (1982): 23–41; George E. Lankford, "Trouble at Dancing Rabbit Creek: Missionaries and Choctaw Removal," *JPH* 62 (1984): 51–66; Edgar W. Moore, "The Kierkempers, Navajos, and the Ganado Presbyterian Mission, 1901–1912," *JPH* 64 (1986): 125–35; Stephen Valone, "Samuel Kirkland, Iroquois Missions, and the Land, 1764–1774," *JPH* 65 (1987): 187–94; Keith R. Widder, "The Missionaries of the Mackinaw Mission, 1823–1837: Presbyterians and Congregationalists on the American Frontier," *JPH* 67 (1989): 273–82. Missions among Native Americans were the focus of an entire issue: *JPH* 77 (1999): 141–206.

23. John R. Crawford, "Pioneer African Missionary: Samuel Phillips Verner," *JPH* 60 (1982): 42–58; Herbert R. Sawnson, "The Kengtung Question: Presbyterian Mission and Comity in Eastern Burma, 1896–1913," *JPH* 60 (1982): 59–80; Loren W. Crabtree, "Andrew P. Happer and Presbyterian Missions in China, 1844–1891," *JPH* 62 (1984): 19–34; Michael V. Metallo, "Presbyterian Missionaries and the 1911 Chinese Revolution," *JPH* 62 (1984): 153–68; Ralph R. Covell, "God's Footprints in China: W. A. P. Martin and Interfaith Dialogue," *JPH* 71 (1993): 233–42; G. Thompson Brown, "Through Fire and Sword: Presbyterians and the Boxer Year in North China," *JPH* 78 (2000): 193–206; Stephen G. Craft, "American Isaiah in China: Frank W. Price, Chiang

Kai-Shek, and Reforming China, 1941–49," *JPH* 82 (2004): 180–203; Wi Jo Kang, "The Presbyterians and the Japanese in Korea," *JPH* 62 (1984): 35–50; Stanley H. Skrestlet II, "The American Presbyterian Mission in Egypt: Significant Factors in Its Establishment," *JPH* 64 (1986): 83–96; Robert Benedetto, "The Presbyterian Mission Press in Central Africa, 1890–1922," *JPH* 68 (1990): 55–72; David C. Etheridge, "Educational Ministry in Brazil: The Potent Agency of Samuel Rhea Gammon," *American Presbyterians* 72 (1994): 23–32; Frank L. Arnold, "From Sending Church to Partner Church: The Brazil Experience," *JPH* 81 (2003): 178–92. An entire issue of *JPH* was dedicated to missions in India: see *JPH* 62 (1984): 189–282; another issue was dedicated to missions more generally: see *JPH* 65 (1987): 71–170.

24. See *JPH* 81 (2003): 77–118.

25. Andrew E. Murray, "Bright Delusion: Presbyterians and African Colonization," *JPH* 58 (1980): 224–37; James H. Smylie, "The Bible, Race, and the Changing South," *JPH* 59 (1981): 197–218; R. Milton Winter, "James A. Lyon: Southern Presbyterian Apostle of Progress," *JPH* 60 (1982): 314–35; Robert Bruce Mullin, "Biblical Critics and the Battle over Slavery," *JPH* 61 (1983): 210–26; Peter J. Wallace, "The Defense of the Forgotten Center: Charles Hodge and the Enigma of Emancipation in Antebellum America," *JPH* 75 (1997): 165–78; Jewel L. Spangler, "Proslavery Presbyterians: Virginia's Conservative Dissenters in the Age of Revolution," *JPH* 78 (2000): 111–24; Stephen Haynes, "Race, National Destiny, and the Sons of Noah in the Thought of Benjamin M. Palmer," *JPH* 78 (2000): 125–44; Vivien Sandlund, "Robert Breckinridge, Presbyterian Antislavery Conservative," *JPH* 78 (2000): 145–54. For twentieth-century reflections on race, see John F. Piper Jr., "Robert E. Speer on Christianity and Race," *JPH* 61 (1983): 227–47.

26. R. Douglas Brackenridge, "Equality for Women? A Case Study in Presbyterian Polity," *JPH* 58 (1980): 142–65; Page Putnam Miller, "Women in the Vanguard of the Sunday School Movement," *JPH* 58 (1980): 311–25; Mary Faith Carson and James J. H. Price, "The Ordination of Women and the Function of the Bible," *JPH* 59 (1981): 245–66; R. Douglas Brackenridge and Lois A. Boyd, "United Presbyterian Policy on Women and the Church—An Historical Overview," *JPH* 59 (1981): 383–407; Rick Nutt, "Robert Lewis Dabney, Presbyterians, and Women's Suffrage," *JPH* 62 (1984): 339–53; Carol Lakey Hess and Estelle Roundtree McCarthy, "A Life Lived in Response: Rachel Henderlite, Christian Educator, Advocate for Justice, Ecumenist, and First Woman Ordained in the PCUS," *JPH* 69 (1991): 133–44; Frederick J. Heuser Jr., "Presbyterian Women and the Missionary Call, 1870–1923," *American Presbyterians* 73 (1995): 23–34. Two entire issues were dedicated to women in the life of the church: see *JPH* 65 (1987): 1–60; and 68 (1990): 221–85. Women were first ordained as ministers of Word and Sacrament in the northern UPCUSA in 1956 and the southern PCUS in 1964.

27. Gary S. Smith, "The Spirit of Calvinism Revisited: Calvinists in the Industrial Revolution," *JPH* 59 (1981): 481–97; David Murchie, "Charles Hodge and Jacksonian

Economics," *JPH* 61 (1983): 248–56; Douglas Firth Anderson, "Presbyterians and the Golden Rule: The Christian Socialism of J. E. Scott," *JPH* 67 (1989): 231–43; Gary S. Smith, "Conservative Presbyterians: The Gospel, Social Reform, and the Church in the Progressive Era," *JPH* 70 (1992): 93–110.

28. Simon P. Newman, "The Hegelism Roots of Woodrow Wilson's Progressivism," *JPH* 64 (1986): 191–202; Arthur S. Link, "The Higher Realism of Woodrow Wilson," *JPH* 76 (1998): 151–58; Mark G. Toulouse, "Working toward Meaningful Peace: John Foster Dulles and the FCC, 1937–1945," *JPH* 61 (1983): 393–410; Mark G. Toulouse, "The Development of a Cold Warrior: John Foster Dulles and the Soviet Union, 1945–1952," *JPH* 63 (1985): 309–22; Monroe Billington and Cal Clark, "Presbyterian Clergy and the New Deal," *JPH* 64 (1987): 249–58; R. Douglas Brackenridge, "'A Beginning Has Been Made': Eugene Carson Blake and the Soviet Union, 1956," *JPH* 68 (1990): 89–98. An entire issue was devoted to Blake's legacy: *JPH* 76 (1998): 251–316.

29. James H. Smylie, "American Presbyterians—*Journal of Presbyterian History*: Continuity and Change, 1902–1992," *American Presbyterians* 70 (1992): 67–68; Virginia F. Rainey, *Stewards of Our Heritage: A History of the Presbyterian Historical Society* (Louisville: Geneva, 2002). A brief survey of dissertations published between 2000 and 2006 bears this out. Only the following would qualify as serious historical investigations of some aspect of Presbyterian history: Anthony Blair, "Fire across the Water: Transatlantic Dimensions of the Great Awakening among Middle-Colony Presbyterians" (Ph.D. diss., Temple University, 2000); Jeffery Charles Burke, "The Establishment of the American Presbyterian Mission in Egypt, 1854–1940: An Overview" (Ph.D. diss., McGill University, 2000); Daniel J. Earheart-Brown, "Baptism in the Theologies of Horace Bushnell, Charles Hodge, and J. W. Nevin" (Ph.D. diss., Union Theological Seminary and Presbyterian School of Christian Education, 2000); Sean Michael Lucas, "'Hold Fast That Which Is Good': The Public Theology of Robert Lewis Dabney" (Ph.D. diss., Westminster Theological Seminary, 2002); Deborah Flemister Mullen, "Bound Together in Christ's Name? United Presbyterians and Racial Justice, 1967–1972" (Ph.D. diss, University of Chicago, 2003); David Torbett, "Theology and Slavery: Charles Hodge and Horace Bushnell on the Slavery Question" (Ph.D. diss., Union Theological Seminary and Presbyterian School of Christian Education, 2002); Peter J. Wallace, "The Bond of Union: The Old School Presbyterian Church and the American Nation, 1837–1861" (Ph.D. diss., University of Notre Dame, 2004).

30. This use of "evangelicalism" as a historical construct has not been entirely positive: see, for example, D. G. Hart, *Deconstructing Evangelicalism: Conservative Protestantism in the Age of Billy Graham* (Grand Rapids, MI: Baker, 2004).

31. George M. Marsden, "My OPC Upbringing," *New Horizons* 27, no. 6 (2006): 6–7, 11; George M. Marsden, *The Evangelical Mind and the New School Presbyterian Experience* (New Haven: Yale University Press, 1970), 241. Marsden teased out the connec-

tions between New School Presbyterianism and American fundamentalism in "The New School Heritage and Presbyterian Fundamentalism," *Westminster Theological Journal* 32 (1970): 129-47. Presbyterians also factored largely in his *Fundamentalism and American Culture: The Shaping of Twentieth Century Evangelicalism, 1870–1925* (New York: Oxford University Press, 1980).

32. Mark A. Noll, *Princeton and the Republic, 1768–1822: The Search for a Christian Enlightenment in the Era of Samuel Stanhope Smith* (Princeton: Princeton University Press, 1989), 294. Noll also traced this argument in "The Irony of the Enlightenment for Presbyterians in the Early Republic," *Journal of the Early Republic* 5 (1985): 150-75. He would extend the argument he made in these works to encompass colonial and antebellum American theology more generally in *America's God: From Jonathan Edwards to Abraham Lincoln* (New York: Oxford University Press, 2002).

Noll has also devoted a great deal of attention to other Presbyterian topics. For example, on Princeton theology: see Mark A. Noll, ed., *The Princeton Theology, 1812–1921: Scripture, Science, and Theological Method from Archibald Alexander to B. B. Warfield,* 2nd ed. (Grand Rapids, MI: Baker, 2001); Livingstone and Noll, "B. B. Warfield: A Biblical Inerrantist as Evolutionist"; Charles Hodge, *What Is Darwinism? And Other Writings on Science and Religion,* ed. Mark A. Noll and David N. Livingstone (Grand Rapids, MI: Baker, 1994); B. B. Warfield, *Evolution, Science, and Scripture: Selected Writings,* ed. Mark A. Noll and David N. Livingstone (Grand Rapids, MI: Baker, 2000). On Presbyterian devotional theology: Mark A. Noll, "A Precarious Balance: Two Hundred Years of Presbyterian Devotional Literature," *American Presbyterians* 60 (1990): 207-19; Mark A. Noll, "Charles Hodge as an Expositor of the Spiritual Life," in *Charles Hodge Revisited: A Critical Appraisal of His Life and Work,* ed. John W. Stewart and James H. Moorhead (Grand Rapids, MI: Eerdmans, 2002), 181-216; Charles Hodge, *The Way of Life and Other Writings,* ed. Mark A. Noll (New York: Paulist, 1987).

33. D. G. Hart, *Defending the Faith: J. Gresham Machen and the Crisis of Conservative Protestantism in Modern America* (Baltimore: Johns Hopkins University Press, 1994); D. G. Hart and John Muether, *Fighting the Good Fight: A Brief History of the Orthodox Presbyterian Church* (Philadelphia: OPC, 1995), 191; D. G. Hart and John Muether, *Seeking a Better Country: 300 Years of American Presbyterianism* (Phillipsburg, NJ: P&R, 2007), 2. These basic themes also show up in his *The Lost Soul of American Protestantism* (Lanham, MD: Rowman and Littlefield, 2002).

Like Noll, Hart has written widely on Presbyterian topics: on the limits of Presbyterian ecumenism, "J. Gresham Machen, Confessional Presbyterianism, and the History of Twentieth Century Protestantism," in *Re-forming the Center: American Protestantism, 1900 to the Present,* ed. Douglas Jacobsen and William Vance Trollinger Jr. (Grand Rapids, MI: Eerdmans, 1998), 129-49; "The Tie That Divides: Presbyterian Ecumenism, Fundamentalism, and the History of Twentieth-Century American

Protestantism," *Westminster Theological Journal* 60 (1998): 85–107; on the contribution of J. Gresham Machen, "J. Gresham Machen, Inerrancy, and Creedless Christianity," *Themelios* 25, no. 3 (2000): 20–34; "When Is a Fundamentalist a Modernist? J. Gresham Machen, Cultural Modernism, and Conservative Protestantism," *Journal of the American Academy of Religion* 65 (1997): 605–33; "Christianity, Modern Liberalism, and J. Gresham Machen," *Modern Age* 39 (1997): 233–45; "J. Gresham Machen, the Reformed Tradition, and the Transformation of Culture," *Evangelical Quarterly* 68 (1996): 305–27; on the "spirituality of the church" doctrine and Presbyterian worship, *Recovering Mother Kirk: The Case for Liturgy in the Reformed Tradition* (Grand Rapids, MI: Baker, 2003). Hart has also edited an important resource, *Dictionary of the Presbyterian and Reformed Tradition in America* (Downers Grove, IL: Intervarsity, 1999).

34. See Clifford Geertz, *The Interpretation of Cultures* (New York: Basic, 1973). Not coincidentally, both Noll and Hart have served on the editorial board of the *Journal of Presbyterian History* for a number of years.

35. Erskine Clarke, *Wrestlin' Jacob: A Portrait of Religion in Antebellum Georgia and the Carolina Low Country* (1979; repr., Tuscaloosa: University of Alabama Press, 2000); Erskine Clarke, *Dwelling Place: A Plantation Epic* (New Haven: Yale University Press, 2005). It is important to recognize that Clarke is professor of American religious history at Columbia Theological Seminary, an institution of the PC (USA). Nevertheless, it has been among historians of the American South where "Presbyterian historiography" has experienced the greatest renaissance: see, for example, Christine Leigh Heyrman, *Southern Cross: The Beginnings of the Bible Belt* (New York: Knopf, 1997); James O. Farmer, *The Metaphysical Confederacy: James Henley Thornwell and the Synthesis of Southern Values* (Macon: Mercer University Press, 1986); and the numerous books by Eugene Genovese and Elizabeth Fox-Genovese, especially their magisterial *The Mind of the Master Class: History and Faith in the Slaveholders' Worldview* (New York: Cambridge University Press, 2005). Often, insights about Presbyterianism are secondary to the larger historical concerns represented in these works.

36. See, for example, Sean Michael Lucas, *Robert Lewis Dabney: A Southern Presbyterian Life* (Phillipsburg, NJ: P&R, 2005); and Sean Michael Lucas, *For a Continuing Church: Southern Presbyterians and Fundamentalism, 1934–74* (forthcoming).

4

From the Margin to the Middle to Somewhere In Between

An Overview of American Baptist Historiography

Keith Harper

"History is a problem for Baptists." So says J. Gordon Melton in the sixth edition of the *Encyclopedia of American Religions,* and when the issue is measured by any objective standard, it is apparent he is right. The *Handbook of Denominations in the United States* lists thirty-one different types of Baptists, while Melton's *Encyclopedia* identifies some sixty different North American Baptist groups, not counting the Christian Church and its related traditions, which he identifies with the Baptist family. These sundry Baptists claim no single theological tradition; they share no common creed. They have no long-standing ties to any specific institution. They are fiercely independent, but they will readily associate with whomever they choose. Perhaps Walter B. Shurden put it best when he said, "Baptists do not agree on where they came from, who they are, or how they got that way. In other words, Baptists do not agree on their historical origins, their theological identity, or their subsequent denominational identity."[1]

If conceptualizing Baptist history is a chore, assessing the course of Baptist historiography is no less difficult. This essay will focus on select works that chart the way historians have interpreted the Baptist experience in the United States. There are hundreds of works that address some aspect of Baptist life in America, many biographical. While biographies are excellent ways to investigate how individuals meet social, political, and theological challenges, space forbids their inclusion in this essay. Neither will this essay include textbook treatments of Baptist history. The literature cited herein, however, suggests a clear trajectory. America's Baptists began on society's fringe, they moved slowly to the mainstream, and they are now somewhere between the two.

Early Studies

In the early seventeenth century most people viewed Baptists as little more than a despicable sect. They were often persecuted, and their earliest chroniclers were eager both to tell the world of their struggles against the established order and to use incidents of persecution to call for freedom of conscience. America's first Baptist, Roger Williams, wrote prolifically, but it was two works—*The Bloudy Tenent of Persecution* and *The Bloody Tenent Yet More Bloody,* both decrying the mistreatment dissenters received from Bay Colony Puritans—that forever secured his position as America's prophet for liberty of conscience.[2]

Williams also set the tone for subsequent treatises. John Clarke's *Ill News from New England* underscored Williams's complaints with his graphic account of Obadiah Holmes's beating for preaching contrary to established order. Holmes's ordeal was not an isolated incident, and persecution remained the central theme of Baptist writings until the early twentieth century.

Considering such persecution, it is tempting to see Roger Williams as a champion of personal liberty as understood within contemporary liberal parameters. However, Williams was neither a political theorist nor an anarchist. As James P. Byrd explains in *The Challenges of Roger Williams: Religious Liberty, Violent Persecution, and the Bible,* Williams was a theologian who framed his political thought around biblical texts. While some studies may have demythologized aspects of Williams's career, Byrd reminds readers that whatever else Roger Williams may have been, he was staunchly committed to biblicism.[3]

Over time Baptists gained a toehold in North America, but for many they remained a loathsome, sometimes persecuted sect. The middle colonies, especially Pennsylvania and New Jersey, proved fairly hospitable for Baptists, and like-minded congregations ultimately formed associations for fellowship and mutual encouragement. The best-known association, the Philadelphia Association, began in 1707. The association's *Minutes* offer a glimpse of the way some Baptists conducted their business in the late colonial and revolutionary eras.[4]

Baptists may have rejected state authority in religious matters, but they were not ultraindividualistic libertarians. Francis Sacks's *The Philadelphia Baptist Tradition of Church and Church Authority: An Ecumenical Analysis and Theological Interpretation* argues that the Philadelphia Association wielded considerable influence over member churches. He also maintains that the Philadelphia Association differentiated between "association" and "council." Whereas the association existed to promote fellowship and harmony, the council carried more clout. The association was an ongoing entity that called councils to address specific issues like ministerial ordination or disputes between churches. A council decision, while not infallible, was more than advisory. He concludes by noting that Baptists in the late twentieth century tended to be far less "connectional" than their Philadelphia forebearers. Thus, Baptists in early America practiced congregational church government that allowed for a "soft centralization." That is, churches conducted their own business at the congregational level, but associational church councils spoke with a measure of authority in an effort to maintain purity of faith and practice.[5]

Associations welcomed others of "like faith and order." By 1765 there was a sufficient number of Baptists for Morgan Edwards, a prominent pastor from Philadelphia, to begin thinking about Baptist history in narrative terms. Considered by many to be the first historian of American Baptists, Edwards wanted to write a comprehensive history that would identify fellow Baptists and promote unity throughout the continent. Edwards did not complete his task, but he did collect and publish *Materials toward a Baptist History*. While he did not ignore persecution, Edwards's *Materials* differs from earlier treatments because it focuses on identifying Baptist preachers and congregations scattered throughout colonial America. Edwards's *Materials* and the *Minutes of the Philadelphia Baptist Association,* his "home" association, suggest that by the mid- to late eighteenth century American Baptists were strongly associational. They worked cooperatively to start churches, and they generally enjoyed a far-reaching fellowship throughout the eighteenth century.[6]

Tensions between authority and structure became apparent during the Great Awakening. If some Baptists adopted "soft centralization" to define power and set the proper bounds of ecclesiastical authority beyond individual congregations, the Great Awakening forced them to consider it all the more carefully. Granted, some scholars question whether there was an "awakening," but eighteenth-century revivalism led to schism in American churches, and Baptists, while not significant participants in the awakening itself, benefited from its results.

Two works focus on the Separate Baptists in the Great Awakening. William Lumpkin's *Baptist Foundations in the South: Tracing through the Separates the Influences of the Great Awakening, 1754–1787* argues that Separate Baptists brought the awakening's revivalism to the South, provided religious leadership to the frontier, and offered a less structured, more emotional alternative to either the staunchly Calvinistic Regular Baptists or the Anglican establishment. While it is informative, Lumpkin's work is based largely on secondary sources and lacks the analytical edge that C. C. Goen's *Revivalism and Sepa-*

ratism in New England, 1740–1800: Strict Congregationalists and Separatist Baptists in the Great Awakening possesses. *Revivalism and Separatism* remains the standard treatment of Separatism and the Great Awakening. Goen maintains that revival preaching did more than win converts; it revived the quest to establish purpose and church purity. Thus, the Great Awakening influenced Baptists *ecclesiologically,* a point Goen makes abundantly clear in the introduction to the Wesleyan University Press edition of *Revival and Separatism,* issued in 1987.[7]

If Goen is right about the Separatists introducing Baptists to a new style, that style played itself out in stunning fashion in the South. To date, Rhys Isaac's *The Transformation of Virginia, 1740–1790* offers the most probing inquiry into Separate Baptist influence in the mid- to late eighteenth century. It is also one of the most important works on American Baptists ever written. Isaac argues that Separate Baptists posed a formidable challenge to the Commonwealth's gentry on behavioral issues ranging from horse racing to cock fighting. By 1790, Isaac claims, Virginia had been "transformed" from within through evangelical leaven.[8]

Eighteenth-century revivalism fueled existing social tensions and fed into the increasing hostilities between America and Great Britain. After all, few of America's leading citizens appreciated supposed "religious fanatics" labeling them "sinners." In some quarters these hostilities led to renewed persecution, which, in turn, rekindled calls for religious liberty. In Massachusetts, Isaac Backus reminded readers that persecution was still a regular feature of life for some Baptists. A prolific writer and Jonathan Edwards's contemporary, Backus penned the two-volume *History of New England, with Particular Reference to the Denomination of Christians Called Baptists,* a detailed diary, and numerous pamphlets.[9] Meanwhile, in Virginia John Leland joined Backus in calling for a separation of church and state.

The Baptist call for liberty of conscience may not be as clear-cut as some pundits suggest. Most late twentieth-century studies suggest that colonial Baptists did not desire unrestricted religious liberty for all. William G. McLoughlin's two-volume *New England Dissent, 1630–1833: The Baptists and the Separation of Church and State* along with his single-volume *Soul Liberty: The Baptists' Struggle in New England, 1630–1833* remind readers that the concept of religious liberty developed slowly and, theological presuppositions notwithstanding, it was an essentially pragmatic venture.[10]

Whether the Separate Baptists changed society may be open for further study, but at least two things seem certain. First, by the revolutionary era much had changed in North America, and the Separate Baptists along with others challenged authority from a different ideological and social perspec-

tive than had Roger Williams and John Clarke. Second, the political circumstances that led to the Revolution renewed the call for religious liberty, a
topic that has received considerable attention. The existing work on Backus
and Leland indicates that they had differing views on what religious freedom
would look like. Leland advocated absolute separation of church and state,
much as Thomas Jefferson would articulate to the Danbury Baptists. Backus,
however, called for a more measured separation, one that allowed for political
give-and-take.[11] By the end of the eighteenth century Baptists were still on
society's margins, but that was about to change.

The Nineteenth Century

Baptists entered the nineteenth century with a measure of optimism. The Bill
of Rights promised religious liberty, and western land was cheap and readily
available. Beginning with the great revivals on the frontier, Americans were
forced to ponder what the separation of church and state, along with religious liberty, really meant.

As pioneers pushed west, American Christians entered the modern mission movement and became determined to win the world for Christ. Baptists became energized by the missionary enterprise, but sending missionaries abroad made unprecedented demands on resources and led to new levels
of organization. Reaching the masses suddenly became a competitive venture as "missions," broadly defined, pulled Baptists into a mold that went beyond associationalism in scope. Missionary work at home and abroad called
for new policies, new programs, and established new objectives. These organizational shifts reshaped American Baptist life.[12]

As Baptists adjusted to their changing emphases, their historians began
taking a different approach to telling the Baptist story. In 1813 David Benedict launched what might be deemed the "golden age of grand narrative
Baptist history." Benedict's *A General History of the Baptist Denomination
in America and Other Parts of the World* emphasized advancement in spite
of persecution. As religious freedom allowed rival religious groups to compete
openly, often intensely, among themselves for new members, Baptist historians began using their history as an apologia, or defense. By claiming certain
Baptist "distinctives" like regenerate church membership and adult baptism
by immersion, they tried to link these distinctives to the New Testament era
through dissenting groups like the Waldenses, Novationists, and Donatists.
They had suffered persecution through the ages because they were different
from other groups and, in their estimation, more like Christ and the apostles
than any other group.[13]

The thrust for comprehensive, apologetic Baptist history continued throughout the nineteenth century, culminating with Thomas Armitage's *History of the Baptists* in 1886. Like most nineteenth-century writers of Baptist history, Armitage was not a professional historian. Rather, he served as pastor of New York's Fifth Avenue Baptist Church. Armitage acknowledged that Baptists had endured their share of persecution but, like many of his predecessors, he maintained that the real danger for Baptists came from departing from their core principles, particularly the commitment to the Bible.[14]

Benedict and Armitage form "bookends" to a remarkable period of consensus among Baptist historians. Throughout the better part of the nineteenth century, Baptists used their history to distinguish themselves from other groups, like the Methodists and Presbyterians and ultimately the Disciples of Christ, led by Alexander Campbell. Moreover, by emphasizing their distinctiveness, Baptists used their history as a powerful platform for polemics against their rivals.

Organizational shuffling and early nineteenth-century growth called for new associations, new state conventions, and new mission societies. Thus, as consensus emerged on the large scale, writing history became somewhat more manageable on the smaller scale. Numerous associations and state conventions began recording their stories and some, like William Fristoe's *A Concise History of the Ketocton Baptist Association* and Robert B. Semple's *History of the Baptists in Virginia,* became classics.[15]

By the middle of the nineteenth century Baptists had established their place in American religious life. But the same organizational revolution that fostered missionary work and evangelism also reinforced "otherness" as a theme in subsequent Baptist historiography. Some Baptists, notably the so-called Landmarkers, resented what they perceived as condescension and chicanery on the part of new denominational leaders. They argued that missionary boards and societies were helpful but subject to authoritarianism and high-handedness.[16] Others went one step further and refused to affiliate with the missionary movement. These Baptists placed themselves outside the emerging "mainstream" and earned the unfortunate and somewhat misleading label "antimissionary." They soon formed new associations, claiming they followed New Testament principles, and hence they are known as Primitive Baptists.[17]

The most comprehensive history of Primitive Baptists is C. B. Hassell and Sylvester Hassell's *History of the Church of God.* This work reads much like the other nineteenth-century Baptist histories, with one significant difference: the Hassells did not embrace the mission movement, and neither did their Baptists. More recent studies focus on the emergence of Primitive

Baptists as a unique segment of nineteenth-century Baptist life. James R. Mathis's *The Making of the Primitive Baptists: A Cultural and Intellectual History of the Anti-Mission Movement, 1800–1840* offers a corrective to the common misconception that Primitives are in some way victims of modernization. Mathis claims that Primitive Baptists see themselves as "preservers" of a pure form of ancient Christianity rather than as "restorationists." Further, he argues that Joshua Lawrence led Primitives to organize into distinct groups in the 1840s and articulated the emerging movement's theological underpinnings.[18]

There are numerous types of Primitive Baptists, but John Crowley's *Primitive Baptists of the Wiregrass South* concentrates on one group, the Ochlocknee Association in southern Georgia and northern Florida. Crowley claims that Primitive Baptists are distinct among other Baptists because they have traditionally internalized social, cultural, and political conflicts and cast them in ecclesiological terms. As such, Crowley sees them as a synthesis of Calvinistic theology and a form of church government that encourages associationalism. Despite their desire to remain pure, Crowley notes that contemporary Primitives face the same sorts of problems as other Baptists—divorce, urbanization, and "worldliness."[19]

As Mathis and Crowley suggest, there is considerable diversity among Primitive Baptists. In fact, Howard Dorgan notes that not all Primitives endorse a strongly Calvinistic theology. His *In the Hands of a Happy God: The "No-Hellers" of Central Appalachia* details the history of the Primitive Baptist Universalists. His other works, *The Old Regular Baptists of Central Appalachia: Brothers and Sisters in Hope* and *Giving Glory to God in Appalachia: Worship Practices of Six Baptist Subdenominations,* attest to Baptist diversity in the region.[20]

Baptist growth and diversification occurred against a backdrop of increasing sectional hostility. In 1845 many of the nation's Baptists split along sectional lines as southerners formed the Southern Baptist Convention (SBC), a breach that was not mended after the Civil War. Thus, the Civil War and Reconstruction era also marks the beginning of another transitional phase in Baptist historiography. From the 1880s onward, Baptist histories began to assume a more regional emphasis. This trend continued throughout the twentieth century, especially among Southern Baptists, who boast three different histories since their founding in 1845.[21]

Once the Civil War ended, Baptists, unlike the nation's other leading denominations, failed to achieve reconciliation. In 1980 Charles Reagan Wilson's *Baptized in Blood: The Religion of the Lost Cause, 1865–1920* offered an interpretive motif of postwar religion that immediately captured the academy's imagination. Wilson maintains that many former Confederates, unable to accept defeat, began extolling the virtues of the "Lost Cause." That is, southern leaders, many of whom were ministers, embraced the myth that the Old South was virtuous and noble. Wilson claims that southerners relied on this backward-looking, fictionalized version of southern virtue as a coping mechanism until well into the twentieth century.[22]

Whether Lost Cause-ism best characterizes postwar southerners may be an open question. It is fairly certain, however, that postwar Baptists wanted to reestablish order for their religious lives. Gregory A. Wills's *Democratic Religion: Freedom, Authority, and Church Discipline in the Baptist South, 1785–1900* explodes at least two myths about nineteenth-century Baptists. As he sees it, nineteenth-century Baptists, at least in the South, maintained strong ties to their churches. Moreover, they had no real aversion to creeds and they held their members to high moral and doctrinal standards. Churches punished offenders by exercising disciplinary actions ranging from mild rebuke to excommunication. Thus, Wills maintains that prior to the twentieth century, many if not most of the nation's Baptists had a limited understanding of individualism. Moreover, they believed that creeds, when voluntary, infringed on no one's liberty of conscience. In other words, belief and behavior were defined and mediated within given communities of like-minded individuals.[23]

Recent Trends

By the twentieth century, America was fast on its way to becoming an urban nation. Immigration was making the United States increasingly pluralistic. As the American economy grew, the nation's cities expanded at an unprecedented—to many alarming—rate. Some preachers wondered what would become of their "Christian" America as immigrants, mostly Catholics and Jews, arrived by the thousands.

America's cultural and intellectual climate also changed in the latter nineteenth century. Anxious Baptists fretted about "modernism," a broad term that encompassed a host of "ills" ranging from Darwinism to higher criticism. Whether one should embrace or reject America's changing social, cultural, and economic structures led to one of the more protracted battles in American Baptist life and ultimately fragmented denominational life in the North. Evolution quickly became a metaphor for all that was either good or bad in America, depending on one's perspective. As the evolution controversy gained momentum, Harry Emerson Fosdick became famous for his sermon, "Shall the Fundamentalists Win?" Fellow New Yorker and pastor of Calvary

Baptist Church John Roach Straton responded with his own broadside, "Shall the Funnymonkeyists Win?"[24]

By 1930 dissention and various palace intrigues had led to new organizations, and it became increasingly difficult to write broadly about Baptists, unless within a textbook. In fact, there were few noteworthy books written about Baptist history between 1930 and 1960 apart from William Warren Sweet's *The Baptists, 1783–1830: A Collection of Source Material*, which was more of a document collection than an analytical study.[25] This situation changed in the late twentieth century as a new generation of historians with new methods began revisiting old questions and asking some new questions of their own. Broadly speaking, inquiries into Baptist life since World War II have either combined Baptists with other evangelical groups or focused specifically on region, race, gender, politics, or Southern Baptist turmoil in the late twentieth century.

Baptists and Evangelicalism

In *Religion in the Old South* Donald G. Mathews argues that beginning in the early nineteenth century, evangelicalism became the dominant religious motif of the Protestant American South. Scholars since the mid-1970s have followed Mathews's lead, and studies comparing Baptists, Methodists, and Presbyterians are instructive. For instance, Anne Loveland's *Southern Evangelicals and the Social Order, 1800–1860* captures the essence of southern evangelical clergymen—their concerns, their involvement in social issues, and their general conformity to the region's status quo—prior to the Civil War. Randy Sparks's *On Jordan's Stormy Banks: Evangelicalism in Mississippi, 1773–1876* is an excellent state study of evangelical cultural interaction prior to and after the Civil War. Nathan Hatch's *The Democratization of American Christianity* is even more ambitious. Hatch argues that evangelicalism literally "democratized" American Christianity.[26]

Distinctives notwithstanding, evangelicals certainly agreed on select theological and cultural issues while maintaining their differences along denominational lines. Thus, as Paul Conkin's aptly titled work suggests, an "uneasy center" formed as denominations struggled to accommodate their theological presuppositions to the nation's rapidly changing social and cultural landscape. Moreover, when it came to politics, Richard Carwardine argues that evangelicals, notably Baptists, influenced the antebellum political process in unexpected ways, not the least of which by forging an "ecclesiastical sectionalism" that tracked closely with the nation's emerging sectional politics. As Carwardine puts it, evangelical church members "instigated political discussion, mobilized voters, pressured vote-seeking politicians, and variously made

their marks on the political cultures of the different parties." Beyond pitting
North against South, Carwardine further maintains, "evangelicalism, more
than any other element, provided the core of these divergent moral perceptions of the appropriate social and economic direction of the union."[27]

Baptists and Region

Baptists and regionalism became increasingly important beginning in the
1960s, as evidenced by Samuel S. Hill Jr. and Robert G. Torbet's *Baptists North
and South* and Edward L. Queen II's *In the South the Baptists Are the Center
of Gravity: Southern Baptists and Social Change, 1930–1980.* Hill and Torbet
explore regional differences and similarities among Baptists, while Queen
maintains that Southern Baptists built an empire in the South by tapping the
region's emotional core and fusing it with theology and politics. State studies also experienced a brief revival, at least in Texas and Alabama, as H. Leon
McBeth's *Texas Baptists: A Sesquicentennial History* and Wayne Flynt's *Alabama Baptists: Southern Baptists in the Heart of Dixie* made their way into
print. State histories prior to the mid- to late twentieth century tended to be
laudatory recitations of denominational advancement within the state and
lacked any substantive analysis. McBeth, and even more so Flynt, concentrate
on the social, political, and cultural contexts for their studies.[28]

    The extent to which Baptists in the South engaged in social ministries
generated considerable scholarly attention. Rufus Spain's *At Ease in Zion: A
Social History of Southern Baptists, 1865–1900* argues that Southern Baptists
were well aware of the region's social problems but failed to develop a high
degree of social awareness for reasons ranging from the Social Gospel's pre-
sumed roots in theological liberalism to their own "extreme southernness."
In a similar vein, John Lee Eighmy's *Churches in Cultural Captivity: A History of the Social Attitudes of Southern Baptists* claims that the Social Gospel challenged the region's social inequities, and even though Southern Baptists fashioned a form of social ministry, they failed to do more because they
were prisoners of a culture that stressed social conservatism, cultural folkways, and volunteerism.[29]

    Other scholars see more social activity among Southern Baptists. Wayne
Flynt maintains that between 1900 and 1914 Southern Baptists addressed numerous social issues, especially those they thought might help the southern
economy. Likewise, John W. Storey's *Texas Baptist Leadership and Social
Christianity, 1900–1980* maintains that Baptist leaders in the Lone Star State
embraced social Christianity on a number of levels. He even notes that while
some Southern Baptists read Rauschenbusch favorably, social Christianity
in Texas arose from state issues, not northern urban problems. In short, they

believed the only way to improve society was by improving its people. This theme also resonates in Keith Harper's *The Quality of Mercy: Southern Baptists and Social Christianity, 1890–1920,* where the author stresses Southern Baptist commitment to social ministries through organizations like schools and orphanages.[30]

Baptists and Race

Assessing the role slavery played in nineteenth-century denominational life has received considerable attention from the scholarly community. C. C. Goen's *Broken Churches, Broken Nation* and Mitchell Snay's *The Gospel of Disunion* discuss how slavery became an issue of righteousness among northerners and southerners. Also, John McKivigan and Mitchell Snay's collection of essays *Religion and the Antebellum Debate over Slavery* is an excellent resource for this ongoing debate. Deborah Bingham Van Broekhoven's essay "Suffering with Slaveholders: The Limits of Francis Wayland's Antislavery Witness" discusses Wayland's struggle to balance his friendship with slaveholders with his personal aversion to slavery. Finally, Robert Gardner's *A Decade of Debate and Division* is equal parts analysis and tabular information that demonstrates the overwhelming influence slaveholders exerted in the SBC's formation.[31]

In one way or another, all subsequent works on religion and race in the American South are indebted to Samuel S. Hill's *Southern Churches in Crisis.* Writing as a Baptist, Hill noted the difficulty in implementing the Bible's mandate to love one another, race notwithstanding. Some of the best recent scholarship in Baptist studies discuss race. Paul Harvey's *Redeeming the South: Religious Cultures and Racial Identities among Southern Baptists, 1865–1925* explores the interconnectedness of black and white Baptists in the post–Civil War South. Harvey argues that while Baptists may have developed separate institutions along racial lines, they still influenced one another. Both faced similar issues in building their respective denominational structures, especially in managing changing concepts of ministerial professionalism. As the biracial South emerged in the late nineteenth and twentieth centuries, its supreme irony, at least in religious terms, may have been that blacks and whites usually had more in common than not.[32]

Overcoming divisive issues like segregation was not easy. In *Getting Right with God: Southern Baptists and Desegregation, 1945–1995,* Mark Newman demonstrates precisely how difficult it can be to reconcile Jesus's mandate to "love thy neighbor as thyself" with white southern folkways and mores. Of course, not all Southern Baptists embraced desegregation, but neither did the majority approve of interracial conflict that led to lawlessness and violence. Southern Baptists came to accept desegregation, albeit reluctantly. Another study of roughly the same period, Alan Scot Willis's *All According to God's Plan: Southern Baptist Missions and Race, 1945–1970,* points out that Southern Baptists pride themselves on being a mission-minded folk. Ultimately, they came to see that racism hindered their mission efforts at home and abroad.[33]

As some scholars examined white Baptist life, others examined the African American community. Albert J. Raboteau's *Slave Religion: The "Invisible Institution" in the Antebellum South* and Leroy Fitts's *A History of Black Baptists* recount African American Baptist life from the colonial era until the nineteenth century. These overviews offer background for a now-familiar pattern of black resistance and/or accommodation to white control. More specific studies, like Mechal Sobel's *Trabelin' On: The Slave Journey to an Afro-Baptist Faith,* detail the ways American slaves created distinct religious communities based on their recollections of African ritual.[34]

Gaining acceptance and establishing credibility in America's nineteenth-century religious world was no mean feat. Sandy D. Martin's *Black Baptists and African Missions: The Origins of a Movement, 1880–1915* details the development of a missionary awareness among African Americans that mobilized their meager resources for African missionary efforts. James Melvin Washington's *Frustrated Fellowship: The Black Baptist Quest for Social Power* chronicles the depth of African American frustration with the white community as well as the difficulties in creating national structures like the National Baptist Convention. But if African American men were frustrated with the status quo, so were the women. Evelyn Brooks Higginbotham's *Righteous Discontent: The Women's Movement in the Black Baptist Church, 1880–1920* tells the story of African American women who organized to advance women's causes. Both Washington and Higginbotham observe that African Americans in the late nineteenth and early twentieth centuries were frustrated with America's social and political inequalities. But they both attest that their frustrations were sometimes leveled at those "within the camp." All told, the existing scholarship indicates that black Baptist churches exhibited tendencies as diverse as white churches.[35]

Baptists and Gender

The emergence of women's history in the late twentieth century provided an opportunity to reassess the role women played in shaping denominational life. H. Leon McBeth was among the first to discuss the role women played in shaping denominational life and character. Subsequent works found much to praise in Baptist women. Denominational heroines like Lottie Moon inspired an entire generation of men and women to become missionaries in Asia. Meanwhile, Annie Walker Armstrong searched for ways to support the Southern Baptist missionary effort. Moon and Armstrong both challenged prevailing stereotypes about southern women in the late nineteenth and early twentieth centuries. Both were strong willed and well educated. Both were dedicated to their denomination. Neither woman ever married.[36]

If Moon and Armstrong served as strong role models for Southern Baptist women, the missionary societies like Woman's Missionary Union (WMU), auxiliary to the Southern Baptist Convention offered women opportunities to serve. Catherine Allen's *A Century to Celebrate: History of Woman's Missionary Union* details the rise of WMU from modest beginnings to a powerful agency in Southern Baptist life, and T. Laine Scales's *All That Fits a Woman: Training Southern Baptist Women for Charity and Mission, 1907–1926* chronicles the story of the Woman's Missionary Training School. On a more individual level, David Morgan's *Southern Baptist Sisters: In Search of Status, 1845–2000* and Pam Durso and Keith Durso's *Courage and Hope: The Stories of Ten Baptist Women Ministers* recount the challenges women have faced in establishing meaningful ministries in a denomination dominated by male leadership.[37]

Establishing ministry parameters is one thing; managing one's family is another matter. In an excellent example of social history applied to a missionary context, Joan Brumberg's *Mission for Life: The Story of the Family of Adoniram Judson* recounts the story of the first American Baptist missionary and his family's history. In a similar vein, Gerald W. Berkley and Wayne Flynt's *Taking Christianity to China: Alabama Missionaries in the Middle Kingdom, 1850–1950* details the struggles missionaries encountered over time. While Berkley and Flynt do not focus exclusively on Baptists, they provide considerable insight into everyday life on the mission field.[38]

Baptists and Politics

Baptists exhibited an increasing tendency to become openly involved in politics in the latter twentieth century. Oran P. Smith's *The Rise of Baptist Republicanism* sketches the shift from Southern Baptists' traditional ties to the Democratic Party to their open affiliation with the Republican Party, not to mention the SBC's newfound role as political power broker in state and national politics. On the local level, Clifford Grammich Jr.'s *Local Baptists, Local Politics: Churches and Communities in the Middle and Uplands South* argues that well-defined voting patterns are hard to discern, but the Baptists in his study are active in the political process.[39]

Of course, Jerry Falwell is the Baptist most often associated with the fusion of religion and politics. In 1979 Falwell, senior pastor of Thomas Road Baptist Church in Lynchburg, Virginia, helped forge a broad-based coalition of dissatisfied Protestants, along with a few Catholics and Mormons, that he hoped would "clean up" America's moral act. Falwell's Moral Majority called for political action at the state and national levels on issues like the Equal Rights Amendment and efforts to overturn *Roe v. Wade*. This movement summoned a new catchphrase in America's cultural vocabulary, "the Religious Right." There are numerous works about Falwell, ranging from his own *Strength for the Journey* and *Listen, America!* to critical and probing assessments like Susan Friend Harding's *The Book of Jerry Falwell: Fundamentalist Language in Politics*.[40]

SBC Controversy

As Falwell railed against America's moral ills, Southern Baptists found themselves embroiled in their own denominational infighting. Between 1979 and 1991 rival factions fought for control of the Southern Baptist Convention in what came to be known as the "fundamentalist takeover of the SBC" or the "conservative resurgence," depending on one's perspective. Essentially, "fundamentalists" (theological conservatives) accused rival "moderates" of theological compromise, while moderates countered with accusations that conservative leaders were only out to control the SBC's political machinery.

There are numerous accounts of the controversy, but three general works are especially noteworthy. Nancy Tatom Ammerman's *Baptist Battles: Social Change and Religious Conflict in the Southern Baptist Convention* remains the best analysis of the issues that framed the controversy. Other notable works include David Morgan's *The New Crusades, the New Holy Land: Conflict in the Southern Baptist Convention, 1969–1991* and Bill J. Leonard's *God's Last and Only Hope: The Fragmentation of the Southern Baptist Convention*. While sympathetic with moderate interests, these accounts offer useful assessments of the controversy. Both note that Southern Baptists did not enter their well-publicized conflict suddenly. Morgan suggests that the controversy most likely began in 1969 with the so-called Broadman commentary controversy, but Leonard cautions that conflict and Southern Baptists are seemingly inseparable. James Hefley's multivolume *The Truth in Crisis* and Jerry Sutton's *The Baptist Reformation: The Conservative Resurgence in the Southern Baptist Convention* are the most comprehensive accounts of the controversy from the conservative viewpoint.[41]

Other works offer useful takes on the controversy from autobiographical perspectives. Ralph Elliott's *The Genesis Controversy and Continuity in Southern Baptist Chaos: A Eulogy for a Great Tradition* chronicles the au-

thor's odyssey from seminary professor of the Old Testament to denominational pariah. In addition to Elliott, Duke McCall, Grady Cothen, and Paul
Pressler have each recorded their reflections on life as a Southern Baptist and
how the controversy affected them.[42]

By the mid-1990s it was clear that the conservatives had won. Serious
scholarly inquiry into Southern Baptist thought and life began moving beyond the political power play versus restoration of theological integrity debate that characterizes much of the existing literature. David Strickland's
Genealogy of Dissent notes that theological and political liberals in the SBC
felt increasingly alienated from the denomination and became, for a time,
allies with their fundamentalist cohorts. Even more important, Barry Hankins's *Uneasy in Babylon: Southern Baptist Conservatives and American Culture* maintains that Southern Baptists have established themselves as America's most vocal foot soldiers in the country's so-called culture wars. In so
doing, Hankins claims, they may have sacrificed key elements of their own
identity, as the leaders of the SBC since the early 1990s have appeared more
like "Yankee evangelicals" than traditional Southern Baptists.[43]

New Directions

Is there a future for Baptist history? Consider this: America's three largest
Baptist groups all experienced significant strife throughout the twentieth century. The National Baptist Convention, the largest group of African American Baptists, split in 1915 and again in 1961. Baptists in the North changed
their name and aspects of their polity in 1908, 1950, and 1973. Southern Baptists affirmed three different confessions of faith: in 1925, 1963, and 2000.
Obviously, for all that has been said about Baptists, much still remains to
be studied.

Toward the end of the twentieth century there were indications that
"large-scale" Baptist history might be making a comeback. No single author
has written as widely about Baptists as William Henry Brackney, and he, too,
finds Baptist history a difficult matter. His 1988 work, *The Baptists,* emphasizes certain doctrinal distinctives as identifying characteristics of Baptists,
but unlike the comprehensive histories from a century earlier, Brackney uses
identifying characteristics for analysis rather than apologetics or polemics.
In a subsequent volume, *A Genetic History of Baptist Thought,* Brackney uses
human genetics as a metaphor to explain Baptist development. As such, Baptist "genes" convey Christ-centeredness, the centrality of the Bible, Christian
experience, a modified Reformed soteriology, a distinct ecclesiology, a sense
of mission, and freedom as heredity characteristics.[44]

Understanding Baptists theologically seems logical, but it may be the most difficult approach of all. Bill J. Leonard is probably close to the truth when he suggests that Baptists are not the world's best consensus builders. Leonard sees Baptists as a people in tension with themselves as well as others. The main point of contention, especially over the past generation, may well be "conversionist particularism" versus "pluralistic libertarianism," or the need to defend the exclusivity of Christian (Baptist) faith claims or remain open to interfaith dialogue. Either way, Leonard maintains that there is more than one way to be a Baptist, and he anticipates more schism in the Baptist family in the future.[45]

Beyond large-scale history, numerous issues in Baptist life deserve a fresh perspective. Scholars might want to revisit state Baptist histories, especially if they follow Flynt's model in *Alabama Baptists*. Baptist associations, especially the older ones, deserve renewed inquiry, and scholars would do well to explore the complex web of interconnectedness that existed between the association ministers and the churches they served. Obviously, more can and should be said about women in Baptist life, and the existing literature remains deficient on the African American Baptist experience, as well as that of Freewill and General Baptists. One might also ask, whatever became of northern Baptist history?

Even the staple themes of Baptist historiography should be carefully reexamined. For example, to what extent has individualism shaped American Baptist life? Curtis Freeman's provocative article "Can Baptist Theology be Revisioned?" challenges the oft-repeated dictum that American Baptists have always been staunch individualists. Rather, Freeman contends, radical individualism is a by-product of the Enlightenment that seeped into Baptist life in the eighteenth and nineteenth centuries.[46]

Going further, Freeman and a number of like-minded scholars maintain that Baptist history should be reenvisioned along with theology. The so-called Baptist Manifesto that accompanied Freeman's article suggested that Baptist history be recast with a particular emphasis on balancing notions of individual freedom with personal faithfulness within one's "faith community." These scholars are on to something. At the height of the Southern Baptist controversy, R. Albert Mohler, president of the Southern Baptist Theological Seminary, observed that the SBC was divided into two rival camps. According to Mohler, the "Truth Party" claimed belief or theology as their defining characteristic, while the "Liberty Party" looked to behavior as the key to their self-understanding. Mohler may also have unwittingly articulated the single greatest myth undergirding most inquiries into Baptist history. If Freeman is correct, neither characteristic by itself adequately describes Baptist life—and it never has. Baptist identity is a function of structure—that is, the local church, associations of churches, or even the larger denomination itself. Hence "freedom" and "truth" are balanced, interpreted, and nuanced through some structure or organization.[47]

Baptist organizational structures offer possibilities for future scholars who want to investigate the role "community" plays in shaping faith and practice. Precisely how do churches shape individual religious experience? On a larger scale, how do churches form associations? What mechanisms, formal or informal, do associations/denominations use to create consensus, and how do organizations handle dissent? How did denominational publications shape denominational development?[48]

Baptist commitment to congregational polity allowed for flexibility, and their numbers increased rapidly in the nineteenth century largely because of their organizational efficiency. That same denominationalism spurred the professionalization of Baptist clergy. Paul Harvey addresses this issue in *Redeeming the South* and a perceptive article titled "The Ideal of Professionalism and the White Southern Baptist Ministry, 1870–1920." Likewise, Beth Barton Schweiger's remarkable study *The Gospel Working Up* raises issues like standardization of "church experience" that need more analysis over a longer period of time.[49]

In the nearly four hundred years since Roger Williams and John Clarke, Baptists have experienced numerous changes. Perhaps the single greatest change is their metamorphosis from despised sect to culture warriors, at home in the political arena they once eschewed. Yet Baptists are a fragmented people. Most scholars concede that Baptists are frequently in conflict with their social, cultural, and political surroundings. They also suggest that Baptists are often in conflict with one another over matters ranging from theological integrity to procedural issues. Where their disputes will carry them in the future is anyone's guess. America's Baptists began as persecuted outsiders; now they are no longer on the periphery, but neither are they completely in the mainstream. As they enter the twenty-first century, they are somewhere in between.

Notes

1. J. Gordon Melton, *Encyclopedia of American Religions,* 6th ed. (Detroit and London: Gale Research, 1999), 97, 477–98; Frank S. Mead, Samuel S. Hill, and Craig Atwood, *Handbook of Denominations in the United States,* 12th ed. (Nashville: Abingdon 2005), 181–216; Walter B. Shurden, "The Baptist Identity and the Baptist *Manifesto,*" *Perspectives in Religious Studies* 25 (Winter 1998): 321–40.

2. Roger Williams, *Bloudy Tenent of Persecution* and *The Bloody Tenent Yet More Bloody*, ed. Samuel L. Caldwell, in *The Complete Writings of Roger Williams*, vols. 3 and 4 (n.p.: Russell and Russell, 1963).

3. James P. Byrd, *The Challenges of Roger Williams: Religious Liberty, Violent Persecution, and the Bible* (Macon: Mercer University Press, 2002).

4. A. D. Gillette, *Minutes of the Philadelphia Baptist Association, 1707–1807* (Philadelphia: American Baptist Publication Society, 1851).

5. Francis Sacks, *The Philadelphia Baptist Tradition of Church and Church Authority: An Ecumenical Analysis and Theological Interpretation* (Lewiston, NY: Edwin Mellen, 1989). For another study of associationalism, see Walter B. Shurden, *Associationalism among Baptists in Early America, 1707–1814*, The Baptist Tradition, ed. Edwin S. Gaustad (New York: Arno, 1980)

6. Thomas R. McKibbens Jr. and Kenneth L. Smith, *The Life of Morgan Edwards*, The Baptist Tradition, ed. Edwin S. Gaustad (New York: Arno, 1980).

7. William Lumpkin, *Baptist Foundations in the South: Tracing through the Separates the Influences of the Great Awakening, 1754–1787* (Nashville: Broadman, 1961); C. C. Goen, *Revivalism and Separatism in New England, 1740–1800: Strict Congregationalists and Separatist Baptists in the Great Awakening* (New Haven: Yale University Press, 1962). See also the Wesleyan University Press edition of 1987.

8. Rhys Isaac, *The Transformation of Virginia, 1740–1790* (Chapel Hill: Institute of Early American History and Culture, Williamsburg, Virginia, and University of North Carolina Press, 1982). Not everyone believes Isaac is entirely convincing. See John B. Boles, "The Discovery of Southern Religious History," in *Interpreting Southern History: Historiographical Essays in Honor of Sanford W. Higginbotham*, ed. John B. Boles and Evelyn Thomas Nolen (Baton Rouge and London: Louisiana State University Press, 1987), 526–28. Boles admires Isaac's methodological sophistication but raises several important questions. He observes that Separate Baptists moved into areas where Anglicanism was weak and offered the citizenry a new type of religious community that supported and affirmed individuals in an evangelical context. Also, Boles suggests that Separate Baptists may have "changed" society by "reclassifying" certain behavior that had previously gone unquestioned as "sinful."

9. Isaac Backus, *History of New England, with Particular Reference to the Denomination of Christians Called Baptists*, 2nd ed. (Newton, MA: Backus Historical Society, 1871); *The Diary of Isaac Backus*, 3 vols., ed. William G. McLoughlin (Providence: Brown University Press, 1979); *Isaac Backus on Church, State, and Calvinism: Pamphlets, 1754–1789*, ed. William G. McLoughlin (Cambridge: Harvard University Press, Belknap, 1968).

10. William G. McLoughlin, *New England Dissent, 1630–1833: The Baptists and the Separation of Church and State*, 2 vols. (Cambridge: Harvard University Press, 1971), and *Soul Liberty: the Baptists' Struggle in New England, 1630–1833* (Hanover and

London: Brown University Press, 1991); see also Theodore Dwight Bozeman, "John Clarke and the Complications of Liberty," *Church History* 75, no. 1 (2006): 69–93. According to Bozeman, John Clarke, Williams's colleague and fellow Rhode Islander, also advocated a limited, pragmatic understanding of religious liberty.

11. See L. F. Greene, *The Writings of the Late Elder John Leland* (New York: G. W. Wood, 1845; repr., Gallatin, TN: Church History and Archives, 1985); see also Bradley J. Creed, "John Leland: American Prophet of Religious Individualism" (Ph.D. diss., Southwestern Baptist Theological Seminary, 1986). For a comparison of Leland's and Backus's views of church and state, see Joe L. Coker, "Sweet Harmony vs. Strict Separation: Recognizing the Distinctions between Isaac Backus and John Leland," *American Baptist Quarterly* 16 (Spring 1997): 241–50; and Edwin S. Gaustad, "The Backus-Leland Tradition," *Foundations* 2 (April 1959): 131–52.

12. John Boles, *The Great Revival, 1787–1805: The Origins of the Southern Evangelical Mind* (Lexington: University Press of Kentucky, 1972); Ellen Eslinger, *Citizens of Zion: The Social Origins of Camp Meeting Revivalism* (Knoxville: University of Tennessee Press, 1999). See also Donald G. Mathews, "The Second Great Awakening as an Organizing Process," *American Quarterly* 21 (Spring 1969): 23–43. For a discussion of interdenominational competition, see Roger Finke and Rodney Stark, *The Churching of America, 1776–1990: Winners and Losers in Our Religious Economy* (New Brunswick: Rutgers University Press, 1992).

13. David Benedict, *A General History of the Baptist Denomination in America and Other Parts of the World* (Boston: Lincoln and Edmands, 1813).

14. *History of the Baptists* is a shortened title for Thomas Armitage, *History of the Baptists: Traced by Their Vital Principles and Practices, from the Time of Our Lord and Savior Jesus Christ to the Year 1886* (New York: Bryan, Taylor, 1886). Arguably, one could extend the "golden age" to W. A. Jarrell's *Baptist Perpetuity* (1894) or even John T. Christian's *A History of the Baptists* (1922). However, by 1886 Baptists had already begun to struggle with a host of issues that would lead to future schisms and Armitage's tone suggests as much.

15. William Fristoe, *A Concise History of the Ketocton Baptist Association* (Staunton, VA: William Gilman Lyford, 1808); Robert B. Semple, *A History of Rise and Progress of the Baptists in Virginia* (Richmond: Author/John Lynch, 1810).

16. James E. Tull, *A History of Southern Baptist Landmarkism in Light of Historical Baptist Ecclesiology* (New York: Arno, 1980). See also James E. Tull, *High-Church Baptists in the South: The Origin, Nature, and Influence of Landmarkism,* ed. Morris Ashcraft (Macon: Mercer University Press, 2000). For a brief historiographical appraisal of Landmarkism, see Keith Harper, "Old Landmarkism: An Historiographical Appraisal," *Baptist History and Heritage* 25 (April 1990): 31–39.

17. See John Taylor, *Thoughts on Missions* (n.p., 1819); Daniel Parker, *A Public Address to the Baptist Society, and Friends of Religion in General, on the Principle and*

Practice of the Baptist Board of Foreign Missions for the United States of America (Vincennes, IN: Stout and Osborn, 1820); *The Black Rock Address: Put Forth at Black Rock Maryland, by the Particular or Old School Baptists While Assembled in Convention, September 28–28, 1832.*

18. Cushing Biggs Hassell, *History of the Church of God, from the Creation to A.D. 1885: Including the History of the Kehukee Primitive Baptist Association,* revised and completed by Sylvester Hassell (Middletown, NY: Gilbert Bebee's Sons, 1886); James R. Mathis, *The Making of the Primitive Baptists: A Cultural and Intellectual History of the Anti-Mission Movement, 1800–1840,* Studies in American Popular History and Culture, ed. Jerome Nadelhaft (New York and London: Routledge, 2004).

19. John Crowley, *Primitive Baptists of the Wiregrass South* (Gainesville: University Press of Florida, 1998).

20. Howard Dorgan, *In the Hands of a Happy God: The "No-Hellers" of Central Appalachia* (Knoxville: University of Tennessee Press, 1997); *The Old Regular Baptists of Central Appalachia: Brothers and Sisters in Hope* (Knoxville: University of Tennessee Press, 1989); *Giving Glory to God in Appalachia: Worship Practices of Six Baptist Subdenominations* (Knoxville: University of Tennessee Press, 1987).

21. William Wright Barnes, *The Southern Baptist Convention, 1845–1953* (Nashville: Broadman, 1954); Robert A. Baker, *The Southern Baptist Convention and Its People, 1607–1972* (Nashville: Broadman, 1974); Jesse C. Fletcher, *The Southern Baptist Convention: A Sesquicentennial History* (Nashville: Broadman and Holman, 1994).

22. Charles Reagan Wilson, *Baptized in Blood: The Religion of the Lost Cause, 1865–1920* (Athens: University of Georgia Press, 1980).

23. Gregory A. Wills, *Democratic Religion: Freedom, Authority, and Church Discipline in the Baptist South, 1785–1900,* Religion in American series, ed. Harry S. Stout (New York: Oxford University Press, 1997).

24. Harry Emerson Fosdick, "Shall the Fundamentalists Win?" *Christian Work,* June 10, 1922, 716–22; John Roach Straton, "Shall the Funnymonkeyists Win?" (sermon preached September 24, 1922), available online at www.Baptiststudiesonline.com/primary sources/sermons&tracts.

25. William Warren Sweet, *The Baptists, 1783–1830: A Collection of Source Material* (Chicago: University of Chicago Press, 1931).

26. Donald G. Mathews, *Religion in the Old South,* Chicago History of American Religion, ed. Martin Marty (Chicago and London: University of Chicago Press, 1977); Anne Loveland, *Southern Evangelicals and the Social Order, 1800–1860* (Baton Rouge and London: Louisiana State University Press, 1980); Randy J. Sparks, *On Jordan's Stormy Banks: Evangelicalism in Mississippi, 1773–1876* (Athens and London: University of Georgia Press, 1994); Nathan O. Hatch, *The Democratization of American Christianity* (New Haven and London: Yale University Press, 1989).

27. Paul K. Conkin, *The Uneasy Center: Reformed Christianity and Antebellum*

America (Chapel Hill and London: University of North Carolina Press, 1995); Richard Carwardine, *Evangelicals and Politics in Antebellum America* (New Haven: Yale University Press, 1993; repr., Knoxville: University of Tennessee Press, 1997), 319.

28. Samuel S. Hill Jr. and Robert G. Torbet, *Baptists North and South* (Valley Forge, PA: Judson, 1964); Edward L. Queen II, *In the South the Baptists Are the Center of Gravity: Southern Baptists and Social Change, 1930–1980* (Brooklyn: Carlson, 1991). For another regionally focused work, see Walter Brownlow Posey's *The Baptist Church in the Lower Mississippi Valley, 1776–1845* (Lexington: University of Kentucky Press, 1957). H. Leon McBeth, *Texas Baptists: A Sesquicentennial History* (Dallas: Baptistway, 1998); Wayne Flynt, *Alabama Baptists: Southern Baptists in the Heart of Dixie* (Tuscaloosa and London: University of Alabama Press, 1998).

29. Rufus Spain, *At Ease in Zion: A Social History of Southern Baptists, 1865–1900* (Nashville: Vanderbilt University Press, 1967); John Lee Eighmy, *Churches in Cultural Captivity: A History of the Social Attitudes of Southern Baptists*, with revised introduction, conclusion, and bibliography by Samuel S. Hill (Knoxville: University of Tennessee Press, 1987).

30. Wayne Flynt, "Dissent in Zion: Alabama Baptists and Social Issues, 1900–1914," *Journal of Southern History* 35 (Winter 1969): 523–42; John W. Storey, *Texas Baptist Leadership and Social Christianity, 1900–1980* (College Station: Texas A&M University Press, 1986); Keith Harper, *The Quality of Mercy: Southern Baptists and Social Christianity, 1890–1920* (Tuscaloosa: University of Alabama Press, 1996).

31. C. C. Goen, *Broken Churches, Broken Nation: Denominational Schisms and the Coming of the American Civil War* (Macon: Mercer University Press, 1985); Mitchell Snay, *The Gospel of Disunion: Religion and Separation in the Antebellum South* (Chapel Hill and London: University of North Carolina Press, 1997); Deborah Bingham Van Broekhoven, "Suffering with Slaveholders: The Limits of Francis Wayland's Antislavery Witness," Beth Barton Schweiger, "The Restructuring of Southern Religion: Slavery, Denominations, and the Clerical Profession in Virginia," John R. McKivigan, "The Sectional Division of the Methodist and Baptist Denominations as Measures of Northern Antislavery Sentiment," all in *Religion and the Antebellum Debate over Slavery*, ed. John R. McKivigan and Mitchell Snay (Athens and London: University of Georgia Press, 1998); Robert G. Gardner, *A Decade of Debate and Division: Georgia Baptists and the Formation of the Southern Baptist Convention* (Macon: Mercer University Press, 1995).

32. Samuel S. Hill, *Southern Churches in Crisis* (New York: Holt, Rinehart and Winston, 1967); Paul Harvey, *Redeeming the South: Religious Cultures and Racial Identities among Southern Baptists, 1865–1925* (Chapel Hill and London: University of North Carolina Press, 1997).

33. Mark Newman, *Getting Right with God: Southern Baptists and Desegregation, 1945–1995* (Tuscaloosa and London: University of Alabama Press, 2001); Alan Scot

Willis, *All According to God's Plan: Southern Baptist Missions and Race, 1945–1970* (Lexington: University Press of Kentucky, 2005).

34. Albert J. Raboteau, *Slave Religion: The "Invisible Institution" in the Antebellum South* (Oxford and New York: Oxford University Press, 1978); Leroy Fitts, *A History of Black Baptists* (Nashville: Broadman, 1985); Mechal Sobel, *Trabelin' On: The Slave Journey to an Afro-Baptist Faith* (Westport, CT: Greenwood, 1979).

35. Sandy D. Martin, *Black Baptists and African Missions: The Origins of a Movement, 1880–1915* (Macon: Mercer University Press, 1989); James Melvin Washington, *Frustrated Fellowship: The Black Baptist Quest for Social Power* (Macon: Mercer University Press, 1986); Evelyn Brooks Higginbotham, *Righteous Discontent: The Women's Movement in the Black Baptist Church, 1880–1920* (Cambridge and London: Harvard University Press, 1993).

36. See McBeth, *Texas Baptists;* Catherine B. Allen, *The New Lottie Moon Story* (Birmingham: Woman's Missionary Union, 1980); and Bobbie Sorrill, *Annie Armstrong: Dreamer in Action* (Nashville: Broadman, 1984).

37. Catherine B. Allen, *A Century to Celebrate: History of Woman's Missionary Union* (Birmingham: Woman's Missionary Union, 1987); T. Laine Scales, *All That Fits a Woman: Training Southern Baptist Women for Charity and Mission, 1907–1926* (Macon: Mercer University Press, 2000); David Morgan, *Southern Baptist Sisters: In Search of Status, 1845–2000* (Macon: Mercer University Press, 2003); Pamela R. Durso and Keith E. Durso, *Courage and Hope: The Stories of Ten Baptist Women Ministers* (Macon: Mercer University Press and the Baptist History and Heritage Society, 2005).

38. Joan Jacobs Brumberg, *Mission for Life: The Story of the Family of Adoniram Judson, the Dramatic Events of the First American Foreign Mission, and the Course of Evangelical Religion in the Nineteenth Century* (New York: Free Press, 1980); Gerald W. Berkley and Wayne Flynt, *Taking Christianity to China: Alabama Missionaries in the Middle Kingdom, 1850–1950* (Tuscaloosa and London: University of Alabama Press, 1997).

39. Oran P. Smith, *The Rise of Baptist Republicanism* (New York and London: New York University Press, 1997); Clifford A. Grammich Jr., *Local Baptists, Local Politics: Churches and Communities in the Middle and Uplands South* (Knoxville: University of Tennessee Press, 1999).

40. Jerry Falwell, *Strength for the Journey: An Autobiography* (New York: Simon and Schuster, 1987) and *Listen, America!* (Garden City, NY: Doubleday, 1980); Susan Friend Harding, *The Book of Jerry Falwell: Fundamentalist Language in Politics* (Princeton: Princeton University Press, 2000).

41. Nancy Tatom Ammerman, *Baptist Battles: Social Change and Religious Conflict in the Southern Baptist Convention* (New Brunswick: Rutgers University Press, 1990); David Morgan, *The New Crusades, the New Holy Land: Conflict in the Southern*

Baptist Convention, 1969–1991 (Tuscaloosa and London: University of Alabama Press, 1996); Bill J. Leonard, *God's Last and Only Hope: The Fragmentation of the Southern Baptist Convention* (Grand Rapids, MI: Eerdmans, 1990); James C. Hefley, *The Truth in Crisis: The Controversy in the Southern Baptist Convention*, 5 vols. (Dallas: Criterion, 1986/Hanibal, MO: Hannibal, 1987–90); Jerry Sutton, *The Baptist Reformation: The Conservative Resurgence in the Southern Baptist Convention* (Nashville: Broadman and Holman, 2000).

42. Ralph Elliott, *The Genesis Controversy and Continuity in Southern Baptist Chaos: A Eulogy for a Great Tradition* (Macon: Mercer University Press, 1992); Duke McCall and A. Ronald Tonks, *Duke McCall: An Oral History* (Nashville: Baptist History and Heritage Society and Fields Publishing, 2001); Grady C. Cothen, *What Happened to the Southern Baptist Convention? A Memoir of the Controversy* (Macon: Mercer University Press, 1993); Paul Pressler, *A Hill upon Which to Die: One Southern Baptist's Journey* (Nashville: Broadman and Holman, 1999).

43. David Strickland, *Genealogy of Dissent: Southern Baptist Protest in the Twentieth Century*, Religion in the South, ed. John B. Boles (Lexington: University Press of Kentucky, 1999); Barry Hankins, *Uneasy in Babylon: Southern Baptist Conservatives and American Culture* (Tuscaloosa and London: University of Alabama Press, 2002).

44. William Henry Brackney, *The Baptists* (Westport, CT: Greenwood, 1988); see also Brackney's *A Genetic History of Baptist Thought* (Macon: Mercer University Press, 2004), 527–38. In *The Baptists*, Brackney claims that Baptists are a "denominational family" that shares five common "vertices": "the Bible, the church, the ordinance/sacraments, volunteerism and religious liberty" (xiii). For recent works bearing on Baptist identity, see Cecil P. Staton Jr., ed., *Why I Am a Baptist: Reflections on Being Baptist in the Twenty-first Century* (Macon, GA: Smyth and Helwys, 1999); Tom J. Nettles and Russell D. Moore, eds., *Why I Am a Baptist* (Nashville: Broadman and Holman, 2001); R. Stanton Norman, *More Than Just a Name: Preserving our Baptist Identity* (Nashville: Broadman and Holman, 2001); and R. Stanton Norman, *The Baptist Way: Distinctives of a Baptist Church* (Nashville: Broadman and Holman, 2005).

45. Bill J. Leonard, *The Baptists*, Columbia Contemporary American Religion series (New York: Columbia University Press, 2005), 257. See also Leonard's Baptist history text, *Baptist Ways: A History* (Valley Forge, PA: Judson, 2003).

46. Curtis Freeman, "Can Baptist Theology be Revisioned?" *Perspectives in Religious Studies* 24 (Fall 1997): 273–310.

47. See Curtis Freeman, "Re-envisioning Baptist Identity: A Manifesto for Baptist Communities in North America," *Baptists Today*, June 26, 1997, 8–10; R. Albert Mohler, "A Call for Baptist Evangelicals & Evangelical Baptists: Communities of Faith

and a Common Quest for Identity," in *Southern Baptists & American Evangelicals: The Conversation Continues,* ed. David S. Dockery (Nashville: Broadman and Holman, 1993), 224–39.

48. Samuel P. Hays, *The Response to Industrialism, 1885–1914* (Chicago and London: University of Chicago Press, 1957); Robert H. Wiebe, *The Search for Order, 1877–1920* (New York: Hill and Wang, 1967).

49. Paul Harvey, "The Ideal of Professionalism and the White Southern Baptist Ministry, 1870–1920," *Religion and American Culture* 5 (Winter 1995): 99–123; Beth Barton Schweiger, *The Gospel Working Up: Progress and the Pulpit in Nineteenth Century Virginia* (New York and Oxford: Oxford University Press, 2000).

5

"Everything Arose Just as the Occasion Offered"

Defining Methodist Identity through the History of Methodist Polity

Jennifer L. Woodruff Tait

One of John Wesley's favorite ways of justifying Methodist theology was by telling the Methodist story. Beginning with Wesley, this essay addresses that Methodist story, first of all from the inside out.[1] What have Methodists, at least the American variety, been telling themselves for the past two hundred and some score years? And how has that story intersected with the mainstream narrative of American religion?

The official Methodist narrative was most often one of providential response to the movement of God, through means both pragmatic and primitive. Furthermore, this narrative often resolved into the claim that pragmatism is itself providential, that Methodism's practical nature—which more and more came to be defined as being exemplified through its connectional polity—was a sign that God had particularly blessed it as an instrument of his purpose.[2] Other American church historians, largely "discovering" Methodism in the twentieth century, have used its pragmatism as a key to both understanding and critiquing the American religious experience. The penetration of their insights into denominational narratives has so far been mixed at best. Providential pragmatism is certainly not the only theme that could be traced through Methodist history, but it illumines Methodists and their self-definition better than any other.

Methodism as a movement is much bigger than United Methodism as a denomination, encompassing the British Methodist story as well as African American Methodist denominations, many nineteenth-century Holiness groups, and even, in its broadest reading, the Pentecostal movement.[3] This essay focuses on white Methodist historiography, although a providential triumphalism also characterized the self-portraits of African American Methodist denominations.[4] Furthermore, the official United Methodist denominational narrative has always had a northern, Methodist Episcopal Church

(MEC) slant; and, after the 1968 merger between the Methodist Church and the Evangelical United Brethren (EUB), the latter's history was mostly swallowed up by the larger body.[5] The pre-1968 EUB has a right to have its own historiographical narrative told, but it is not the focus of this essay.

Wesley and Methodist Inevitability

In terms of daily practice, American Methodism has frequently honored Wesley more in the breach than in the observance. Nevertheless, his description of Methodism's providential and pragmatic appearance on the historical scene was profoundly formative for Methodist historiography. Most of his writings on the subject have been collected in volume 9 of the ongoing critical edition of his works.[6] *A Plain Account of the People Called Methodists* opened with the assertion, "As they [Methodists] had not the least expectation at first of anything like what has since followed, so they had no previous design or plan at all, but everything arose just as the occasion offered." Wesley named the criteria they used to judge their actions as those of "*common sense* and *Scripture*—though they generally found, in looking back, something in *Christian antiquity*, likewise, very nearly parallel thereto."[7] He then traced God's providence in the specific events leading to Methodism's rise. The same theme was found throughout his historical writings—from the opening of the *Nature, Design, and General Rules of the United Societies*, which rooted Methodism's beginning as a response to a few seekers in 1739 who desired that Wesley "would spend some time with them in prayer, and advise them how to flee from the wrath to come," to *A Short History of the People Called Methodists*, whose meticulous reproduction of Wesley's early journals continued to find God in the particulars.[8] For Wesley, Methodism's providential essence was discovered in pragmatic response to the evils of the day, born out by a plain study of common sense and the Bible, and measured up pretty well against the standards of the early church. Later historians would retain his enthusiasm even when the essence under discussion had greatly altered.

Methodist Historians in the Nineteenth Century: Guided by Providence

Methodism came to America in the 1760s, was officially chartered as a denomination in 1784, and published its first major history about a quarter of a century later, Jesse Lee's *Short History of the Methodists in the United States of America*. Even while arguing that Methodists were pragmatically right to reject Wesley's final authority in matters of church government and lit- urgy, Lee rang the changes on Wesley's theme that the rise and structure of Methodism—as exemplified both in Wesley's life and in the American Methodist experience—were divinely appointed and practically responsive to changing circumstances. "We have changed the economy and discipline of our church at times," he said, "as we judged for the benefit and happiness of our preachers and people; and the Lord has wonderfully owned and pros- pered us. It may be seen from the following account how the Lord has, from very small beginnings, raised us up to be a great and prosperous people." This prosperity was particularly due to Methodism's itinerant structure and to "the goodness of our doctrine and discipline," which "has greatly con- tributed to the promotion of religion, the increase of our societies, and the happiness of our preachers." Lee's history also set the structural paradigm for later nineteenth-century works: a straightforward, detailed narrative of growth in numbers and godliness, year by year, conference by conference, evidencing everywhere a love for quoting statistics that Methodist histo- rians have never lost. Though he noted disagreements such as the O'Kelley schism (where, tellingly, the church government developed by the Repub- lican Methodists was "found to be defective" when compared with the Meth- odist Episcopal Church), they fell by the wayside while his story marched on, concluding, "In this HISTORY there is such a collection of facts, and such a clear, plain, and full account of the Methodists, that he that runs may read, and he that reads may understand that the Lord has done great things for us, whereof we are glad."[9]

Some thirty years after Lee, book agent and magazine editor Nathan Bangs produced the first of Methodism's magisterial multivolume histories with his four-volume *History of the Methodist Episcopal Church*. Marking Meth- odism's progress, like Lee, by the onward march of General Conferences and the upward march of statistics, Bangs focused on official pronouncements and reports of bishops and of the General Conference. Bangs concluded, like Lee, that the "success and influence of Methodism" had "one true original cause, namely, the divine agency"—particularly as that agency had worked through Methodist institutions, praising "the aptitude of the means which divine wisdom saw fit to employ to produce the desired results, and the suit- ableness of the instruments, and their plans of operation, to the condition and tendencies of human society."[10]

As American Methodism approached in 1867 the centenary of its arrival in America, it produced various self-congratulatory historical reflections. Most influential were the writings of *Christian Advocate* editor Abel Stevens, who considered that he was picking up where Bangs had left off. Stevens published a three-volume history of Methodism, a four-volume *History of the Methodist Episcopal Church,* a condensed version of the latter called *A Compendious History of American Methodism,* and several smaller biographies, including *The Women of Methodism* and *Life and Times of Nathan Bangs.*[11] He was perhaps the single greatest advancer of the providentialist narrative, with a robust faith in Methodism's inevitability. Methodism's success was for Stevens once again explained not by theological argument but by a simple statement of the events of history: "I do not admit the conditions of its success to be a secret; the question receives frequent attention at appropriate points in these three volumes, but no chapter is devoted to it. Why should the narrative pause for the discussion of a question which it answers on almost every page?"[12]

Stevens connected Methodism strongly with the primitive church and thus justified its pragmatic bent—a common nineteenth-century theme that would largely vanish after the turn of the century: "A true Christian Church is a collective or organic form of this spiritual life; its external institutions . . . are valuable only so far as they can be means to this end. And therefore any new practical matters which may be rendered expedient, by the ever-varying conditions of human history, for the effectiveness of the Church in the moral regeneration of individual men, are admissible, being in harmony with the original purpose and simplicity of the Gospel, however much they may contravene ecclesiastical precedents or traditions." Furthermore, Stevens proclaimed Methodism as the culmination of Christian development, a theme that would not vanish so quickly in the twentieth century. Methodism completed what the Reformation had left unfinished in both its Continental and English forms. These had been "ecclesiastical" attempts to overthrow Catholicism that were not "an evangelical revival of the spiritual life of the Church," and therefore retained within Lutheranism and Anglicanism "many papal errors."[13] His Bangs biography also described Methodism as the best example of modern Christianity in all its particulars; its successful founders proclaimed its doctrines "anew, and almost exclusively" through the agency of their providential polity: "Wesley did not devise his system; he adapted it, as, from time to time, its principal facts were evolved in the 'movement,' that is to say, providentially suggested, as he believed."[14] Such trust in providence and polity should be a model for Wesley's successors.

As Stevens's works make clear, mid-nineteenth-century writers loved to narrate Methodism's progress through heroic biography, imprinting the image of the circuit rider firmly on the American historical imagination. The most famous circuit rider story was the *Autobiography of Peter Cartwright,* which narrated Cartwright's sinful youth, conversion to Methodism as a young man, and difficult but entertaining and ultimately successful career in the itinerant ministry. Distrustful of Methodism's growing respectability, Cartwright approached providentialism in a minor key, emphasizing the theme of Methodism's fall from a more heroic age when it better understood its purpose. He strongly linked Methodism's early providential success with its primitive simplicity: "In reference to the MEC, when we consider that her ministers were illiterate, and not only opposed and denounced by the Catholics, but by all Protestant churches; that we were everywhere spoken against, caricatured, and misrepresented; without colleges and seminaries, without religious books or periodicals, without missionary funds . . . and a Methodist preacher's library almost entirely consisted of a Bible, Hymn Book, and a Discipline, may we not, without boasting, say with one of old, 'What hath God wrought?'"[15]

Nineteenth-century Methodists approached Wesley and his family through the lens of heroic biography as well. Most nineteenth-century biographical treatments of Wesley emphasized his tireless travels and countless sermons and drew a sharp dichotomy between his pre- and post-Aldersgate experience, narrated as the moment when he cast off a constricting Anglican approach to church tradition and practice in favor of one more in line with a primitive, spiritual, and pragmatic religion. The most influential stand-alone biographies of Wesley circulating in America during the nineteenth century were British—Thomas Coke and Henry Moore's *The Life of the Rev. John Wesley, A.M.*, Robert Southey's *Life of Wesley*, and Luke Tyerman's *The Life and Times of the Rev. John Wesley, M.A.*—but they were used thoroughly and hagiographically as source material by American Methodist historians.[16] We owe to Southey the most dramatic description of Wesley's providential deliverance from the Epworth fire, which later biographers made much of.[17] But while the Anglican Southey placed Wesley in opposition to Voltaire as one of the most influential forces of his age, he was also critical of Wesley's tendencies toward separation from the Established Church and some of the "enthusiasm" of his doctrine and behavior. For American Methodists, on the other hand, such developments were divinely appointed.[18]

The later nineteenth century saw a continual explosion of Methodist histories as various centenary celebrations prompted historical consciousness. One of the most formative, though not as a straight narrative, was Bishop Matthew Simpson's *Cyclopedia of Methodism*.[19] Simpson's compendium of theological, historical, and biographical articles, illustrated with copious line drawings, was on every bookshelf of those interested in Methodist history next to Lee and Stevens, and remains among the most valuable sources on nineteenth-century American Methodism. Although Simpson admitted his

MEC emphasis, he attempted to cover other branches of Methodism fairly. He emphasized Methodism's growing respectability as well as its growing numbers—the *Cyclopedia*'s articles focused on colleges, bishops, educators, large churches, and leading laymen. Bishop Holland McTyeire of the Methodist Episcopal Church, South (MECS) also weighed in with an important centenary history in 1884 that was as much a narrative of Wesley's providential life as it was of later church developments. While maintaining the MECS perspective on the issues that had split the church in 1844—slavery and the powers of the bishops in relation to the General Conference—McTyeire sounded the same major notes as his northern brethren in the theme of Methodism's God-ordained rightness. He asserted that Methodism began with a desire to "realize in the hearts and conduct of men the true ideal of Christianity" and that "their system of government grew up out of this, and was accordingly shaped by it." He chose to end his story on a high point, positioning Methodism to move from strength to strength in the next century—particularly ecumenically, a theme that *would* be reiterated in the twentieth century. McTyeire saw ecumenical hope first in the fraternal agreement reached by the MEC and MECS in 1876 and then in the first Ecumenical Methodist Conference (1881), precursor to today's World Methodist Council—where, he notes, one of the speakers commented, "Methodism is admitted to be, in its ground-plan and in its structure, of all Church systems the closest in texture and most cohesive. . . . No other Church has such a concatenation of appliances for binding its members together."[20] The idea that its polity was Methodism's gift to the greater church would only grow stronger.

On the MEC side, one of the most influential late nineteenth-century histories was editor and church bureaucrat James Buckley's two-volume *A History of Methodism in the United States,* which situated Methodism firmly within the history of English Protestantism.[21] Again here, Wesley was the "Man of Providence," with his delivery from the fire at Epworth prominently foregrounded, whose "providential preservation . . . led his mother to devote great pains to him."[22] When he organized the Methodist societies, it was around "a standard of spiritual life and conduct to which comparatively few Christians in any age have attained." Buckley claimed that it was no longer necessary to argue for Wesley's greatness, since "his fame may be trusted safely to Macaulay, Lecky, Green, and every modern church historian of rank, who have placed him upon a pedestal apart, agreeing with one of the most recent of them, Dr. Philip Schaff, that he was 'the most apostolic man since the apostolic age.'" Buckley's assessment of Methodism's apostolic character was equally sunny. Noting that Methodism was the largest Protestant denomination in the United States, he attributed this to "the power of the fundamental principles of Christianity as taught and preached by it" and claimed that "by its stimulus and its example it has powerfully affected other religious bodies," as those converted among Methodists returned with renewed zeal to their own denominations. As had McTyeire, Buckley laid great stress upon the ecumenical convergence of various Methodisms and of Protestantism in general, hoping for closer fraternity and perhaps even organic union. Though Methodism's enterprises were more varied, complex, and worldly than in its infancy, he claimed the denomination was still producing conversion of the ungodly and devotion to the cause.[23]

One of the last great heroic Methodist histories was Bishop John Fletcher Hurst's seven-volume *The History of Methodism,* which included British and worldwide Methodism in the story. Hurst's was the culmination of a line of illustrated histories for lay consumption that also included W. H. Daniels's *The Illustrated History of Methodism in Great Britain and America* and James Wideman Lee's *The Illustrated History of Methodism.*[24] Again, Hurst argued that Methodism was a "moral and spiritual force that has wrought mightily during the last sixteen decades of human history" and had "asserted its primitive and apostolic character as a renewal of Christianity." Hurst also emphasized his ecumenical desire for the reunion of Methodism in the twentieth century, and claimed Methodism as a guiding influence not only on "souls in other communions" but on American culture and civilization itself as Methodism went in "its rapid march across the continent, leavening each new community with industry and righteousness, and planting its strongholds of piety in every village."[25]

The Twentieth Century

Twentieth-century Methodist historiography began in that heroic vein with Halford Luccock and Paul Hutchinson's optimistic, missions-minded *The Story of Methodism,* which was confident of Methodism's continuing contribution to Christianizing the twentieth century and the world.[26] But Methodism soon found itself challenged with maintaining this providentialist narrative in the face of social turmoil and declining membership. This was particularly true after the 1968 merger with the Evangelical United Brethren. What was the essence of Methodism? If the heroic visions of the nineteenth century had not been realized, and if primitivism was dead, was pragmatism still alive? Methodist historians found their exceptionalism harder to explain in an age of declension and often advanced it in a more nuanced fashion, but it did not stop them from producing a deluge of self-studying historical treatments near the end of the twentieth century. More and more, Methodist structure and polity, rather than Methodism's apostolic message, was foregrounded as the most providential characteristic of the denomination.

At the same time, outsiders were beginning to discover the clues to American church history that the study of Methodists could provide. The denomination was first mined for insights into the frontier and appreciated for its populist character; by the late twentieth century, this had bred a more nuanced study of exactly what made Methodism the most American of denominations and how it had formed the American religious consciousness. Polity played a role here, but not always the providential one which insiders had assigned it.

Insiders Looking In

The first part of the twentieth century was dominated by the work of William Warren Sweet, professor of church history at the University of Chicago. As a Methodist church historian read by the professional guild, his works were instrumental in presenting Methodism's face to the world, particularly in *Religion on the American Frontier: The Methodists* and *Methodism in American History.*[27] Sweet attempted to apply Frederick Jackson Turner's famous frontier thesis to Methodist history. He knew that Methodists had so far been either ignored or stereotyped as uneducated and devoted to emotional camp meetings. Instead, he wanted to give them their due prominence alongside the Puritans in the story of American Christianity—which meant, to some extent, trying to explain Methodism in terms dictated by Puritan sensibilities: emphasizing Methodist support of higher education and claiming that camp meetings were "an extra occasion" in the Methodist economy, not its essential part. Sweet was captivated, like his predecessors, by the heroic figure of the circuit rider, but emphasized not his evangelistic mission but his civilizing one: "the influence he exerted in bringing the refining influence of religion to bear upon a rough, uncouth society." Sweet's understanding of Wesley's life and early Methodism was more nuanced than that of his nineteenth-century predecessors. Still, he found Methodists' pragmatic adaptability to have been providential even on secular terms: "It was a fortunate circumstance, from the standpoint of the propagation of Methodism in America, that the movement was not handicapped by rigid views in regard to church government."[28] In fact, the Methodist adoption of itinerancy was perfectly suited for a frontier ministry.

The Methodists was a collection of source material aimed at outsiders, designed to illustrate the life and work of the circuit rider within the Methodist system. *Methodism in American History,* on the other hand, was a history for insiders published by the Methodist press. It aimed at a calm and factual summary of Methodist events that presented both sides of controversial topics; it strongly emphasized Methodism's increasing education and refinement along with its numerical and economic growth; and it concluded by celebrating not only white Methodism's 1939 union among its three major branches but its leadership in the peace process and the ecumenical movement. Like his predecessors, Sweet found Methodism poised to conquer, only now it would do so in union with other Protestant churches: "The vast destruction—physical, spiritual, and moral—wrought by World War II has created in American Protestantism a sense of world mission such as it has never known before, and Methodism in America shares with all the great sister churches a world task which demands, as never before, a united Protestantism."[29]

The last gasp of self-consciously magisterial Methodist historiography came with the three-volume *History of American Methodism* (*HAM*), officially enjoined by the 1956 General Conference, edited by Emory Stevens Bucke and published just before merger. This work, a product of both Methodist and non-Methodist scholars, aimed, even more than Sweet had, to tell Methodists their own story while making it understandable and respectable in the eyes of secular historians. *HAM* critiqued Methodist exceptionalism while still maintaining it, especially in its concluding essays, "Methodism's Contribution to America" (Jaroslav Pelikan) and "American Methodism: An Experiment in Secular Christianity" (F. Gerald Ensley). The term *secular* was meant to describe Methodism's worldly orientation as well as its pragmatic spirit: "the gospel of Jesus filtered through the activistic temperament of John Wesley and habituated to the American frontier." Ensley saw pragmatism as key to Methodist success, sounding familiar themes: the adaptability of the itinerant system to the frontier where, "unbound by centuries-long traditions the Methodists met the need for clergy in pragmatic fashion," and the ability to unite "democracy and efficiency in rare fashion." This ethos was crucial to American democracy as well, a theme non-Methodist historians would adopt: "The Methodist preachers for a century and a half have helped keep freedom alive in America simply by refusing to be intimidated. . . . Methodism has sought a perfection like God's—a perfection, be it noted, that consists in treating all men, the unjust as well as the just, impartially." Ensley saw some problems with pragmatism, but still thought Methodists held the key to advancing the ecumenical movement beyond theological debates to practical results: "The church needs someone to insist—as we believe John Wesley would do—that the ecumenical tree be judged by its fruits. There is no form of church union, polity, order of ministry, or sacrament that is intrinsically superior. Each is to be tested by whether it furthers or retards the kingdom." However, this test proved for Ensley that Methodist polity was in fact superior, "the most effective form of church government in Protestantism" and "a flexible, efficient, finely tempered instrument for kingdom purposes."[30]

More inwardly focused than *HAM* but equally magisterial, the *Encyclopedia of World Methodism* succeeded in being the *Cyclopedia* for the twentieth century, incorporating EUB history and making sense of the postmerger Methodist landscape in the United States and abroad through stories of notable men, educational and benevolent institutions, large churches, and theological distinctives.[31] The *Encyclopedia* was recently updated in briefer fashion by Charles Yrigoyen Jr. and Susan Warrick's *Historical Dictionary of Methodism*.[32]

Also published in 1974, Frederick Norwood's *Story of American Methodism* quickly became a popular brief history of the denomination and remains the most commonly assigned textbook in denominationally required seminary courses on Methodist history. Norwood, like Ensley, saw Methodism as the most quintessentially American of denominations and subsumed its theology in its polity: "Sometimes other Christians have looked on with disapproval as they mistakenly thought Methodists were so busy doing things that they had no time for theological understanding. What they didn't realize was that the understanding was there all along in the doing." Norwood recognized and critiqued earlier historians' easy assumption "that the history of the United Methodist Church is the same as the history of American Methodism," and so incorporated chapters on women, minorities, and the EUB heritage. But he still maintained the basic triumphalist narrative, tracing Methodism's progress through revival, frontier movement, and growing Americanization, leaving postmerger Methodism poised to do great things in the late twentieth century—hopefully through ecumenical merger, the "highest dream of our generation."[33]

Joining Norwood's book as a brief popular history was John McEllhenney's edited volume, *United Methodism in America: A Compact History*. McEllhenney's outlook was more dire than Norwood's, concluding not with the heady optimism of merger but with the 1990 Cartwright-like declarations from the evangelical Good News movement, which called on Methodism to return to its past glories through an renewed emphasis on doctrine. Unlike many of his twentieth-century colleagues, McEllhenney rooted the problem of modern Methodist apathy in its structure and polity: "No Anglican council of bishops penned a pastoral letter that warmed John Wesley's heart. . . . No think tank of Lutheran bureaucrats prioritized goals, voted evangelism number-one, and appointed Jacob Albright." This theme was later expanded on by Riley Case, whose *Evangelical and Methodist: A Popular History* firmly repudiated the polity-as-providential argument of many of his denominational colleagues. Case billed his history as the story of populist, "unofficial" Methodism, "an 'unmediated' Christianity, one not needing to be filtered by educated clergy or annual conferences."[34] It was mostly a history of the emergence of the conservative Good News movement, but it rooted that development firmly in the revivalist, Holiness branch of Methodist tradition. In terms Cartwright would understand, Case was explicitly critical of growing denominational respectability and magisterial providentialism, particularly as typified by Bishop Matthew Simpson and the *Cyclopedia*. He preferred the nondenominational take on Methodism of outsider scholars like Nathan Hatch and John Wigger, which focused on the populist energy of early Methodism.

In the thirty or so years since Norwood's work, United Methodist denominational historiography has been mainly the work of a small group of scholars, all professors at denominational seminaries: Russell Richey, James Kirby, Jean Miller Schmidt, and Kenneth Rowe.[35] Their influential works include Richey's *Early American Methodism* and *The Methodist Conference in America,* Schmidt's *Grace Sufficient,* Rowe's bibliographical guide *United Methodist Studies: Basic Bibliographies,* the jointly authored *The Methodists* and *The Methodist Experience in America,* and the jointly edited essay collections *Rethinking Methodist History* and *Perspectives on American Methodism.*[36] Richey also served as one of the general editors of the five-volume United Methodism and American Culture series, a polity-heavy Methodist self-study funded by the Lilly Endowment.[37] Of these, *Perspectives* is the most valuable as a historiographical introduction to the field: its thirty-two essays treat Methodist doctrine and practice from a largely social-history standpoint, with a focus on the concerns of women and African Americans, on Methodist social activism, and on the continuing struggle over Methodist self-definition.

Perhaps more than any other modern Methodist historian, Russell Richey was responsible for the continued emphasis on Methodist polity as its most providential characteristic. *Early American Methodism* saw in Methodism's founding period the tensions between vernacular/experiential, Wesleyan, episcopal, and republican languages, and attempted to explain Methodism mostly in terms of the first. Richey concluded that Methodists experienced conference as a supreme means of grace, but they never seized the opportunity to wrestle with what this meant theologically and ecclesiologically, thus allowing the camp meeting to take over some of conference's spiritual functions.[38] *The Methodist Conference in America,* a more closely grained history of Methodist polity, argued that Methodists should understand their commitment to the idea of conference spiritually, not just politically.[39] The

United Methodism and American Culture volumes that Richey edited, particularly the first, *Connectionalism,* and the last, *Marks of Methodism,* focused on the spiritual and bureaucratic aspects of Methodist polity as a key to its uniqueness among American denominations. *Marks of Methodism* argued that Methodism was best defined as "connectional, itinerant, disciplined, and catholic," the first three being different aspects of Methodist polity and the last one representing its participation in the ecumenical movement. *Connectionalism* continued to advance Richey's argument that Methodism ought to define itself ecclesiologically through its connectional polity rather than in the more formal terms of the Articles of Religion: "Connectionalism represents a/the distinctive Methodist manner of being the church, a multifaceted, not simply political, mode of spirituality, unity, mission, governance, and fraternity that Methodists lived and operated better than they interpreted."[40]

Rowe focused on caucuses and the controversies they provoke as the defining feature of twentieth-century polity and (closely following in the footsteps of *HAM*) on Methodism's relation to ecumenism. We still lack the narrative framework, but the documents volume of *The Methodist Experience in America,* which Rowe edited with Richey and Schmidt, made a conscious effort to define Methodism, clearly articulated as *United* Methodism, through primary source documents relating to its polity controversies, liturgical expressions, minority witness, and the rise of the caucus tradition. The influence of *United Methodist Studies: Basic Bibliographies* in making these issues the concerns of a generation of seminarians and researchers should not be underrated. The function of a bibliography is, after all, to define which works on a given topic are important, and consequently to marginalize others. *Basic Bibliographies* places particular stress on Methodism as structure, Methodism at worship, and Methodism as ecumenical dialogue partner.

These works approached Methodist history with a mournfulness that nineteenth-century triumphalists such as Stevens, Buckley, and Hurst lacked. They admitted that Methodism had a great deal to answer for, especially in its treatment of women and minorities, and that subsequent Methodist history needed to include these groups in the denominational story.[41] They also looked back to early Methodism as a golden age—not so much, as Cartwright had argued, because early Methodists were uneducated yet energetic and successful, but because in those early ages Methodism was so foundational in the shaping of American religious attitudes. "It was not that all Protestants had become Methodists, but that most Protestants had become so very much like Methodists in certain significant ways," Donald Mathews wrote of nineteenth-century Christianity in the opening essay of *Perspectives.*[42] Yet these historians also maintained that Methodism was not done offering its gifts to the church, and that after all the crises of the past two hundred-odd years had shaken themselves out, one of those major gifts was its structure: "This gracious vision, this notion of structure as grace."[43]

Although Methodists never left off viewing Wesley as a providential instrument of God, the twentieth century saw a renaissance in Wesley studies that elevated him as a providential theologian as well. This was spearheaded by the work of theologian Albert Outler of Perkins and historian Frank Baker of Duke, both influential in the Wesley Works project: a thirty-five-volume critical edition of the works of John Wesley, begun with Oxford University Press in 1975 and, since 1984, ongoing with Abingdon as the *Bicentennial Edition of the Works of John Wesley*.[44] Outler's edited collection of Wesley's writings, *John Wesley*, introduced what has since become known as the "Wesleyan Quadrilateral" to the Methodist world: the idea that Wesley's theological method was grounded in scripture as dynamically interpreted through the lenses of reason, tradition, and experience.[45] In more recent years, the quadrilateral has come under criticism, both as an accurate representation of Wesley's method and as a sufficient guide for modern Methodist theologizing.[46]

The preeminent Wesley scholar after Outler was Richard Heitzenrater, now the general editor of the Wesley Works project. Heitzenrater's works, which include *The Elusive Mr. Wesley* and *Wesley and the People Called Methodists*, served as an antidote to the providential reading, attempting to situate Wesley firmly in his historical context as well as debunking some hagiographic myths of earlier biographers. Randy Maddox and Kenneth Collins carried on a continuing theological debate over the influences of Catholic and Eastern Orthodox thought on Wesley versus the Protestant cast of eighteenth-century Anglicanism. Maddox's *Responsible Grace* argued for a strong connection in Wesley's thought to the Eastern Church's concept of theosis or divinization, while Collins responded with a more Protestant Wesley in *The Scripture Way of Salvation*, the biography *A Real Christian*, and *John Wesley: A Theological Journey*. Henry Rack's "Some Recent Trends in Wesley Scholarship" is the best recent evaluation of the current state of the field and future trends in Wesley studies.[47]

Outsiders Looking In

William Warren Sweet had sounded a call for American historians to look at Methodism as a key to interpreting American religious history. Among the first works to meet his challenge was Richard Hofstadter's *Anti-intellectualism in American Life*.[48] Hofstadter turned the providentialist narrative inside out. He easily recognized the "crude pietistic pragmatism" of the early Methodists, and the adaptability of their itinerant policy to the new American situation, but for him that influence contributed to a problem of his own time—the suspicion of the life of the mind he saw as characteristic of the McCarthy era.[49] Charles Ferguson's *Organizing to Beat the Devil* took Methodism's polity as both its most characteristic feature and its most salient, if ambivalent, contribution to American history, asking, "How far is aggregate Methodism responsible for the worship of methodology in American life?" His answer was, considerably, and he did not see that influence fading: "Preoccupation with organization, besides helping to establish the priceless principle that means are more important than the end, may prove to be a prophetic form of efficiency suited to a complex and conglomerate society."[50]

It was not until the 1990s that what might be called "objective" studies of Methodism exploded—ones that neither celebrated nor feared the providential Methodist juggernaut, but simply described both its progress and its decline. Ironically, though these studies did not share the denominational presupposition that Methodism's success was due to its providential gift of a pragmatic and adaptable polity, they largely gained for the study of Methodism the respectability on its own terms that many denominational historians had longed for. By and large, these studies have focused on the antebellum period, when Methodism's pragmatic energy was most obvious, and have not yet struggled with Methodism in the twentieth century. Many end just as Methodism was evolving into respectability, though a few crucial studies do track that evolution. This has meant that, with the notable exception of David Hempton, the guild has yet to wrestle with modern Methodism's focus on its polity and its ecumenical commitments as the remaining evidence of its providential mission.

Nathan Hatch's *The Democratization of American Christianity* opened the door. Hatch argued that religious populism was one of the strongest and oldest impulses in American church life, and discussed Methodists as one of five understudied movements, along with Baptists, Disciples, the black churches, and Mormons, that showed this impulse rooted deep in the founding of the Republic. Methodism's rise to respectability left a space for other populist movements to arise and contain this energy, a trend he traced into twentieth-century evangelicalism. Hatch found it necessary to add a postscript pointing out that the history of Methodism had, until that point, largely been left to the Methodists by contemporary religious historians, who retained "a bias towards elite churches." While Sweet had brought Methodists— and Baptists—to the attention of the guild, he had done so on the guild's terms, committed "to a vision of these groups as bearers of civilization to the uncouth, unrestrained society of the frontier." The same point was made in *Methodism and the Shaping of American Culture,* which Hatch edited with John Wigger.[51] The volume's essays attempted to read Methodism back into American church history through a focus on by now familiar ground—women, African Americans, and zealous itinerants in early American Methodist history—as well as some new territory—politics, economic questions, and regionalism.

Hatch's work inaugurated a focus on Methodism among Americanists—particularly in the antebellum period. Wigger's *Taking Heaven by Storm* pictured Methodism as the single most formative influence on American evangelicalism and popular religion, making both of them far more "enthusiastic, individualistic, egalitarian, entrepreneurial, and lay oriented." Yet he noted that influence could be a two-way street, with Methodism losing much of its distinctive energy as it became a dominant force in American culture. Dee Andrews's *The Methodists and Revolutionary America, 1760–1800* challenged the classless, prejudice-free, and democratic myths that Methodists peddled of their beginnings, yet still found the denomination crucial to the growth of the early Republic as it "revolutionized American culture by popularizing the confessional religious life, making religious regeneration the great American equalizer." Lester Ruth's *A Little Heaven Below* focused on questions of worship, picturing camp meeting spirituality as a natural outgrowth of the intense encounters with God that Methodists built into their early polity via the quarterly meeting.[52] Ruth's study helped suggest why current Methodist historians continue to try to find in their structure the same fervor their ancestors found.

Methodism's contributions to, and oppositions to, southern culture have also recently received attention. Richey's "The Formation of American Methodism: The Chesapeake Refraction of Wesleyanism," in *Methodism and the Shaping of American Culture,* challenged the traditional opposition of North and South in Methodist history, arguing that Methodism should be seen as an expansion outward from the Chesapeake area with an Upper South flavor, but without the later baggage the Civil War assigned to the North-South division. Christine Leigh Heyrman's *Southern Cross* described an assimilation of Methodist and Baptist countercultural ideas to conventional southern attitudes toward war, family, patriotism, and honor during the course of the nineteenth century. Like Wigger, she thought that the result had formatively shaped contemporary evangelicalism, whether southern or not. Cynthia Lynn Lyerly's *Methodism and the Southern Mind* also noted Methodism's countercultural challenge to southern culture, but focused on their earlier opposition rather than their later rapprochement.[53]

Two works that did delineate Methodism's evolution from populist en-

ergy to respectable Americanism were A. Gregory Schneider's *The Way of
the Cross Leads Home* and Mark Noll's edited volume *God and Mammon.*[54]
Schneider traced the shift in Methodist piety as Methodism grew more bureaucratic and respectable, and the "family of God" more and more came to
mean not the public ritual of the class meeting but the domestic ideology of
the Christian home: "Methodists learned the way of the cross in class meeting, and they learned that this way led to a home that was ordered on patterns similar to the class meeting. Once home was ordered along those lines,
they found that it was a more appropriate agency than class meeting for inculcating the moral individualism and self control that were the outcome of
Methodist discipline and piety."[55] *God and Mammon* contained several essays that pictured nineteenth-century Methodist interaction with the market as complex and shaped by theological as well as economic forces; particularly notable was David Hempton and John Walsh's "E. P. Thompson and
Methodism," which noted how Thompson's lack of sympathy with Methodist
spirituality prevented him from fully understanding Methodist motives in
his seminal *The Making of the English Working Class.*[56]

Historians have also begun the long overdue process of looking at Methodism transatlantically, a theme somewhat ignored since Stevens and Hurst.
David Hempton, a British Methodist, has led in this, first with "Methodist
Growth in Transatlantic Perspective, ca. 1770–1850," in *Methodism and the
Shaping of American Culture,* and more recently in his *Methodism: Empire of
the Spirit.*[57] Hempton focused on the sets of complementary forces that characterized the Methodist ethos and drove its expansion: competition and sym-
biosis, enlightenment and enthusiasm, opposition and conflict, money and
power, medium and message, boundaries and margins, mapping and mission.
He pictured Methodism as constantly in tension between the "authoritarian
ecclesiology" of its top-down government and the "noisy, populist, and eclec-
tic" lived experience of its adherents—making polity as much a problem as a
solution. One of the few to wrestle with Methodism's modern decline, Hempton rejected simplistic explanations of that decline, whether the mournful
providentialism of Cartwright or the religion-inevitably-fades narrative of
secularization theory. But like the mournful providentialists, he attributed it
in part to the closing of tensions between Methodism and the larger society,
an insight shared by sociologists such as Roger Finke and Rodney Stark.[58]
American Methodists Kenneth Cracknell and Susan White's *An Introduction
to World Methodism* took not only a transatlantic but a global view in their
survey of Methodist history, theology, worship, polity, social ethics, and ecumenical commitments. While focusing on Britain and America, their work
also contained a brief survey of worldwide Methodist churches that helped

update the information found in the *Encyclopedia*. Cracknell and White were sharply critical of the providentialist tradition: "Methodism's failures will become as apparent in the following pages as its successes. Triumphalism in Methodist writings is a prevailing tendency that goes back to the earliest years of the movement, but we hope to avoid any suggestion that Methodism is a normative pattern for all Christians."[59]

From a sociological standpoint, Finke and Stark made nineteenth-century Methodist and Baptist growth a large part of their groundbreaking argument in *The Churching of America, 1776–1990*. They maintained that up-start, high-requirement sects survive while mainline, low-requirement denominations decline, that the first almost invariably turn into the second and leave room for new upstarts, and that mainline ecumenism is doomed, in part because growing churches are precisely those that wish to maintain their distinctiveness.[60] Finke and Stark's economic model, which attributed denominational success solely to religious competition, not to any theological superiority, was in some ways as far as possible from Methodist claims that providence had particularly gifted them for success. Yet at the same time, by not sharing that presupposition, Finke and Stark went a long way toward explaining why and how Methodists had succeeded.

Future Directions

There remain many riches to mine in the Methodist movement, both on its own terms and as a window into American religious history. While denominational historians have brought the story down to the present day, more detailed studies need to be done from an "outsider" perspective to situate post-bellum and twentieth-century Methodism in the larger contours of American church history. What does Methodist polity (and Methodist love of Methodist polity) say about the American religious experience after 1900? How does the Methodist focus on ecumenism illuminate the successes and failures of the modern ecumenical movement? How do modern polity controversies on social issues like homosexuality relate to earlier ones? How does Methodism relate to the rise of twentieth-century fundamentalism and evangelicalism, a development often explained from a more "Presbygational" perspective?[61] And, what else is there to say about Methodism if scholars stop talking about Methodists as defined by their commitment to connectionalism?

Future inquiries might also probe the Evangelical United Brethren tradition—its pietistic roots, its distinctive ecclesiology(ies), its denominational evolution from ethnic to mainline, and its twentieth-century consumption by Methodism. African American Methodist denominations have received some attention, but work remains to be done, especially regarding African Methodists in the North and in the twentieth century, as well as a scholarly treatment of the Christian Methodist Episcopal Church. White Methodist historiography still needs to wrestle with the challenges posed to it by the African American story (though denominational efforts to describe and assert minority traditions have opened the door a bit), and would benefit by engaging with the rich historiographical traditions of African Methodist churches. Continuing exploration of Methodism as a transatlantic tradition and as a global church would also shed light on the influence America and Methodism have exerted on each other.[62] And while modern historians have gone a long way toward understanding the role of women in the Methodist story as well, much more remains as the story is brought down to the present—particularly women's complex involvement with home and foreign missions, which occurred both within and around denominational structures, and the twentieth-century role of feminist concerns in Methodist debates.

Both insiders and outsiders have repeatedly labeled Methodism the most American of denominations. It remains for both insiders and outsiders to continue exploring—and critiquing—what that meant and means, both in the days of Methodism's triumph and of its decline. "Everything arose just as the occasion offered" remains a powerful explanatory paradigm for the Methodist story. It will shape future expressions and explanations of that story as well.

Notes

1. No serious student of Methodism should be without Kenneth Rowe's *United Methodist Studies: Basic Bibliographies,* 4th ed. (Nashville: Abingdon, 1998), available online at http://www.gcah.org/UMStudies.pdf. Also helpful are Charles Yrigoyen Jr. and Susan Warrick's *Historical Dictionary of Methodism* (Lanham, MD: Scarecrow, 2005); Susan Warrick's *Women in the Wesleyan and United Methodist Traditions: A Bibliography* (Madison, NJ: General Commission on Archives and History, 2003), online at http://www.gcah.org/Bibliography.pdf; and Elmer O'Brien's *Methodist Reviews Index, 1818–1985* (Nashville: Board of Higher Education and Ministry, 1989).

2. Russell Richey makes a similar point in the essay "History as a Bearer of Denominational Identity: Methodism as a Case Study," in *Perspectives on American Methodism: Interpretive Essays,* ed. Russell Richey, Kenneth Rowe, and Jean Miller Schmidt (Nashville: Kingswood, 1993), 480–97. See also L. Dale Patterson, "The Ministerial Mind of American Methodism: The Course of Study for the Ministry of the MEC, the MECS, and the MPC, 1876–1920" (Ph.D. diss, Drew University, 1984).

3. The best introduction to providential pragmatism in Pentecostalism is Grant Wacker's *Heaven Below: Early Pentecostals and American Culture* (Cambridge: Harvard University Press, 2001).

4. See Jennifer L. Woodruff, "True and Capable Heirs: A.M.E. Church Historiography and Intellectual Responsibility," *A.M.E. Church Review,* July–September 2002, 17–25, for a survey of the African Methodist Episcopal Church's providential role as seen through official denominational histories.

5. One exception to this generalization was the ongoing denomination-published United Methodist History of Mission Series. Volumes issued so far (all New York: General Board of Global Ministries) are J. Steven O'Malley, *On The Journey Home: The History of Mission of the Evangelical United Brethren, 1946–1968* (2003); Ruth A. Daugherty, *The Missionary Spirit: The History of Mission of the Methodist Protestant Church, 1830–1939* (2004); Robert Sledge, *Five Dollars and Myself: The History of Mission in the MECS, 1845–1939* (2005); Linda Gesling, *Mirror and Beacon: The History of Mission of the Methodist Church, 1939–1968* (2005); and Robert J. Harman, *From Missions to Mission: The History of Mission of the United Methodist Church, 1968–2000* (2005). See Rowe, *United Methodist Studies,* 43, for a brief summary of EUB histories. The basic EUB history is J. Bruce Behney and Paul Eller, *The History of the Evangelical United Brethren Church* (Nashville: Abingdon, 1979). For historical context, see J. Steven O'Malley, *Pilgrimage of Faith: The Legacy of the Otterbeins* (Lanham, MD: Scarecrow, 1973) and *Early German-American Evangelicalism: Pietist Sources on Discipleship and Sanctification* (Lanham, MD: Scarecrow, 1992).

6. Rupert Davies, ed., *The Bicentennial Edition of the Works of John Wesley,* vol. 9, *The Methodist Societies: History, Nature, and Design* (Nashville: Abingdon, 1989).

7. Ibid., 252–80 (the quotes are from 254). The *Plain Account* was ostensibly written as a letter to Anglican priest and Methodist sympathizer Vincent Perronet.

8. Ibid., 67–75 (the quote is from 69), 425–503. Wesley's published journals were *not* his personal diaries, but were consciously shaped and edited for the public to promote the Methodist movement.

9. Jesse Lee, *Short History of the Methodists in the United States of America* (Baltimore: Magill and Cline, 1810), vii, viii, 367.

10. Nathan Bangs, *History of the Methodist Episcopal Church,* 4 vols. (New York: Mason and Lane, 1838–41), 4:436. Bangs's work is most easily accessed today online at the Christian Classics Ethereal Library, http://www.ccel.org/b/bangs/.

11. Abel Stevens's many works included: *History of the Religious Movement of the Eighteenth Century, Called Methodism,* 3 vols. (New York: Hunt and Eaton/Phillips and Hunt, 1858–61); *History of the Methodist Episcopal Church in the United States of America,* 4 vols. (New York: Carlton and Porter, 1864–67); *A Compendious History of American Methodism: Abridged from the Author's History of the Methodist Episcopal Church* (New York: Carlton and Porter, 1867); *The Women of Methodism: Its Three*

Foundresses, Susanna Wesley, the Countess of Huntingdon, and Barbara Heck; with Sketches of Their Female Associates and Successors in the Early History of the Denomination (New York: Carlton and Porter, 1866); *Life and Times of Nathan Bangs, D.D.* (New York: Carlton and Porter, 1863).

12. Stevens, *History of the Religious Movement*, 3:3, 6.

13. Ibid., 1:19–20.

14. Stevens, *Life and Times of Nathan Bangs*, 66–67.

15. W. P. Strickland, ed., *Autobiography of Peter Cartwright, the Backwoods Preacher* (New York: Carlton and Porter, 1856), 242–43. See also Abel Stevens, *Sketches and Incidents; or, A Budget from the Saddle-Bags of a Superannuated Itinerant* (New York: Lane and Tippet, 1847); Robert Paine, *Life and Times of William M'Kendree: Bishop of the Methodist Episcopal Church* (Nashville: Southern Methodist Publishing House, 1869); and Edward Eggleston's novel, *The Circuit Rider: A Tale of the Heroic Age* (New York: J. B. Ford, 1874). Francis Asbury received the heroic treatment as well; see W. P. Strickland, *The Pioneer Bishop; or, The Life and Times of Francis Asbury* (New York: Carlton and Porter, 1858); Ezra Squier Tipple, *Francis Asbury: The Prophet of the Long Road* (New York: Methodist Book Concern, 1916). The modern edition of Asbury's journal is Elmer T. Clark, ed., *The Journal and Letters of Frances Asbury*, 3 vols. (Nashville: Abingdon, 1958).

16. Thomas Coke and Henry Moore, *The Life of the Rev. John Wesley, A.M.* (Philadelphia: John Dickins, 1793); Robert Southey, *The Life of Wesley; and the Rise and Progress of Methodism* (New York: W. B. Gilley, 1820); Luke Tyerman, *The Life and Times of the Rev. John Wesley, M.A., Founder of the Methodists* (New York: Harper and Brothers, 1872). I have cited the earliest American printings.

17. Coke and Moore also treated the incident, but in a more matter-of-fact manner, simply reprinting letters of Susanna and John on the subject (*Life of the Rev. John Wesley*, 42–46).

18. See Southey, *Life of Wesley*, chap. 29. Criticisms of Southey were common in American Methodist historiography; see particularly theologian Richard Watson's *Observations on Southey's "Life of Wesley": Being a Defence of the Character, Labours, and Opinions of Mr. Wesley, against the Misrepresentations of That Publication* (New York: Bangs and Mason, 1821).

19. Matthew Simpson, *Cyclopedia of Methodism* (Philadelphia: Everts and Stewart, 1876).

20. Holland McTyeire, *A History of Methodism* (Nashville: Publishing House of the MECS, 1884), 13, 686. A modern, and less sanguine, history of the MECS is Robert Wilson Sledge's *Hands on the Ark: The Struggle for Change in the MECS, 1914–1939* (Lake Junaluska, NC: Commission on Archives and History, 1975).

21. James Buckley, *A History of Methodism in the United States*, 2 vols. (New York: Harper and Bros., 1898). It was published as one volume of the American Church His-

tory series, *A History of Methodists in the United States* (New York: Scribner, 1900). The American Church History series was edited by Philip Schaff, who discussed Methodism himself briefly and somewhat critically in *America: A Sketch of Its Political, Social, and Religious Character* (New York: Scribner, 1855).

22. Buckley, *A History of Methodists*, 55, 57. "Man of Providence" is Buckley's chapter title for the narrative of Wesley's early life.

23. Ibid., 103, 324–27, 439–41.

24. John Fletcher Hurst, *The History of Methodism*, 7 vols. (New York: Eaton and Mains, 1902); W. H. Daniels, *The Illustrated History of Methodism in Great Britain and America: From the Days of the Wesleys to the Present Time* (New York: Methodist Book Concern, 1879); James Wideman Lee, *The Illustrated History of Methodism: The Story of the Origin and Progress of the Methodist Church, from Its Foundation by John Wesley to the Present Day* (St. Louis: Methodist Magazine, 1900).

25. Hurst, *History of Methodism*, 3:v–vi.

26. Halford Luccock and Paul Hutchinson, *The Story of Methodism* (New York: Methodist Book Concern, 1926).

27. William Warren Sweet, *Religion on the American Frontier*, vol. 4, *The Methodists* (Chicago: University of Chicago Press, 1946), a collection of source documents with an introductory essay; William Warren Sweet, *Methodism in American History* (Nashville: Abingdon, 1954).

28. Sweet, *The Methodists*, 3, v, 32.

29. Sweet, *Methodism*, 427–28.

30. Emory Stevens Bucke, ed., *The History of American Methodism in Three Volumes* (Nashville: Abingdon, 1964), 3:618, 620–23, 626–27.

31. Nolan Harmon, ed., *Encyclopedia of World Methodism* (Nashville: United Methodist Publishing House, 1974). The *Encyclopedia* contains a number of valuable appendixes listing significant Methodist and EUB leaders, institutions, and statistics.

32. See note 1. The *Historical Dictionary* contains a chronology of Methodist history, a brief history of the movement, and a bibliographical essay surveying the fields of Methodist and Wesley studies.

33. Frederick Norwood, *Story of American Methodism* (Nashville: Abingdon, 1974), 17, 21; see also chap. 38. This work was soon joined by a collection of documents edited by Norwood, *Sourcebook of American Methodism* (Nashville: Abingdon, 1982).

34. John McEllhenny, ed., *United Methodism in America: A Compact History*, rev. ed. (Nashville: Abingdon, 1992), 162; Riley Case, *Evangelical and Methodist: A Popular History* (Nashville: Abingdon, 2004), 14.

35. Rowe was also for thirty years head of the library at the UMC archives on the campus of Drew University.

36. Russell Richey, *Early American Methodism* (Bloomington: Indiana University Press, 1991); Russell Richey, *The Methodist Conference in America* (Nashville: Kings-

wood, 1996); Jean Miller Schmidt, *Grace Sufficient: A History of Women in American Methodism* (Nashville: Abingdon, 1999); James Kirby, Russell Richey, and Kenneth Rowe, *The Methodists* (Westport, CT: Greenwood, 1996); Russell Richey, Kenneth Rowe, and Jean Miller Schmidt, *The Methodist Experience in America* (Nashville: Abingdon, 2000), of which only the second volume (containing source documents) has appeared—the first volume, a narrative history, is still in process; Russell Richey, Kenneth Rowe, eds., *Rethinking Methodist History: A Bicentennial Historical Consultation* (Nashville: Kingswood, 1985). For *Perspectives,* see note 2.

37. Along with Dennis Campbell and William Lawrence, he edited *Connectionalism: Ecclesiology, Mission, and Identity* (Nashville: Abingdon, 1997); *The People(s) Called Methodist: Forms and Reforms of Their Life* (Nashville: Abingdon, 1998); *Doctrines and Discipline* (Nashville: Abingdon, 1999); *Questions for the Twenty-first Century Church* (Nashville: Abingdon, 1999); and *Marks of Methodism: Theology in Ecclesial Practice* (Nashville: Abingdon, 2005).

38. Richey, *Early American Methodism,* chap. 5.

39. Richey, *The Methodist Conference in America,* 13–20, 199–204. See also Kirby, Richey, and Rowe, *The Methodists,* which was structured around Methodism's ways of structuring itself, with major sections on the episcopacy, on conference, and on membership procedures and processes.

40. See Richey's introductions to Richey, Campbell, and Lawrence, *Connectionalism,* 1–20 (the quote is from p. 3), and to Richey, Campbell, and Lawrence, *Marks of Methodism,* 1–15. The modern polity textbook is Thomas Frank's *Polity, Practice, and the Mission of the United Methodist Church* (Nashville: Abingdon, 1997, 2000, 2006) (revised after every General Conference). See also Nolan Harmon, *The Organization of the Methodist Church* (Nashville: UMPH, 1962).

41. The problems that minority histories represent to the triumphal Methodist narrative were particularly foregrounded in several denomination-sponsored histories of Methodist ethnic groups: Homer Noley, *First White Frost: Native Americans and United Methodism* (Nashville: Abingdon, 1991); Justo Gonzàlez, *Each in Our Own Tongue: A History of Hispanic United Methodism* (Nashville: Abingdon, 1991); Grant Shockley, *Heritage and Hope: The African-American Presence in United Methodism* (Nashville: Abingdon, 1991); Artenio R. Guillermo, ed., *Churches Aflame: Asian Americans in United Methodism* (Nashville: Abingdon, 1991).

42. Donald G. Mathews, "Evangelical America—The Methodist Ideology," in Richey, Rowe, and Schmidt, *Perspectives on American Methodism,* 17–30 (the quote is from 17).

43. Richey, Campbell, and Lawrence, *Connectionalism,* 4.

44. John Wesley, *The Bicentennial Edition of the Works of John Wesley,* ed. Frank Baker and Richard Heitzenrater (Nashville: Abingdon, 1976–). In the tradition of he-

roic biography, Outler was recently the subject of a ten-volume "life and works" edited by former student Bob Parrott. The biography volume was *Albert Outler: The Gifted Dilettante* (Anderson, IN: Bristol House, 1999).

45. Albert Outler, ed., *John Wesley*, Library of Protestant Thought (New York: Oxford University Press, 1964). See also Outler's "The Wesleyan Quadrilateral—In Wesley," in *Doctrine and Theology in the United Methodist Church*, ed. Thomas Langford (Nashville: Kingswood, 1991), 75–88, or in *Wesleyan Theological Journal* 20, no. 1 (1985), http://wesley.nnu.edu/wesleyan_theology/theojrnl/16–20/20–01.htm. Outler and the quadrilateral had a strong influence on the theological statement of the 1972 *Book of Discipline* (Nashville: UMPH, 1972), para. 68, 68–72.

46. See Ted Campbell, "The 'Wesleyan Quadrilateral': The Story of a Modern Methodist Myth," in Langford, *Doctrine and Theology*, 154–61; and W. Stephen Gunter et al., *The Wesleyan Quadrilateral: Renewing the Conversation* (Nashville: Abingdon, 1997). William J. Abraham's *Canon and Criterion in Christian Theology* (Oxford: Oxford University Press, 1988) and *Waking from Doctrinal Amnesia* (Nashville: Abingdon, 1995) attacked the quadrilateral as a theological method. The theological statement in the 1988 *Discipline* (Nashville: UMPH, 1988), para. 69, 77–90, was revised to reflect a much clearer stress on the primacy of scripture, both for Wesley and for his modern heirs.

47. Richard Heitzenrater, *The Elusive Mr. Wesley*, 2nd ed. (Nashville: Abingdon, 2003) and *Wesley and the People Called Methodists* (Nashville: Abingdon, 1995). Heitzenrater was the scholar who finally broke the shorthand code of Wesley's private diaries. Randy Maddox, *Responsible Grace: John Wesley's Practical Theology* (Nashville: Kingswood, 1994); Kenneth Collins, *The Scripture Way of Salvation: The Heart of John Wesley's Theology* (Nashville: Abingdon, 1997); Kenneth Collins, *A Real Christian: The Life of John Wesley* (Nashville: Abingdon, 1999); Kenneth Collins, *John Wesley: A Theological Journey* (Nashville: Abingdon, 2003); Henry Rack, "Some Recent Trends in Wesley Scholarship," *Wesleyan Theological Journal* 41, no. 2 (2006): 182–99.

48. Richard Hofstadter, *Anti-intellectualism in American Life* (New York: Vintage, 1962), 95–104. Also see Bernard Weisberger, *They Gathered at the River: The Story of The Great Revivalists and Their Impact upon Religion in America* (Boston: Little, Brown, 1958).

49. Hofstadter, *Anti-intellectualism*, 3–23; see also his treatment of fundamentalism, 117–36.

50. Charles Ferguson, *Organizing to Beat the Devil: Methodists and the Making of America* (Garden City, NY: Doubleday, 1971), viii, 427.

51. Nathan Hatch, *The Democratization of American Christianity* (New Haven: Yale University Press, 1989), 221, 223; Nathan Hatch and John Wigger, eds., *Methodism and the Shaping of American Culture* (Nashville: Kingswood, 2001). See p. 11 of *Methodism*

and the Shaping of American Culture for a brief survey of the state of Methodist research in the 1990s.

52. John Wigger, *Taking Heaven by Storm: Methodism and the Rise of Popular Christianity in America* (New York: Oxford University Press, 1998), 7; Dee Andrews, *The Methodists and Revolutionary America, 1760–1800: The Shaping of an Evangelical Culture* (Princeton: Princeton University Press, 2000), 244; Lester Ruth, *A Little Heaven Below: Worship at Early Methodist Quarterly Meetings* (Nashville: Kingswood, 2000). See also Ruth's *Early Methodist Life and Spirituality: A Reader* (Nashville: Kingswood, 2005).

53. Russell Richey, "The Formation of American Methodism: The Chesapeake Refraction of Wesleyanism," in Hatch and Wigger, *Methodism and the Shaping of American Culture*, 197–222; Christine Leigh Heyrman, *Southern Cross: The Beginnings of the Bible Belt* (New York: Alfred Knopf, 1997); Cynthia Lynn Lyerly, *Methodism and the Southern Mind* (Oxford University Press, 1998).

54. A. Gregory Schneider, *The Way of the Cross Leads Home: The Domestication of American Methodism* (Bloomington: Indiana University Press, 1993); Mark Noll, ed. *God and Mammon: Protestants, Money, and the Market, 1790–1860* (Oxford: Oxford University Press, 2002).

55. Schneider, *Way of the Cross,* xxvii. Methodist construals of religious experience in the nineteenth century also made frequent appearances in Ann Taves's *Fits, Trances, and Visions: Experiencing Religion and Explaining Experience from Wesley to James* (Princeton: Princeton University Press, 1999).

56. David Hempton and John Walsh, "E. P. Thomson and Methodism," in Noll, *God and Mammon,* 99–120. See also other essays in this collection: Richard Cawardine, "Charles Sellers' 'Antinomians' and 'Arminians': Methodists and the Market Revolution," 75–98, and "Trauma in Methodism: Property, Church Schisms, and Sectional Polarization in Antebellum America," 195–216; David Hempton, "A Tale of Preachers and Beggars: Methodists and Money in the Great Age of Transatlantic Expansion, 1780–1830," 123–46.

57. David Hempton, *Methodism: Empire of the Spirit* (New Haven: Yale University Press, 2005); Hempton's *Methodism and Politics in British Society, 1750–1850* (Stanford: Stanford University Press, 1984) and *The Religion of the People: Methodism and Popular Religion, c. 1750–1900* (London: Routledge, 1996) focused solely on the British story.

58. Hempton, *Methodism: Empire of the Spirit,* 206–7.

59. Kenneth Cracknell and Susan White, *An Introduction to World Methodism* (Cambridge: Cambridge University Press, 2007), viii.

60. Roger Finke and Rodney Stark, *The Churching of America, 1776–1990: Winners and Losers in Our Religious Economy* (New Brunswick: Rutgers University Press, 1992). This book was issued in a revised edition in 2005 as *The Churching of America,*

1776–2005. Finke and Stark's method and presuppositions were more extensively explained in *Acts of Faith: Explaining the Human Side of Religion* (Berkeley: University of California Press, 2000).

61. See George Marsden's seminal *Fundamentalism and American Culture: The Shaping of Twentieth-Century Evangelicalism* (New York: Oxford University Press, 1980). This work was issued in a revised edition in 2006.

62. One work that did this admirably for the African Methodist Episcopal Church tradition was James Campbell's *Songs of Zion: The African Methodist Episcopal Church in the United States and South Africa* (New York: Oxford University Press, 1995).

6

Black Protestantism

A Historiographical Appraisal

Paul Harvey

America once was called the nation with the soul of a church; riffing on that, one scholar has referred to the black church as the "church with the soul of a nation." Black Protestant parishioners, for example, empowered the civil rights movement, the most important social movement of twentieth-century American history. During the civil rights era—"the King years," as Taylor Branch has expressed it—they seemed to be the most powerful body of Christians in America in terms of being able to move a nation socially and politically. At the same time, black church organizations have formed, in the words of the late seminary professor James Melvin Washington, a "frustrated fellowship."[1]

Washington's concept of a frustrated fellowship may be applied more broadly to black Protestants in American history. On the one hand, the very singularity of the term *black church*—however questionable it may be to singularize such a multifarious set of institutions—suggests a unified force that crested during the civil rights movement. Historically, black Christians in America have overwhelmingly been identified with Protestant denominations, a legacy of the simultaneous rise of slavery and Protestant evangelicalism in the Deep South. Black Protestants, moreover, historically have been overwhelmingly Baptist and Methodist. African Americans, then, historically have been per capita one of the most Protestant ethnic groups in the country. On the other hand, "the black church" and its leaders have been the constant subject and target of relentless criticism. From the repeated attempts to reform the ritual behavior of African American worshippers through the repression of shouting and other emotionally enthusiastic practices to the frequent parodying of "jackleg" ministers in black music and literature and film to the steady drumbeat of criticisms of "otherworldly" ministers and church organizations more devoted to inward-looking institution building than to

practical programs of social reform, black Protestantism has been as beleaguered as it has been powerful. Its most eloquent and elegiac defenders and
its fiercest critics have come from within the black community. In short, the
church with the soul of a nation has been, for much of its history, a frustrated
fellowship. This is a fundamental paradox of the history of black Protestantism in America.

Another fundamental paradox is this: white Americans spread Christianity, specifically Protestantism, among black Americans, intending not only
to evangelize people of color but also to make them more secure and con-
tented in their enslavement. The end result was precisely the opposite: ultimately, African American Christianity provided the language and the spirit
of African American survival under slavery, and of African American freedom
movements toward the destruction of apartheid.

And a final paradox: black Protestants empowered the social revolution of
the civil rights movement, and have become associated with a powerful and
solid voting bloc for liberal-left candidates in politics, *even though* the theology of the black church historically has been conservative and devoutly
evangelical. In the civil rights years, by rejecting the fundamental premises
of mid-twentieth-century optimism, returning instead to the prophetic and
jeremiadic tradition of biblical texts, black Protestants—in that moment, at
least—became the church that cleansed the soul of a nation.

General Studies

African Americans had to create their own history and historiography within
a context of American history writing that ignored, patronized, or demon-
ized Negroes. The history of the history of black Protestantism begins with
in-house denominational narratives from the nineteenth century, especially
from writers in the African Methodist Episcopal tradition. They wrote to
heroize their founders and predecessors and to exhort the faithful in building denominational institutions. A good bibliography of many of these older
documents may be found in Albert Raboteau et al., "Retelling Carter Woodson's Story." More modern scholarship on the subject may be dated from
Carter Woodson's classic *History of the Negro Church,* a general survey focusing on the rise of denominations, the biographies of prominent clergymen, and the achievements of individuals coming from church traditions.
As Albert Raboteau summarized its contents, "it moves briskly toward the
history of black evangelicalism. Baptists and Methodists abound in Woodson's pages—and they are mostly male and usually clergy, and they are generally busy building institutions, conducting educational and social service en-

terprises, and fighting the good fight politically. One reads little there about the missionary societies of black women or the special performance styles of black preaching and worship." While obviously dated, Woodson's narrative remains a starting point, if only because few have tried to duplicate a general short narrative history in that form since. Some years later, the famous black sociologist E. Franklin Frazier produced *The Negro Church in America,* but his critical sociological treatise lacks the solid historical research that graced Woodson's work.[2]

Between the pioneering efforts of Woodson and the more contemporary accounts dating from the 1960s forward, a generation of scholars—sociologists, historians, public policy activists, cultural anthropologists, and others—provided a consistent, and mostly negative, picture of "the Negro" in church and of "the Negro Church," by which they meant black Protestantism. Psychological theories of "compensatory" religion, a kind of psychologized "opiate of the masses" theory, abound in these works. Gunnar Myrdal's *American Dilemma,* Hortense Powdermaker's *After Freedom,* and Benjamin Mays and Joseph Nicholson's *The Negro's Church* depicted black religion as being as politically inert as it was psychologically "compensatory." The basically pathological condition of Negro life in America, created by the gross violation of the "American creed" of equality as applied to black people, engendered a religious culture dependent on excesses of emotionalism—seen in the screaming, shouting, and crying in church—to symbolically and emotionally fill what could not be realized in an everyday world designed to relentlessly degrade Negroes.[3]

Coming from a deeply religious background in South Carolina, a student of divinity at Howard as well as a professor at Morehouse College, Benjamin Mays was more sympathetic than other scholars to the richness of African American religious life, but his basic interpretation relied on the psychological model pervasive in academia during the interwar years. In *The Negro's God, as Reflected in His Literature,* he found most black ideas of God historically to be of the "traditional, compensatory" type: "The masses, on the whole, see no connection between God and social and economic reconstruction." Ironically, this was even more the case in the twentieth century than before, when (for example) the spirituals at least vaguely limned a better world. Mays concluded: "the Negro is not interested in any fine theological or philosophical discussions about God. He is interested in a God who is able to help him bridge the chasm that exists between the actual and the ideal. The Negro's life has been too unstable, too precarious, too uncertain, and his needs have been too great for him to become sufficiently objective to theologize or philosophize about God."[4]

In the 1960s, the civil rights and black power movements compelled a fundamental rethinking of African American history. As academia, at first begrudgingly and later with more alacrity, responded to these trends, at last scholars found intellectual and financial resources to reenvision the entire subject of African American religious history. One early scholarly production, Gayraud Wilmore's *Black Religion and Black Radicalism,* provided a new narrative synthesis. Looking for heroes rather than villains, and tying together disparate subjects into a story that highlighted a march toward freedom at nearly all stages, Wilmore's text fit with a historiography that was overturning old racist vestiges of demonization as well as more recent reliance on the kind of psychological theorizing famously employed by Stanley Elkins in his hypothesis of the slave plantation as a kind of totalizing concentration camp that broke people so completely that they became the "Sambo" personality of lore. Of Presbyterian training, Wilmore became part of the same coterie of black intellectuals as James Cone, whose seminal text *Black Theology and Black Power* launched the contemporary "black theology" movement of the 1960s and 1970s. Wilmore's historical work was one of the earliest attempts to provide an interpretive survey history of black religious life and to connect African American religious history with contemporary struggles. It is clear to the reader now how much of this scholarship depended on simply reversing old stereotypes rather than asking newer questions, and how the heroes of the new history were invariably male. In this sense, this early scholarship emerging from the civil rights years unconsciously reproduced the basic outlines of church history as it was still taught.[5]

Ironically, perhaps the most memorable chapters in Wilmore's work are "The Deradicalization of the Black Church" and "The Secularization of Black Radicalism," which examine the apparent retreat of the black church from the public sphere after World War I and leading into the 1950s. At the time of his writing, for example, the largest African American denomination, the National Baptist Convention, was headed by J. H. Jackson, famous for driving Martin Luther King Jr. out of the convention. Jackson represented an older tradition of working for black rights within the system, a midcentury consensus that was in fact characteristic of other major preachers of his era, as Wallace Best makes clear in a recent article on Jackson's career. Nonetheless, from the standpoint of the 1960s, Jackson personified a reactionary and insular church establishment. Even after his excoriating of the frustrated fellowship and deradicalization of the church, Wilmore still concluded that "Black pride and power, Black nationalism and Pan-Africanism have had no past without the Black church and Black religion, and without them it may well have no enduring future."[6]

Since the 1960s, scholars in the growth industry of African American history have fleshed out the history of black Protestantism. Most of this was done through more specific scholarly and monographic studies, to be detailed below. But in 1990, C. Eric Lincoln and Lawrence Mamiya's *The Black Church in the African-American Experience* attempted to provide an overall survey and synthesis of the major black Christian traditions, from both historical and sociological perspectives, along with policy recommendations. As a reasonably comprehensive (if, at times, frustratingly plodding) assessment of black religious sensibility, spirituality, and structural organization, *The Black Church in the African-American Experience* remains an essential reference book for scholars. Lincoln and Mamiya described a black "sacred cosmos," with individual conversion and transformation at its core. Lincoln and Mamiya also proposed a "dialectical" model for interpreting African American religious history, emphasizing particularly tensions between the priestly and the prophetic, between ethnic particularism and Christian universalism, and between public activism and private piety. In short, the black church represents in institutional form the "double consciousness" that DuBois so memorably discussed. Lincoln and Mamiya collected significant amounts of historical and sociological data about the seven major black Protestant denominations and presented their findings together with extensive notes, appendixes, and bibliography. Moreover, Lincoln and Mamiya provide capsule histories of the major black denominations (as good a starting point for black denominational history as exists), an examination of women in the black church, a look at music and the black church, and a survey of black rural and urban clergy. Lincoln and Mamiya's work represented an important accomplishment, if for no other reason than the accumulation of significant data and for proposing some major themes to explore. Their text is limited to the degree it stays within carefully delimited boundaries of "church history."[7]

Scholars have searched for new ways of comprehending and narrating denominational life, including the black denominations. In their work, institutional history remains important, for religious folk live and operate within institutions. And yet much of the most compelling recent work suggests how people create religious life regardless of institutional constraints, and indeed how denominations become focal points for lived religious experience that may bear only a tangential relationship to the particulars of a denomination's history. For African American religious history, this often takes the form of examining tensions between an "assimilated" or "white" religious style, usually endorsed by guardians of institutional orthodoxy, and African-based or "folk" religious forms practiced by local people regardless of or in spite of denominational mandates.[8]

Birth of Black Protestantism

Beginning in the late eighteenth century, black slaves and free people of color converted to Christianity in significant numbers. The most important moment for the birth of black evangelical Protestantism came with the Great Awakening and the evangelical revolutions of the late eighteenth and early nineteenth centuries. The importance of this moment in Afro-American Protestant history can scarcely be overstated, and Sylvia Frey and Betty Wood capture this in the opening paragraph of their work *Come Shouting to Zion:* "The passage from traditional religions to Christianity was arguably the single most significant event in African American history. It created a community of faith and provided a body of values and a religious commitment that became in time the principal solvent of ethnic differences and the primary source of cultural identity. It provided Afro-Atlantic peoples with an ideology of resistance and the means to absorb the cultural norms that turned Africans into African Americans." Black churches then trained "men and women who were to lead the community out of slavery and into a new identity as free African American Christians." Frey and Wood's excellent narrative survey also traces, and implicitly decries, the way the profoundly egalitarian impulse of early southern evangelicalism eventually gave way to church structures that reproduced the very hierarchies they originally challenged, part of the "dichotomous themes" of racial equality and racial submission that formed the dialectic of race and American evangelicalism. Frey and Wood's work, moreover, engages black religious history within the framework of the "Atlantic World," which has for the last generation been the cutting-edge conversation of colonial history. Jon Sensbach, among others, has illuminated the international Afro-Moravian and Afro-Protestant world in the Americas, Europe, and Africa. Frey and Wood, moreover, stress the central role of women in the "reciprocal process" that characterized the relationship of enslaved Africans to Christianity during this initial stage of conversion, providing in the process a model of how to avoid making denominational history a de facto synonym for male history.[9]

After an initial bout of grand historical synthesizing in the vein of Gayraud Wilmore's heroizing of the black radical tradition, and with the explosion of scholarship that came on the heels of the "social history revolution," it became clear that in order to understand the lives of ordinary Americans (as was the quest of the new social historians), one would have to understand their religious expressions and institutions. Thus, a social history revolution that emerged from a context of recapturing the American past from dominance by elites or by "social control" theories ironically, and unintentionally, set the stage for the remarkable rise of American religious history over the last generation. Much of that religious history went back to the sources—to diaries and letters, to church records, to the slave narratives, to tracts and novels, and to hymns and musical records—to understand how people went about creating sacred orders. In no other field has that scholarship been more influential than in African American religious history.

In the 1970s, early in this process of reprobing old sources (especially church records) with new questions, Milton Sernett's pioneering work began to uncover the world of biracial Protestantism. As evangelicalism spread throughout the South, white slave owners often brought slaves to church with them. Many antebellum churches in the South were filled with whites on the main floor and slaves in the balcony. In some cases, especially in southern urban centers such as Richmond and Charleston, black congregants formed a majority of "white" churches. More recently, the essays compiled by John Boles in *Masters and Slaves in the House of the Lord* detail the story further, through a series of local case studies that again show, in instance after instance, how much "southern" religion was biracial. All of this scholarship provided historical understanding for the fascinating juxtaposition of white and black southern evangelicalism, how white and black evangelical churches could look so much alike and so utterly different at the same time.[10]

Beyond this visible church lay the "invisible institution"—slave religion. Few topics in American history have attracted such a body of high-quality and innovative scholarship, ranging from Albert Raboteau's synoptic classic *Slave Religion* to Eugene Genovese's magisterial survey *Roll, Jordan, Roll* to Lawrence Levine's pioneering cultural history *Black Culture and Black Consciousness* to Charles Joyner's intensive study of one plantation community in *Down by the Riverside* and shorter broad survey "Believer I Know" to Mechal Sobel's innovative *The World They Made Together* and intensive exploration of the internal dynamics of slave conversion in *Trabelin' On* to Sylvia Frey and Betty Wood's wide-ranging survey *Come Shouting to Zion* to Eddie Glaude's intellectual history of black notions of religion, race, and nationhood in *Exodus* to Michael Gomez's more skeptical take on the extent of evangelical influence in *Exchanging Their Country Marks*. The civil rights movement energized this scholarship; attention to the sources required that religious history become central to the story.[11]

The bulk of Albert Raboteau's *Slave Religion* takes up where Frey and Wood's *Come Shouting to Zion* chronologically leaves off; and Raboteau still sets the standard for all subsequent studies of the subject. In the initial section of his book, Raboteau depicts the "death of the gods," meaning the inevitable demise of African religions in any systemic form. There were "retentions" and "survivals," fragments of surviving African religious customs, as Melville Herskovits had documented in his older classic *The Myth of the Negro Past*, but the brutal passage to the New World meant that African religions would not survive intact. This latter argument has been pressed to its full logical conclusion in Jon Butler's provocative and controversial piece "The African Spiritual Holocaust," which insists that religious systems be understood as an integral whole and, consequently, that African systems necessarily were killed by the brutalities of the slave trade. Nonetheless, while African religions died, from their remnants African American Christianity took its characteristic cultural forms. In Raboteau's account, enslaved Christians might have attended white-sanctioned and -supervised services, sung Anglo-American hymns, and listened to southern ministers instruct them in the virtues of obedience, patience, and humility. But they also created their own covert religious culture, one with its own distinctive theology and rituals. In services held in slave cabins, in the woods at night, and in "hush arbors," enslaved African Americans developed a religious culture that brought together elements of their African past and their American evangelical training. Before the war, when independent institutions were impossible, black religious life emerged most clearly in religious rituals such as ring shouts, spirituals, and chanted sermons.[12]

Historians of African American life in search of intellectual models to help them comprehend their primary documents found a perfect answer in cultural anthropology, particularly of the kind practiced by Clifford Geertz. In studying people who often left little or no conventional written records of the kind customarily studied by historians but did leave a rich legacy of oral traditions, anthropologically inspired history proved essential in opening up the religious worlds of slaves. For example, the black spirituals, the most memorable cultural product of antebellum slave religious life, have inspired much excellent historical, theological, and musicological scholarship. No one has yet surpassed Lawrence Levine's account of the slave spirituals in the first chapter of *Black Culture and Black Consciousness* in terms of exploring their meaning. The spirituals cannot be attributed to individual authors, but instead emerged as a sort of communal voice of slave believers. More important than the origins of the spirituals are their meaning set within the ritual context—the hush arbors and secret meetings—of slave religion. Much debate has centered on the degree to which the spirituals contained encoded messages. To what degree was the spiritual freedom referred to in so many songs in effect a code for freedom from slavery? For generations of slaves, there was simply no viable hope that freedom would come in this life. But in times of turmoil and war, when the very future of slavery was in question, freedom could take on more obvious meanings. The spirituals exalted Old Testament heroes such as Moses as well as more obscure figures, and often turned New Testament figures such as Jesus into Old Testament avenging heroes. These biblical heroes, moreover, were available in the present. Sacred time merged with real time when President Lincoln came way down in Egypt land at last.

Independent Black Churches in the Antebellum Era

In addition to the invisible institution of slave religion, black Protestantism took on a visible form in the antebellum era as well. In the South, from the 1820s forward, black congregations sometimes were allowed a separate existence from their white parent churches. Over 150 separate black churches were formed, many with separate buildings, pastors, and deacons. The very presence of these congregations testified to the faith of enslaved Baptists in the power of the Christian message to overcome the most unpromising of conditions. The churches were not independent, but they nurtured independent spirits. Mechal Sobel's assiduous research, appearing in the appendixes of her underappreciated book *Trabelin' On,* details the extent and membership strength of the independent black churches in the antebellum South.

Meanwhile, free African Americans in the North created the first independent black denominations, notably the African Methodist Episcopal Church and the African Methodist Episcopal Zion Church. Though formally organized as denominations in 1816 and 1822, both grew out of experiences much earlier, when black Methodist parishioners in Philadelphia and New York were denied equal access to the communion table and generally disrespected and dehumanized in God's house. African American Christians of various denominations organized into separate congregations, as the millennial hopes deriving from the American Revolution and the gradual abolition of slavery in the North gave way to the reality of Jim Crow in northern cities and violent conflict with the Irish and other immigrants for working-class job opportunities on the docks and elsewhere. James Campbell's *Songs of Zion,* discussed further below, is the essential work on the rise of African Methodism, but one may also consult older works on blacks in antebellum cities, such as Leon Litwack's *North of Slavery* and Gary Nash's *Forging Freedom.* Patrick Rael's insightful *Black Identity and Black Protest in the Antebellum North* as well as his important article "Black Theodicy" also emphasize how Christian belief paired with American republicanism and the deeply rooted idea of America as a "chosen nation" fundamentally shaped black expressions of protest against enslavement and oppression in both South and North. The intellectual history of black nationalism, in short, arose from a deeply Protestant context, in spite of the role that Protestantism also played in propagating the ideas that enslaved and oppressed black Americans. The relationship of African Americans to Protestantism, again, formed one of the most fundamental dialectics of American religious history.[13]

African American Protestantism after the Civil War

The Civil War was the central apocalyptic moment for nineteenth-century black believers. Once again, in the process of trying to capture the social history of ordinary Americans, historians (often belatedly) woke up to the significant role of evangelical belief and practice in comprehending such central events of American history as the Civil War and Reconstruction. Reginald Hildebrand's *The Times Were Strange and Stirring* is one of numerous works to capture the depth of the spirit moving through formerly enslaved communities. In taking religion seriously as a central part of the largest stories of the Civil War/Reconstruction era, and in particular of the African American experience during Reconstruction, two themes emerge. One is the active and crucial role of African American ministers and congregations in state- and local-level politics. Another theme, perhaps more intangible but just as important, concerns how religious discourse shaped Reconstruction and Redemption. Black southerners certainly understood the history of their times in the powerful imagery of the Bible, and the numerous ministers involved in Reconstruction-era politics encouraged that. The consultations during Reconstruction between government officials, including the Freedmen's Bureau, and the black clergy suggested the remarkable changes wrought by emancipation, a story told in a number of works, including Andrew Billingsley's *Mighty Like a River.*[14]

After the war, independent churches and denominational organizations sprang up quickly in black communities, including thousands of small local congregations and major national organizations such as the African Methodist Episcopal Church and the National Baptist Convention. Only a decade after the war, hardly any black parishioners still worshipped in the historically white southern churches. Through the last part of the nineteenth century, black church membership grew rapidly. By the 1906 religious census, the National Baptist Convention claimed more than 2 million communicants, or over 61 percent of black churchgoers. The African Methodist Episcopal Church (AME) church numbered some 500,000, the African Methodist Episcopal Zion (AMEZ) denomination about 185,000, the Colored Methodist Episcopal (CME) sect approximately 173,000, and the Methodist Episcopal

Church (MEC) about 60,000 black adherents. Altogether, church member-ship among African Americans rose from 2.6 million to 3.6 million between 1890 and 1906.

Daniel Stowell's *Rebuilding Zion* and William Montgomery's *Under Their Own Vine and Fig Tree* both document extensively the impressive institutional growth of independent black churches after the Civil War. Stowell's work, focusing on religious institutions after the war, is nicely complemented by Montgomery's more culturally analytical account. Montgomery emphasizes the "merging" of the folk religiosity of the slaves with the institutional churches of American denominationalism brought to the South by northern missionaries. The resulting black denominations were "complex and factious" precisely because of their mixed heritage. Overnight, a northern denomination such as the African Methodist Episcopal Church became a predominantly southern institution, as black Methodist leaders welcomed legions of ex-slaves into their ranks and attempted to teach them the ways of "dignified" and "rational" worship. Montgomery offers a compelling look at the controversies over "the spirit of worship" arising out of the continued vitality of folk traditions in countryside churches. Mongtomery finds churches divided within themselves between integrationism and separatism and thus voicing a multiplicity of views from conservative accommodationism to radical separatism. While recognizing the expediently calibrated ecclesiastical response to the rise of Jim Crow, Montgomery nevertheless stresses how the church was "an important instrument for the steady advancement of African Americans."[15]

Black and white missionaries in the post–Civil War South pursued the work of "political evangelization," the securing of religious and political rights for the former bondspeople. Henry McNeal Turner was a powerful evangelist for the African Methodist Episcopal Church. His story is told capably in Stephen Angell's *Henry McNeal Turner and African-American Religion in the South*. Born free in South Carolina in 1834, the young Turner quickly established himself as a prominent AME churchman, missionary, legislator, newspaper editor, and rhetorical firebrand. The AME and its sister competitor the AMEZ sent missionaries to evangelize what they perceived to be waiting masses of freedpeople who needed the leadership of the venerable black ecclesiastical bodies. Clarence Walker's *Rock in a Weary Land* fills out the narrative of African Methodist expansion in the South during Reconstruction. Turner and his fellows saw their religious work as essential to securing full citizenship rights for the freedpeople. When southern-style racism swept the country in the 1890s, Turner's rhetoric grew harsher. As editor of the *Voice of Missions*, the major project in the last two decades of his life, Turner articulated what would later be called black theology.[16]

Turner's career was remarkable, yet throughout the South dozens of black ministers and missionaries forged notable careers in political evangelization. In comparison to Turner, many languish in relative obscurity. One was the Georgia Baptist, educator, newspaper publisher, and outspoken advocate against segregation William Jefferson White, whose career is detailed in an important article by Bobby Donaldson. Other figures who have attracted scholarly interest include Holland Thompson of Alabama, whose career in the black Baptist church has been recounted by Howard Rabinowitz; and Richard Boyd, who rose from slave roots to build the single largest black publishing house in the country, the National Baptist Publishing Board.[17]

In some locales, African Americans joined with some whites in protesting the racial separation and segregation of the major denominations. This was most notably true in New Orleans, as recounted in James Bennett's *Religion and the Rise of Jim Crow*. According to the standard historiography, presented effectively in Katharine Dvorak's *An African-American Exodus*, after the Civil War black Christians in the South, seeking cultural self-determination in their own institutions and offended by the refusal of white Christians to recognize the equality of souls before God, immediately moved into wholly independent African American churches. Bennett provides a fascinating counterpoint by following the saga of the Methodist Episcopal Church and the Catholic Church in New Orleans. He argues that the MEC and Catholic churches resisted the trend toward creating racially separate churches and denominations, but eventually both became "southernized" in terms of their acquiescence to Jim Crow. But this outcome, Bennett forcefully argues, was imposed over the vigorous protests of black Christians in the Crescent City, who fought for a desegregated church in a desegregated society.[18]

As the hopes for Reconstruction dimmed in the darkening reality of postwar apartheid, African American religious leaders continued the tradition of protest that they had developed from the very earliest days of black Protestant resistance to white supremacy in the church. While this essay focuses mostly on historiography, scholars of African American religion, and more generally of American religious history, will be grateful for Stephen Angell's and Anthony B. Pinn's *Social Protest Thought in the African Methodist Episcopal Church, 1862–1939*, which serves for this period the same seminal role of opening up relatively inaccessible documents as Patrick Rael et al.'s *Pamphlets of Protest* does for the antebellum era. This essential volume collects and reprints writings, primarily from the *A.M.E. Church Review* and

secondarily from the *Christian Recorder,* the monthly intellectual periodical
and the weekly newspaper published by the African Methodist Episcopal
Church. This primary source compilation will take its place alongside Milton
Sernett's *Afro-American Religious History: A Documentary Witness* as an in-
dispensable tool for scholars, students, and research libraries.[19]

The primary sources presented by Angell/Pinn and Sernett make a perfect backdrop for James Campbell's essential *Songs of Zion,* which ranks still
as the most significant work in African American religious history to appear since Raboteau's *Slave Religion.* Campbell's story is, he says, "a study of
the complex human and imaginative traffic that binds African and African
American experience." He finds this "traffic" not so much in the realm of culture but instead in "African American intellectual and imaginative life, particularly in the imagination of black Christians. . . . black Christians could
not establish their own identity until they had defined their relationship with
their ancestral continent."[20]

Of the many themes connecting the dots on the triangular intellectual
trade traced in Campbell's study, the paradigm of "respectability" is perhaps
the most important. In recent years historians of African American religion
have pondered deeply the complex issue of respectability. Self-respect was at
the core of the church's identity from the beginning. Just like the white denominations, the African Methodists began the slow march upward toward
respectability through the nineteenth century. They created a professionalized class of bishops to oversee the church hierarchy; they enforced church
discipline in local congregations; they extracted what money they could from
their poor congregants and built impressive temples of worship in the larger
urban areas; and they wrote hymns and preached sermons in a style far removed from the camp meeting excesses of early Methodism. But none of
this drive to respectability could succeed in making African Methodists "respectable" in the eyes of Americans; they were colored people, with no rights
that the white man was bound to respect. Church officials responded to this
by vigorously campaigning against the endless varieties of American racism. In the late nineteenth century, the American AME Church evangelized
among the freedpeople, carrying the message of respectability and racial dignity. "Ultimately," Campbell explains, "African Methodism embodied both
tendencies—rebellion and respectability, freedom and authority. . . . These
twined impulses emerged from the same realities; they represented responses
to the same cruel dilemmas."[21]

The dilemma was indeed cruel. On the one hand, to be respected, blacks
had to engage successfully in the dominant discourse, and individual black
persons had to serve as "representative individuals," icons of race pride who

met all the tests of success by white standards; on the other hand, doing so required adopting a standard of "civilization" that by definition excluded most of the practices that gave African American religion its particular power. DuBois's essays in *Souls of Black Folk* balanced this tension perfectly, as he opened each chapter with a verse from European "high" poetry juxtaposed with a selection from what he called the "sorrow songs" (the spirituals).

In more recent scholarly literature Evelyn Brooks Higginbotham's theoretically informed and influential book *Righteous Discontent* provides the latest and most searching exploration of how the canons of bourgeois respectability both distanced African American church leaders from their own folk and also provided an ideological weapon in the struggle against racism. Hers is, as well, the first serious and extended study that places black women at the center of African American religious life, a subject that will greatly benefit from the ongoing Women and Religions of the African Diaspora project. Higginbotham narrates the remarkable careers of black Baptist women who organized missionary societies, especially Nannie Helen Burroughs. She argues that women in the black Baptist convention forged a space, a "public sphere," for themselves, outside the dictates of the male-dominated convention structures. Organized into the Woman's Auxiliary of the National Baptist Convention, black Baptist women such as Burroughs pursued racial justice politics, progressive reform, and racial uplift. If their distinctly bourgeois agenda sometimes misunderstood or repressed the expressive choices of black working-class women, they nonetheless seized the limited means available to resist the imposition of Jim Crow. They also articulated a nascent but powerful "feminist theology" that challenged the masculinist tone and style of the male church leadership.[22]

From the works canvassed thus far, it is clear that scholarship on black Protestants has generally concentrated in one of three areas: (1) assessing the role of "the black church" (usually singularized like that) in the political life of the Jim Crow South and of apartheid-era America; (2) discussing the growing divide between practitioners of "slave religion" or "folk religion"— with their exuberantly emotional worship rites—and adherents to norms of bourgeois respectability in church; (3) more recently, analyzing the gendered nature of the black church. A fourth category of study has emerged as well, pioneered by Lawrence Levine's *Black Culture and Black Consciousness: Afro-American Folk Thought from Slavery to Freedom*. Scholars have addressed subjects such as ring shouts, conjure rituals, chanted sermonizing, and blues hollers. In such activities, students of religious culture have discovered a rich tradition of black expressive culture percolating underneath the smothering rhetoric of "uplift" and respectability.

One prime example of what might be called the "cultural turn" in African American religious history is John Giggie's *After Redemption: Jim Crow and the Transformation of African-American Religion in the Delta, 1874–1914*. Drawing from ideas about consumption and material culture, Giggie suggestively creates a "feel" for the religious community developing in the postbellum rural Delta region, regarding not only what people did in church settings but also how they acted there, what kinds of things they bought, and what kinds of decorations and items of material culture they considered important. In particular, Giggie focuses on the impact of commercial culture even in the rural and poor Delta region (brought there largely via catalogs from northern cities) and the complicated ways religious folk alternately celebrated, capitalized on, and rejected marketplace impulses.[23]

Giggie's work nicely complements Jon Spencer's *Blues and Evil* and Yvonne Chireau's *Black Magic*. Neither of the latter two is about black Protestantism per se, but they do analyze a religious culture that pervaded black communities and thus deeply influenced the cultural forms of black Protestantism. In *Blues and Evil*, Jon Spencer, a prolific author in the field of black theomusicology, depicts the blues as one medium for older African-derived spiritualities driven underground by the assimilationist tendencies of late nineteenth-century black religious leaders. The power of folk traditions also receives sweeping historical analysis in Yvonne Chireau's study of four centuries of black magic. Chireau shows how for African Americans, both slave and free, religion and magic provided complementary strategies to deal with the most philosophical and long-range (religion) as well as the most immediate and practical (magic) needs of their spiritual and quotidian lives. Additionally, Chireau pulls together research on how the belief patterns and practices of conjure found their way into African American Pentecostalism, the Spiritualist churches in New Orleans and elsewhere, and the blues. Hans Baer's work on black Spiritualism in New Orleans, recently reissued, analyzes the crazy-quilt religious culture of New Orleans–based Spiritualism. Scattered through the Crescent City, Spiritualist churches imported objects and rites from the conjure world—roots, candles, ointments, chants, and notions of bodily possession. The cultural studies of scholars such as Spencer, Chireau, and Baer have understood that religion is, at heart, lived, embodied, and physically expressed, and that embodied religious expressions are not necessarily symptomatic of psychological "compensation" or political "deradicalization." These are studies squarely in the larger academic worlds of cultural history and "lived religion."[24]

In this sense, all these works of cultural history just discussed—by Chireau, Giggie, Spencer, and others—represent an important trend in denominational history: to explore cultural themes that transcend denominations, but may take particular form within church institutions, and provide thick descriptions of lived religion within church bodies regulated by particular denominational rules. Again, this pattern of historiography has influenced much of American religious history, but it has been particularly powerful in ethnoreligious studies of African Americans, Latinos, and immigrants (especially Italian and eastern European Catholics). In this work, denominational institutions remain important, because they are sites where people's individual lived religious experience intersects with, complements, or rubs against communal history and memory.

Transition to Civil Rights Era

Recent scholarship has been focused heavily on the post–Civil War era, and then on the "King years." The in-between times, from World War I to the 1950s, have been relatively neglected and remain rich for study. Significant recent works include Milton Sernett's *Bound for the Promised Land.* Sernett traces how the migration of African Americans from south to north, most famously from the Delta to Chicago, led to the urbanization of African American Christianity, which to that point had been largely rural and small-town. Even more significant, he finds that the migration set the stage for combining the two poles—protest and praise—that Lincoln and Mamiya had set up as central to the dialectic of black church history. The Great Migration, Sernett writes, was the "catalyst for the revitalization of a church doctrine that stressed the importance of more fully understanding the social dimensions" of Christianity. The migration, in short, witnessed the "confluence of praise and protest. The preaching, prayer, music, and shouting of today's urban black churches are shaped by influences born of that generation," when scores of migrants moved north "in need of material assistance but also bearing spiritual gifts." That the churches did as well as they did in this unrealistic task is a testament to the adaptability of black Protestant institutions to the wrenching historical transformations brought on by the migration.[25]

Sernett's work on the black church and urban migration nicely complements the more narrowly focused but fascinating work by Michael Harris on the black gospel pioneer Thomas Dorsey. Harris's *The Rise of the Gospel Blues* documents the way in which southern folk religious forms found their way into northern churches and gradually broke through the walls of respectability that northern black churches put up in an effort to protect their class status. Nick Salvatore's *Singing in a Strange Land,* a superbly written biography of the Reverend C. L. Franklin (father of Aretha Franklin), relates this story in rich detail. A migrant from the Mississippi Delta to Detroit, the Reverend Franklin was a master of "the whoop," the rhythmic and ecstatic style of African American folk sermon delivery. He took it to new heights when he married the African American sermonic form to contemporary themes. Franklin's generation of ministers grew restive with the fundamentalist literalism of their earliest religious training. They understood that "the whoop" would be even more powerful, not less, when linked to the modern African American experience of migration, segregation, and discrimination, as well as of upward mobility.[26]

Black Pentecostalism should prove to be a major source of provocative studies in black Protestant history, particularly insofar as black Protestants (notably William Seymour) were among the primary founders of Pentecostalism itself. Moreover, black Pentecostal groups embraced rather than rejected or limited African-based cultural forms (especially in music and physical expression), enormously influencing all American religious culture in the process. In an earlier generation of scholarship, black Pentecostals stood almost as the archetypical examples of "compensatory" religion, with storefront churches in northern cities offering shouting experiences instead of pragmatic help for urban migrants wandering in a new wilderness. In more recent scholarship, Pentecostals appear in very different guises: as cultural innovators who understood religion's physicality, and as denominational revolutionaries in their willingness to provide ministerial space to anyone who had the call, including women.

Black Pentecostals are only just coming into their own in scholarly studies, but one should consult Wallace Best's recent *Passionately Human, No Less Divine,* a classic example of the way in which Holiness/Pentecostalism opened up space for female religious impresarios and entrepreneurs, and Anthea Butler's dissertation on women in the Church of God in Christ, the single largest black Pentecostal denomination. Work on black Pentecostalism also has provided an ideal opportunity for bringing the cultural emphases of studies of slave religion into the twentieth-century context. Jerma Jackson's *Singing in My Soul,* for example, covers the rise of black gospel music, paying particular attention to the immensely talented but long-neglected figure of Rosetta Tharpe. Tharpe bridged the gap from the obscure Holiness/Pentecostal world that kept alive the exuberant tradition of black religious music from the nineteenth century to the black gospel world of the twentieth, performing onstage, in nightclubs, and on records. "Together," explains Jackson, "the singers and audiences of gospel . . . forged a place for the music at the interstices of church and commerce."[27]

Far removed from the incantatory rites of black Pentecostals, Spiritual-

ists, and conjurers, one finds the world of black intellectuals. They had a conflicted relationship with religion. W. E. B. DuBois, for example, celebrated
the creations of black religious culture, such as the spirituals, while blast-
ing the wasted potential of the church, in one case asking, "[W]hat is this
church doing towards its primary task of teaching men right and wrong, and
the duty of doing right? The flat answer is nothing, if not less than nothing. . . . It was built up a body of dogma and fairy tale, fantastic fables of
sin and salvation." Edward Blum's *W. E. B. Du Bois: American Prophet* provides the definitive interpretation of the relationship of DuBois and religion. Blum reconciles the side of DuBois that was a rationalist, an empiri-
cist, a social scientist and, later in his life, a Communist with the side that
produced those deeply soul-searching essays in *Souls of Black Folk* and *Dark-
water.* Blum shows the consistency and depth of DuBois's spiritual explora-
tions throughout his intellectual career. Clarence Taylor's *Black Religious Intellectuals: The Fight for Equality from Jim Crow to the 21st Century* surveys a
range of figures from various religious traditions. As Blum does with DuBois,
Taylor finds a spiritual sensibility even in those, such as the labor leader A.
Philip Randolph, who expressed hostility to organized religion. Taylor also
includes figures from the Pentecostal tradition, such as Bishop Smallwood
Williams, who generally have been ignored in the scholarship, using them to
show the breadth of black religious thought and social activism.[28]

In terms of the black church and politics, the era from World War I to the
classic civil rights era, dating from *Brown v. Board,* provides rich material
for study. A much older tradition of scholarship, exemplified by Hortense
Powdermaker's *After Freedom* and Charles Johnson's *Shadow of the Plantation,* portrayed African American Protestantism in this era as essentially
otherworldly and ineffectual. As scholars have pushed back the history of
the civil rights movement to incorporate black activism from World War I
to 1950, though, the "hidden transcript" of this time has emerged more evi-
dently. Black religious liberals and radicals, for example, receive extensive
attention in Paul Harvey's *Freedom's Coming.* Harvey emphasizes the lives
of southern religious progressives and radicals who, in relative anonymity
and often under the most difficult of conditions, carried on the struggle for
interracial justice at a time when few were paying much attention, and when
struggling for freedom could come at the cost of one's life.[29]

Civil Rights Era

Born in 1868 and dying just on the eve of the March on Washington in 1963,
W. E. B. DuBois was a true Moses; he lived to see but never enter the Promised

Land. The same might be said for the Reverend Vernon Johns, Martin Luther King's predecessor at Dexter Avenue Baptist Church in Montgomery, Alabama, and one of the least known but more important black religious figures of the twentieth century. The controversial Johns, perhaps best described as a "feisty orator," prepared the way for the young and studious Martin Luther King, in 1954 still a doctoral student at Boston University. King's quiet demeanor contrasted sharply with Johns's penchant for picking fights and pointing out the faults of his congregants, and of the black church generally, too often and too publicly.

As he took over the pulpit of Ebenezer Baptist in Montgomery, Martin Luther King had no idea of the history that was about to overtake him, but longtime community activists quickly recognized the usefulness of the young doctoral candidate. The story in elaborate detail has been told most fully, and for a popular audience, in Taylor Branch's trilogy, especially in his magnificent *Parting the Waters*. David Garrow's *Bearing the Cross* provides a landmark scholarly biography that places King firmly in the context both of his southern religious roots and of his northern theological training and his connections with political organizers outside the church world such as Bayard Rustin. Garrow places much emphasis on King's visionary spiritual experience in the mid-1950s, steeling him for the numerous attempts on his life and the constant internecine struggles within movement organizations.[30]

Another seminal work in black Protestantism and civil rights is Aldon D. Morris's *The Origins of the Civil Rights Movement: Black Communities Organizing for Change*. He begins his story not with Montgomery but with an earlier boycott led by black Baptist pastor T. D. Jemison in Baton Rouge, Louisiana, in 1953, an action that set the stage for mass mobilizations to come. Morris refers to the Southern Christian Leadership Conference (SCLC) as the "decentralized arm of the black church." Morris argues strongly for the central role of churches in organizing and carrying out the black freedom struggle, noting that only an indigenous organization such as the church could have served so effectively as an agent of mass mobilization. The argument advanced by Morris is furthered by Andrew Manis's memorable biography of Fred Shuttlesworth, *A Fire You Can't Put Out*, which shows the longtime Baptist pastor in Birmingham at the forefront of civil rights crusades in this most brutally racist of southern cities long before the more well-known names from SCLC showed up in 1963.[31]

Numerous other civil rights books assess the role of religion in the movement. One of the most interesting interpretations comes from Charles M. Payne's compelling study *I've Got the Light of Freedom: The Organizing Tradition and the Mississippi Freedom Struggle*. Payne suggests that religion provided for women the same kind of organizing and sustaining gumption that landownership gave to men in Mississippi. Because there was more religion than there was landownership, women were largely responsible for keeping the movement alive at the grassroots in Mississippi. Men led, he argues, while women organized, a point since furthered in numerous local studies of civil rights activism, as well as by Charles Marsh's gripping chapter on Fannie Lou Hamer in his theological study of the ideas animating the civil rights struggle in Mississippi, *God's Long Summer.* As one poor Mississippi woman explained her conversion to movement activism, "Something hit me like a new religion." David Chappell's *Stone of Hope: Prophetic Religion and the Death of Jim Crow* provides a provocative analysis of this "new religion." Chappell stresses that "black southern activists got strength from old-time religion, and white supremacists failed, at the same moment, to muster the cultural strength that conservatives traditionally get from religion." Chappell portrays the movement's "nonviolent soldiers" as "driven not by modern liberal faith in human reason" but instead deriving power from a "prophetic tradition that runs from David and Isaiah in the Old Testament through Augustine and Martin Luther to Reinhold Niebuhr in the twentieth century." This prophetic view made the civil rights movement *move.*[32]

Black Protestantism in the Post–Civil Rights Era

An institution that has been so defined by the struggle for civil rights faces both opportunities and dilemmas in the post–civil rights era. On the one hand, the church has been one of the relatively few black institutions to survive and thrive in the post–civil rights era. This is because the church came about not simply as a result of the imposition of Jim Crow but because black Americans nurtured their churches as their own institutions. In recent years, the historic contrast between the conservative theology and the liberal politics of black churches has been narrowing and even closing to some degree, as activists on the religious-political right have exploited ideological affinities, particularly regarding beliefs about abortion and gay rights, to forge interracial alliances, especially around issues of gender and sexuality. Nonetheless, black churches also remained aligned with the civil rights agenda, and black voters still reliably turn out for Democratic and liberal candidates. Thus, the political impact of black Protestants is mixed, and the frustrations of fellowship with white Americans on both left and right remain difficult, as Anthony Pinn observes in *The Black Church in the Post–Civil Rights Era.*[33]

A number of recent studies have taken up the public role and life of black churches in the contemporary era. One of the best is *Long March Ahead,* pub-

lished as volume 2 of *The Public Influences of African American Churches.*
This book demonstrates once again the paradox that, despite the great collective power of African American churches, they have remained a frustrated
fellowship. As editor R. Drew Smith writes, "a consistent refrain is that there is
a potential for—or at least an expectation of—black church public policy influence that has been, to this point, largely unfilled." Admittedly, this is a significant burden to put on churches that are often placed within beleaguered
communities, but one "inherited as a result of their civil rights movement in-
volvements." Drawing from a survey of 1,956 African American churches, the
authors in this collection describe black Christian responses to issues such as
affirmative action controversies in Florida, welfare reform under the Clinton
administration, antiapartheid activism, health issues and the AIDS crisis in
the black community, and the "Boston Miracle" of crime reduction in the
1990s. The authors conclude that, while "a relatively small percentage of African American congregations have been actively engaged in public policy
activism in recent years," nevertheless that activism "has been characterized
by greater diversity with respect to issue orientation," including especially a
"greater emphasis on Africa-related policies and women's rights." But this
very diversification of issues also means that the relatively small core of ac-
tivist churches will have their influence spread thinly, furthering the legacy
of the remarkable power together with the "frustrated fellowship" of black
Protestant history.[34]

Studies of Black Protestantism: A Prospective

Despite the explosion of scholarship on black Protestantism in recent years,
scholars still enjoy many opportunities for significant research. For the early
years of black Protestantism, Jon Sensbach's *Rebecca's Revival* and Frey and
Wood's *Come Shouting to Zion* have placed Afro-Protestantism within the
context of the "Atlantic world," and one hopes this internationalization of
the study of black Protestantism will continue. The interaction of Christianity and Islam through the Atlantic world in the seventeenth and eighteenth
centuries is a vital area of research, as evidenced by Michael Gomez's encyclopedic study *Black Crescent.* Serious archival work on this subject, and on
the history of black religion in the New World generally, will be opened up
by the ongoing project entitled "African-American Religion: A Documentary
History Project," projected for many volumes. A sample of the riches awaiting scholars in African American religious history may be found on the project Web site.[35]

Black Pentecostalism is a second major area for future researchers. Works already cited by Anthea Butler, Wallace Best, and John Giggie, as well as Cecil Robeck's *The Azusa Street Mission and Revival,* all tell compelling stories and have begun to fill in one of the most exciting areas for research in American religious history generally. This is still a wide-open area, especially with the opening of the papers collected by the librarian and bibliographer Sherry Sherrod Dupree, now available for research at the Schomburg Center for Research in Black Culture in New York City. A full-length scholarly study of Church of God in Christ, while a challenge since the church does not have a public archive open for scholars, certainly would be a boon to scholarship.[36]

Next, important work remains to be done in studying the black church in the post–civil rights era. The two volumes in the African American Churches in Public Life project at Morehouse College, Smith's *Long March Ahead* and *New Day Begun,* as well as the recent survey by Anthony Pinn, *The Black Church in the Post–Civil Rights Era,* have provided good beginnings in this regard. "Faith-based activism" in a conservative era remains a critical area for further examination; so does the issue of the black church and sexuality. Finally, black parishioners increasingly are responding to the "megachurch" phenomenon, and assuming this continues, one may ask whether mainline denominations will come to be seen as irrelevant, as they have been in white churches. The "neo-Pentecostal revolution" that Lincoln and Mamiya noted in their 1990 work has exploded since then. In African American religion, this is most evident in the star preacher T. D. Jakes, born to a working-class family in West Virginia and now a preacher in Dallas (and confidant of, among others, George W. Bush), who pushes "prosperity theology" to an integrated crowd of enthusiastic listeners. A generation ago, Martin Luther King was certainly the best-known black minister; twenty years ago, it was Jesse Jackson. Now, it could be one of several figures, but T. D. Jakes and other neo-Pentecostal black ministers would certainly be in the running. To this may be added the impact of black parishioners attending historically "white" churches and the growth of historically black churches within white denominations like the Southern Baptist Convention. Overall, the history of black Protestantism should remain one of the most exciting and creative areas of scholarly research in American religious history.[37]

Notes

1. James Melvin Washington, "The Making of a Church with the Soul of a Nation, 1880–1889," in *African American Religious Thought: An Anthology,* ed. Cornel West and Eddie S. Glaude Jr. (Louisville: Westminster John Knox, 2003), 414–34; James Melvin

Washington, *Frustrated Fellowship: The Black Baptist Quest for Social Power* (Macon: Mercer University Press, 1986).

2. Albert Raboteau et al., "Retelling Carter Woodson's Story: Archival Sources for Afro-American Church History," *Journal of American History* 77, no. 1 (1990): 183–99; Carter Woodson, *History of the Negro Church* (Washington, DC: Associated Publishers, 1921); E. Franklin Frazier, *The Negro Church in America* (New York: Schocken, 1964).

3. Gunnar Myrdal, *An American Dilemma* (1948; repr., New York: McGraw Hill, 1964); Hortense Powdermaker, *After Freedom: A Cultural Study in the Deep South* (New York: Viking, 1939); Benjamin Mays and Joseph Nicholson, *The Negro's Church* (New York: Institute for Social Research, 1933).

4. Benjamin Mays, *The Negro's God, as Reflected in His Literature* (1936; repr., New York: Negro Universities Press, 1969), 96, 254.

5. Gayraud Wilmore, *Black Religion and Black Radicalism: An Interpretation of the Religious History of the Afro-American People,* 2nd ed. (New York: Orbis, 1973); James Cone, *Black Theology and Black Power* (New York: Seabury, 1969).

6. Wallace Best, "The Right Way Achieved and the Wrong Way Conquered: Reverend J. H. Jackson, Martin Luther King, Jr., and the Conflict over Civil Rights," *Religion and American Culture* 16, no. 2 (2006): 195–226; Wilmore, *Black Religion and Black Radicalism,* xiii.

7. C. Eric Lincoln and Lawrence Mamiya, *The Black Church in the African-American Experience* (Durham: Duke University Press, 1990).

8. Larry Murphy's invaluable edited collection *Down by the Riverside* provides an invaluable one-stop shopping resource and excerpts many of the works to be discussed below: *Down by the Riverside: Readings in African-American Religion* (New York: New York University Press, 2000).

9. Sylvia Frey and Betty Wood, *Come Shouting to Zion: African American Protestantism in the American South and the Caribbean to 1830* (Chapel Hill: University of North Carolina Press, 1998), 1; Jon Sensbach, *A Separate Canaan: The Making of an Afro-Moravian World in North Carolina, 1763–1840* (Chapel Hill: University of North Carolina Press, 1998); Jon Sensbach, *Rebecca's Revival: The Making of Afro-Christianity in the Atlantic World* (Cambridge: Harvard University Press, 2005).

10. Milton Sernett, *Black Religion and American Evangelicalism: White Protestants, Plantation Missions, and the Flowering of Negro Christianity, 1787–1865* (Metuchen, NJ: Scarecrow, 1975); John Boles, ed., *Masters and Slaves in the House of the Lord: Race and Religion in the American South, 1740–1870* (Lexington: University Press of Kentucky, 1988). See also Janet Cornelius, *Slave Missions and the Black Church in the Antebellum South* (Columbia: University of South Carolina Press, 1999).

11. Albert Raboteau, *Slave Religion: The "Invisible Institution" in the Antebellum*

South (New York: Oxford University Press, 1978); Eugene Genovese, *Roll, Jordan Roll: The World the Slaves Made* (New York: Viking, 1973); Lawrence Levine, *Black Culture and Black Consciousness: Afro-American Folk Thought from Slavery to Freedom* (New York: Oxford University Press, 1977); Charles Joyner, *Down by the Riverside: A South Carolina Slave Community* (Urbana: University of Illinois Press, 1984) and "Believer I Know: The Emergence of African American Christianity" in *African American Christianity: Essays in History,* ed. Paul Johnson (Berkeley: University of California Press, 1994), 18–46; Mechal Sobel, *The World They Made Together: Black and White Values in Eighteenth-Century Virginia* (Princeton: Princeton University Press, 1997) and *Trabelin' On: The Slave Journey to an Afro-Baptist Faith* (Westport, CT: Greenwood, 1978); Eddie Glaude, *Exodus: Religion, Race, and Nation in Early Nineteenth-Century Black America* (Chicago: University of Chicago Press, 2000); Michael Gomez, *Exchanging Their Country Marks: The Transformation of African Identities in the Colonial and Antebellum South* (Chapel Hill: University of North Carolina Press, 1998).

12. Melville Herskovits, *The Myth of the Negro Past* (New York: Harper Brothers, 1941); Jon Butler, "The African Spiritual Holocaust," in *Awash in a Sea of Faith: Christianizing the American People* (Cambridge: Harvard University Press, 1990).

13. James Campbell, *Songs of Zion: The African Methodist Episcopal Church in the United States and South Africa* (New York: Oxford University Press, 1995); Leon Litwack, *North of Slavery: The Free Negro in the Antebellum North* (Chicago: University of Chicago Press, 1963); Gary Nash, *Forging Freedom: The Formation of Philadelphia's Black Community, 1720–1840* (Cambridge: Harvard University Press, 1989); Patrick Rael, *Black Identity and Black Protest in the Antebellum North* (Chapel Hill: University of North Carolina Press, 2002); Patrick Rael, "Black Theodicy: African Americans and Nationalism in the Antebellum North," *North Star* 3 (Spring 2000), http://northstar.as.uky.edu/volume3/rael.pdf.

14. Reginald Hildebrand, *The Times Were Strange and Stirring: Methodist Preachers and the Crisis of Emancipation* (Durham: Duke University Press, 1995); Andrew Billingsley, *Mighty Like a River: The Black Church and Social Reform* (New York: Oxford University Press, 1999).

15. Daniel Stowell, *Rebuilding Zion: The Religious Reconstruction of the South, 1863–1877* (New York: Oxford University Press, 1998); William Montgomery, *Under Their Own Vine and Fig Tree: The African-American Church in the South, 1865–1900* (Baton Rouge: Louisiana State University Press, 1993), xii, 3, 5, 305. See also Christopher Owen, *The Sacred Flame of Love: Methodism and Society in Nineteenth-Century Georgia* (Athens: University of Georgia Press, 1998); Paul Harvey, *Redeeming the South: Religious Cultures and Racial Identities among Southern Baptists, 1865–1925* (Chapel Hill: University of North Carolina Press, 1997).

16. Stephen Angell, *Henry McNeal Turner and African-American Religion in the*

South (Knoxville: University of Tennessee Press, 1992); Clarence Walker, *Rock in a Weary Land: The African Methodist Episcopal Church during the Civil War and Reconstruction* (Baton Rouge: Louisiana State University Press, 1982).

17. Bobby J. Donaldson, "Standing on a Volcano: The Leadership of William Jefferson White," in *Paternalism in a Southern City: Race, Religion, and Gender in Augusta, Georgia,* ed. Edward J. Cashin and Glenn T. Eskew (Athens: University of Georgia Press, 2001), 135–77; Howard N. Rabinowitz, "Holland Thompson and Black Political Participation in Montgomery, Alabama," in *Southern Black Leaders of the Reconstruction Era* (Urbana: University of Illinois Press, 1982), 249–79; Paul Harvey, " 'The Holy Spirit Come to Us and Forbid the Negro Taking a Second Place': Richard H. Boyd and Black Religious Activism in Nashville, Tennessee," *Tennessee Historical Quarterly* 55 (Fall 1996): 190–201.

18. James Bennett, *Religion and the Rise of Jim Crow in New Orleans* (Princeton: Princeton University Press, 2005); Katharine Dvorak, *An African-American Exodus: The Segregation of the Southern Churches* (Brooklyn: Carlson, 1991).

19. Stephen Angell and Anthony B. Pinn, eds., *Social Protest Thought in the African Methodist Episcopal Church, 1862–1939* (Knoxville: University of Tennessee Press, 2000); Patrick Rael et al., eds., *Pamphlets of Protest: An Anthology of Early African-American Protest Literature* (New York: Routledge, 2001); Milton Sernett, ed., *Afro-American Religious History: A Documentary Witness* (Durham: Duke University Press, 1999).

20. Campbell, *Songs of Zion,* ix.

21. Ibid., 327.

22. Evelyn Brooks Higginbotham, *Righteous Discontent: The Women's Movement in the Black Baptist Church, 1880–1920* (Cambridge: Harvard University Press, 1993).

23. John Giggie, *After Redemption: Jim Crow and the Transformation of African-American Religion in the Delta, 1874–1914* (New York: Oxford University Press, 2007).

24. Jon Spencer, *Blues and Evil* (Knoxville: University of Tennessee Press, 1993); Yvonne Chireau, *Black Magic: Religion and the African American Conjuring Tradition* (Berkeley: University of California Press, 2003); Hans Baer, *The Black Spiritual Movement: A Religious Response to Racism* (1984; repr., Knoxville: University of Tennessee Press, 2001).

25. Milton Sernett, *Bound for the Promised Land: African American Religion and the Great Migration* (Durham: Duke University Press, 1997), 242, 247.

26. Michael Harris, *The Rise of the Gospel Blues: The Music of Thomas Andrew Dorsey in the Urban Church* (New York: Oxford University Press, 1992); Nick Salvatore, *Singing in a Strange Land: C. L. Franklin, the Black Church, and the Transformation of America* (New York: Little Brown, 2005).

27. Wallace Best, *Passionately Human, No Less Divine: Religion and Culture in Black Chicago, 1915–1952* (Princeton: Princeton University Press, 2005); Anthea Butler, "A Pe-

culiar Synergy: Matriarchy and the Church of God in Christ" (Ph.D. diss., Vanderbilt University, 2001); Jerma Jackson, *Singing in My Soul: Black Gospel Music in a Secular Age* (Chapel Hill: University of North Carolina Press, 2004).

28. DuBois, quoted in Phil Zuckerman, "The Sociology of Religion of W. E. B. DuBois," *Sociology and Religion* 63 (Summer 2002): 245; Edward Blum, *W. E. B. Du Bois: American Prophet* (Philadelphia: University of Pennsylvania Press, 2007); Clarence Taylor, *Black Religious Intellectuals: The Fight for Equality from Jim Crow to the 21st Century* (New York: Routledge, 2002).

29. Powdermaker, *After Freedom;* Charles Johnson, *Shadow of the Plantation* (Chicago: University of Chicago Press, 1934); Paul Harvey, *Freedom's Coming: Religious Cultures and the Shaping of the South from the Civil War through the Civil Rights Era* (Chapel Hill: University of North Carolina Press, 2005).

30. Taylor Branch, *Parting the Waters: America in the King Years, 1954–1963* (New York: Simon and Schuster, 1989); David Garrow, *Bearing the Cross: Martin Luther King, Jr., and the Southern Christian Leadership Conference* (New York: Viking, 1988).

31. Aldon D. Morris, *The Origins of the Civil Rights Movement: Black Communities Organizing for Change* (New York: Free Press, 1984), 3; Andrew Manis, *A Fire You Can't Put Out: The Civil Rights Life of Birmingham's Reverend Fred Shuttlesworth* (Tuscaloosa: University of Alabama Press, 2001).

32. Charles M. Payne, *I've Got the Light of Freedom: The Organizing Tradition and the Mississippi Freedom Struggle* (Berkeley: University of California Press, 1995), 231; Charles Marsh, *God's Long Summer: Stories of Faith and Civil Rights* (Princeton: Princeton University Press, 1997); David Chappell, *Stone of Hope: Prophetic Religion and the Death of Jim Crow* (Chapel Hill: University of North Carolina Press, 2004), 3.

33. Anthony Pinn, *The Black Church in the Post–Civil Rights Era* (Maryknoll, NY: Orbis, 2002).

34. R. Drew Smith, ed., *Long March Ahead: African American Churches and Public Policy in Post–Civil Rights America* (Durham: Duke University Press, 2005), 25. See also R. Drew Smith, ed., *New Day Begun: African American Churches and Civic Culture in Post–Civil Rights America* (Durham: Duke University Press, 2003).

35. Michael Gomez, *Black Crescent: The Experience and Legacy of African Muslims in the Americas* (Cambridge: Cambridge University Press, 2004); "African-American Religion: A Documentary History Project," http://www.amherst.edu/~aardoc/menu.html (accessed August 10, 2006).

36. Cecil Robeck, *The Azusa Street Mission and Revival* (Nashville: Thomas Nelson, 2006).

37. Shayne Lee, *T. D. Jakes: America's New Preacher* (New York: New York University Press, 2005).

7
Mormon Historiography

David J. Whittaker

The Church of Jesus Christ of Latter-day Saints was organized on April 6, 1830. It has grown from six members in an obscure village in western New York to a membership of over 13 million worldwide. By 2005 it was ranked as the fourth largest Christian denomination in America. Joseph Smith Jr. (1805–44) claimed personal visits by God the Father and the Son in the spring of 1820, in addition to other heaven-sent messengers who revealed lost scriptures, bestowed priesthood authority, and gave further instructions as to the restoration of the ancient Christian Church. Smith was considered by his loyal followers a "prophet, seer and revelator" from the earliest years of the movement, though his claims to new scripture, authority, and truth evoked hostility from some.[1] Persecution and forced moves were almost yearly events in the church over which Joseph Smith presided. His murder at the hands of a mob in June 1844 was just part of the ongoing reaction of non-Mormon neighbors to what they perceived to be threats to their community and way of life in a young nation still trying to find and stabilize its identity.

The movement of the majority of the followers of Joseph Smith into the American West under Brigham Young's leadership in 1847 was important in the survival and growth of the young religion. In the West Mormons found space for their community building and peace for their religious worship and activities. Before Brigham Young's death in 1877, almost 350 communities had been established in the areas throughout the Great Basin, with newer colonies eventually spreading into southern Canada and northern Mexico in the 1880s. Driving all this activity was a very successful missionary program, particularly in the British Isles and Scandinavia. By 1887 over sixty thousand converts had gathered into Mormon communities in the West, bringing needed skills and new blood to these settlement efforts.

If Mormon claims to new revelation and new scripture were not enough, the Mormon practice of plural marriage seemed to confirm to everyone else that this religion was both non-Christian and a public menace and thus worthy of persecution and prosecution. Much of Mormon history to 1900 was focused on attempts to defend its religious claims, its unique lifestyle, and what appeared to outsiders as Kingdom building that allowed no possibility of the separation of church and state. By the end of the nineteenth century, Mormons had given up polygamy and had moved to soften their institutions that were seen as un-American. While suspicion remains among many, the Latter-day Saints are no longer considered a threat to mainstream America; in fact, Mormons are often portrayed as ideal Americans.[2]

Mormon historiography is the story of the attempts to record and interpret this rich and complex history. This essay will sketch the basic stages and contours of this literature, suggesting the major authors and works that have attempted to explain the history of the Latter-day Saints both to themselves and to those outside the faith.[3]

Mormon Antiquarianism

The keeping of historical records by the Latter-day Saints dates from their organized beginnings. Reinforced and broadened by both their biblical heritage and record keeping in the early American Republic, their Book of Mormon constantly referred its readers to the record-keeping activities of the peoples whose story is told in its pages—records that kept both their knowledge of their Redeemer and their sacred covenants alive and also reinforced the cultural significance of language for the survival of civilization itself (Omni 1:17). In the Book of Mormon, history writing was a sacred responsibility.[4]

Mormons maintain that Joseph Smith received a revelation on the day the church was organized commanding him and his followers to keep a record of their activities.[5] In time, specific individuals were assigned the duties of keeping the church history. While these early efforts were fitful and incomplete by modern standards, they did begin the process of record creation and interpretation in Mormonism. Because these early accounts were recorded by the participants, their value remains high. Additional directions from Joseph Smith broadened and deepened the responsibilities of these initial historical assignments, and these early directives also help in understanding the direct involvement of church leaders in the process of creating and maintaining a history of the church, an involvement that continues to the present day.[6]

Forced moves, growing criticism, and active persecution assured that the earliest histories would be brief, incomplete, and polemical. Some records were lost or stolen, and some of the individuals assigned to keep the history proved incapable or incompetent. By the end of the first decade, following the group's expulsion from Missouri, Joseph Smith democratized Mormon historical efforts by inviting all those who had suffered losses in Missouri to prepare accounts of their own experiences. Such efforts, early members were told, constituted an "imperative duty" they owed their own generation as well as to future generations.[7] It was in these Missouri histories that a real defensiveness emerged in Mormon historiography. The feeling that Mormons had been denied their civil and property rights colored Mormon historical writing for at least a century.

Significant pamphlet histories and hundreds of petitions for redress became important records of the Mormon Missouri experience.[8] But the most significant historical project to emerge during this period was directed by Joseph Smith. Ironically, just as historical writing was democratized among the faithful, the real focus of Mormon history became the telling of Joseph Smith's life.[9] It was primarily the work of the church historian, Willard Richards, and those assigned to work with him, especially George A. Smith and Wilford Woodruff. Titled the "History of Joseph Smith" in manuscript, it was, in reality, a documentary history of the main events of the church over which he presided. The project was not finished until ten years after Smith's death, but this series was the most important historical work in the early church. It was serialized in the church's newspapers (both in the United States and in England) and was eventually edited by B. H. Roberts into a multivolume work entitled the *History of the Church*. In an age when there was no real distinction between historian, editor, or compiler, such a work was really an antiquarian effort in a time before that word took on a pejorative meaning.[10]

Thus, the *History of the Church*, like so many early Mormon historical efforts, was a compilation of documents rather than a crafted historical work. Such works did gather key documents upon which later interpretative studies could be built, and such efforts at record keeping were at their heart record preservation. These foundational efforts help us to understand the reasons for the survival of rich manuscript sources for contemporary historians of the Mormon experience.[11]

Mormon historical writing essentially remained in this documentary tradition throughout the nineteenth century. The individual who carried it the furthest was Andrew Jenson.[12] A convert from Denmark, Jenson eventually found his calling in historical work. By the time he was called to be an assistant church historian in 1891, he had already published several newspapers and periodicals in addition to several other historical projects, the most important of which was his historical magazine, the *Historical Record*. After being called as "a historian in Zion," his compiling activities only increased. Several main projects provided the focus of his work. The first was the preparation of biographies of the founders and officers of the church, many of which were published in his four-volume *L.D.S. Biographical Encyclopedia* (1901–36). The *Encyclopedic History of the Church* (1941) did for church organizations and missions what the *Biographical Encyclopedia* did for individuals.[13]

Jenson's most important project was the compilation of a multivolume scrapbook of church history. Eventually known as the "Journal History," this work of some 518 volumes of legal-size scrapbooks, ranging from three to five inches in thickness, is a gold mine of source material on church history. It represents the apex of the documentary tradition in Mormon historical writing.[14] Though never published, the "Journal History" has been indexed and microfilmed and is available in a number of Utah libraries.

Jenson was also a key figure in the attempts to modernize the church's archives at the turn of the century.[15] His concerns for better and more systematic record keeping led church leaders to establish the Committee on Church Records, which encouraged local units to keep historical and statistical records and which also gave Jenson church support for his frequent travels to various Mormon communities and historic sites to gather documents of historical value. Jenson also worked to gather records and publications about the church in areas beyond the United States, making him a pioneer in documenting the growing internationalization of Mormonism. His indefatigable work in gathering Mormon historical documents and his many compiling, publishing, and copying efforts make Jenson one of the great Mormon historians.

Toward a Synthesis

By the 1870s, a different approach was emerging in Mormon historiography. Still grounded in a documentary effort, some authors began to synthesize these into more interpretive narratives. T. B. H. Stenhouse's *Rocky Mountain Saints* was published in New York in 1873. His work began as a defense of the church, and he was given access to the church's archives, but by the time he was writing his history he had left the church and joined the Reform Church of William S. Godbe. Thus his volume came to offer an anti–Brigham Young and pro-Godbe view of the Mormon experience. But interwoven through this lengthy work were significant contributions to Mormon history. It was reprinted five times by 1905 and was the most read history outside Mormon Utah. It was the first volume to treat the handcart tragedies of 1856 and the

Mountain Meadows Massacre of 1857. It was also the first interpretive history to suggest better ways of viewing Mormon history—arguing, for example, that the conflicts and persecutions of the Latter-day Saints in Missouri might be better understood as cultural conflicts, with both sides contributing to the problems; that the Mormon troubles in Illinois were as much related to politics as to religion; and that the Mormon frustration with governmental leaders in their attempts at redress ought to be considered within the growing conflict of states' rights struggles with the federal government. Thus, Mormon issues were often placed in the context of the larger conflicts and compromises in nineteenth-century American politics. Such ideas planted seeds for future historians, but Stenhouse's excommunication from the church lessened his influence among members.[16]

Another historian who tried to move beyond merely publishing documents was Edward W. Tullidge (1829–94). He held Mormon religion in low esteem, but he admired Mormon culture. While his lifetime ambition was to create the "epic" of the Mormon experience, he generally wrote in the documentary tradition. His most important work was his *History of Salt Lake City* (1886), but here, as in his other works, he offered documents with little analysis and synthesis.[17] He also abandoned the Utah church.

Another attempt at synthesis appeared under the direction of non-Mormon Hubert Howe Bancroft. Having made his fortune as a publisher in gold rush California, he retired and turned to collecting western Americana. His huge collection would later find a home in the library that bears his name at the University of California, Berkeley. But collecting was not enough. He next decided to write the histories of the areas whose documents he had gathered. Thus, Bancroft's *History of the Pacific States,* eventually covering the areas from Alaska to Mexico, with volumes devoted to the Native Americans, grew to thirty-nine volumes. Wishing to include Utah in his project, he sought for and eventually obtained church approval and assistance. His *History of Utah,* volume 26 in the series, covered the years from 1540 to 1889, the year the volume was published. Much of it was actually the work of Alfred Bates, an employee of Bancroft, who assembled his histories like Henry Ford would assemble his cars. The volume's format told the Mormon story in the main text with sources and other points of view in the extensive footnotes. The lengthy bibliography at the front of the volume is still a valuable guide to the contemporary sources he and his coauthors used. And because early Utah territorial history was then understood only within Mormon history, the first 250 pages provide an overview of pre-Utah Mormon history.[18]

A Mormon version of Bancroft's *History* found its author in Orson F. Whitney (1855–1931), whose four-volume *History of Utah* (1892–1904) provided Latter-day Saints with a major narrative history of their own region by one of their own. Whitney had grown up in Utah and was knowledgeable in the history and lore of the territory. He came to history writing later in his life, and he was writing still in the antiquarian tradition, seldom providing footnotes for his work. And, like Bancroft, Whitney used research assistants to prepare drafts of chapters (John Q. Cannon and James H. Anderson). His interest in poetry and theater gave his history a sense of the grand epic, and he gave to his people a story that was their story. He smoothed out the more unfavorable parts of the story, but as the Mormons were coming through a time of intense persecution and forced readjustment to American culture, he presented a stirring epic of this pioneering adventure.[19]

But the most important historian of this genre and period was Brigham Henry Roberts (1857–1933). He was an English convert whose poverty prevented him from learning to read until he was twelve. After that, thanks to caring church leaders and access to private libraries, he devoured all the books he could find. He eventually was called to be a church leader, and by his death in 1933 had become the most prolific author in the church. In addition to biographies and histories, he edited the earlier "History of Joseph Smith" into its multivolume format (1902–12). But his most extensive historical work was the *Comprehensive History of the Church: Century I*. Published in 1930 on the occasion of the church's centennial celebrations, the project had its origin in a series of articles first published in the *Americana* magazine at the invitation of its editor, David Nelke. Clearly influenced by the nineteenth-century romantic historians he loved to read, Roberts painted the history of his people, both their triumphs and their tragedies. He was not afraid to treat events like the Mountain Meadows Massacre (see chapters 100 and 101), and he did not hide from addressing the criticism leveled at the church and its doctrines. This history is still essential reading for serious students of Mormon history.[20]

Professionalization of Mormon History

Even as Roberts was drafting his historical works, Mormon history was moving in new directions. By the 1880s, Mormon students had begun leaving Utah to seek higher education in graduate schools across America. At first concentrating in law, education, and the sciences, these students eventually turned to studying the social sciences. In graduate seminars they learned to evaluate sources, discussed various ways to read the documents, and were influenced by the cross-fertilization of ideas that graduate study encouraged. By the 1910s and 1920s Latter-day Saints were studying history and related subjects.

Such out-migration for education was bound to have an effect on the way they understood their own history.[21]

A number of trends seem obvious as one looks back on the early years of the twentieth century. Mormon history was clearly becoming an interesting subject for non-Mormon scholars. The Mormon involvement in the western American experience was one reason their history could not be ignored by American historians. After 1893, the popularity of the frontier thesis of Frederick Jackson Turner seemed to make the Mormon experience the ideal test case for its validity. Studies by Mormon students like Dean D. McBrien, Joel E. Ricks, and especially Milton R. Hunter suggested that the Mormon experience proved Turner's ideas by focusing on the frontier phases of its history.[22] Others found their topics by looking at Utah and its regional history. Thus Levi Edgar Young, Andrew Neff, and Leland Creer were important early students of these topics.[23] LeRoy Hafen, working with his wife, Ann, focused on the mountain men and fur trappers of the American West, but his 1926 master's thesis at the University of California, Berkeley, was on the Mormon handcart experience, and Hafen would include several important volumes of documents in his series, one on the handcarts and another on the Utah Expedition of 1857–58.[24]

From the 1930 to the 1960s, the study of Mormon history was also influenced by several individuals who were not trained historians (they were English majors, for the most part) but who nevertheless researched and wrote books and reviews that helped bring Mormon history to a national audience. All had roots in small Mormon communities, but most left the faith of their youth. These individuals included Bernard DeVoto, Dale L. Morgan, Juanita Brooks, and Fawn M. Brodie.

Bernard DeVoto (1897–1955) was born in Ogden, Utah. He taught English at Northwest University following his graduation from Harvard University. He became an editor of the *Saturday Review* and eventually wrote a regular column, "The Easy Chair," for *Harper's*.[25] His early published articles poked fun at his Utah origins. For example, in 1926 he wrote cruelly that "[t]he Mormons were staid peasants whose only distinguishing characteristics were their servility to their leaders and their belief in a low-comedy God." By 1945, as national attitudes about the Mormons had softened, DeVoto repudiated his earlier Menckenesque tone. He said of his earlier comments: "they were ignorant, brash, prejudiced, malicious, and, what is worst of all, irresponsible." DeVoto's softened position grew out of his growing interest in the history of the American West. In the 1940s and 1950s, DeVoto wrote three volumes on the history of the West in which he treated the Mormons with great sympathy.[26] Thus his trilogy remains an important study, one that gave the Mormon's westward trek national attention.

Another scholar with Utah roots was Dale L. Morgan (1914–71).[27] He graduated from the University of Utah in 1937, but he was handicapped by deafness after contracting spinal meningitis when he was fourteen. He found employment with the Historical Records Survey of the Works Progress Administration during the Depression. His assignment as the administrator of Utah State Records firmly established his path toward bibliography and history. Before long, few people could match his knowledge of the primary sources, first of Utah and then of the American West. He eventually worked in the Bancroft Library. Morgan authored and edited numerous works on the history of the West, and his work as a bibliographer and compiler continues to serve researchers. In Mormon history he published a number of works that reflected his broad interests. While not a Mormon, he wrote with skill and fairness when he treated the Latter-day Saints.[28] His major works included histories of Ogden, Provo, and Salt Lake City and the 1941 *Utah: A Guide to the State,* which he oversaw. In 1947, he published *The Great Salt Lake,* an interdisciplinary study of a major landmark in Utah and the West. His documentary compilation *The State of Deseret* in the *Utah Historical Quarterly* is the essential work on the initial efforts of the Mormons to achieve statehood in 1849.[29] His own history of the Mormons, originally planned for three volumes, never progressed beyond a few chapters.[30] A lesser-known role Morgan played in the story of Mormon historiography was his work as a correspondent and reviewer of others' work. He regularly reviewed books for the *Saturday Review,* calling national attention to works on Mormon and Utah history.

One of Morgan's correspondents was Juanita Brooks (1898–1989), a Mormon woman of independent spirit with great integrity. Remaining an active Latter-day Saint, she was trained in English and sought her whole life to better understand her southern Utah, southern Nevada roots.[31] While best known for her pioneering study the *Mountain Meadows Massacre* (1950), she also wrote a sympathetic biography of John Doyle Lee, the only individual executed for his participation in the massacre; she also edited Lee's diaries and those of Hosea Stout, to mention only the most important.[32] She also helped collect Mormon manuscripts for the Henry E. Huntington Library in San Marino, California, and she was a regular contributor to the *Utah Historical Quarterly.* Her work helped push the quest for truth in Mormon history to new levels, even when she was ostracized by her Mormon neighbors for treating controversial topics they felt would be better left covered and forgotten. But her historical work, by confronting hard and painful realities of early Mormon history, helped in the healing process and prepared the way for the next generation of Mormon historians, who could build on her insights and her compassionate approach.

Another correspondent of Morgan was Fawn M. Brodie (1915–81), niece of church president David O. McKay.[33] She is best known for her 1945 biography of Joseph Smith, *No Man Knows My History,* which was, as Morgan noted, her act of "liberation and exorcism," her intellectual attempt to be rid of the founder of the religion of her youth.[34] It was, at its heart, a naturalistic biography of a religious man. Brodie was also trained in English, and clearly one of the enduring qualities of her biography is its literary grace. But it was essentially a psychobiography that presented Joseph Smith as a fraud, a "myth-maker of prodigious talent," and a man with an eye for young maidens whose practice of polygamy was just a cover for his lust. Such an explanation was in the tradition of I. Woodbridge Riley's 1902 "The Founder of Mormonism: A Psychological Study of Joseph Smith, Jr.," a Yale University dissertation that sought an explanation of Smith in his environment and especially in the inner workings of his mind.[35] Religion was a mask for other, darker desires. Thus the Book of Mormon was really an autobiography of the young man and could provide insights into the Smith family, its strengths and weaknesses. Like Freud, Brodie treated religion as a negative force in her subject's life. She also failed to consult important manuscript collections that would have altered her account.[36]

Brodie's biography was, however, a major watershed in Mormon studies. While it offered a secular explanation for Mormon origins and a naturalistic handling of the sources, it did suggest an agenda for the next generation of Mormon historians. For Latter-day Saints, it cried out for response and thus more research. For non-Mormons, many felt that at last they had an explanation for Joseph Smith, and with that, no more work was necessary. In a second edition (1972) the volume continues in print and is, unfortunately, often the most recommended biography.

Scholars like DeVoto, Morgan, Brooks, and Brodie wrote in an age of growing secularism and modernity. Such secular scholarship took its toll on Mormons and some of their historians; one student of the period has referred to "Mormondom's Lost Generation," and indeed, other writers with Mormon roots, like Vardis Fisher, Maurine Whipple, and Virginia Sorenson, turned their interest in history to writing historical fiction.[37]

The New Mormon History

By the 1950s, additional changes were becoming obvious in Mormon history. By 1969, these changes were being labeled "the New Mormon History."[38] Whether the label is really the best one, it was clear new kinds of historical studies were appearing that treated Mormon history in ways never imagined by earlier practitioners. Of course, these new histories did not appear in a vacuum, and most were really building upon earlier scholarship. One benchmark for these changes was the 1958 publication of Leonard J. Arrington's *Great Basin Kingdom: An Economic History of the Latter-day Saints, 1830–1900.* Issued by Harvard University Press, it was the revision of his 1952 dissertation. Idaho-born and -raised, he eventually went east to study at the University of North Carolina. Arrington was aware of the important work being published by southern historians as they focused on the South as a region. In time, Arrington decided to apply the same approach to the Mormon region in the Great Basin. He eventually accepted a job teaching economics at Utah State University in Logan, Utah. There he learned much from S. George Ellsworth, a colleague in the history department who critiqued various drafts of the work, drawing upon his own extensive knowledge of Utah and Mormon history.[39]

When *Great Basin Kingdom* appeared in 1958, it was both a summation of earlier Mormon scholarship and a model of what could and should be done. Arrington continued to publish extensively in Utah, Mormon, and western history.[40] He was one of the founders of the Mormon History Association in 1965, and in 1972 was called to serve as the church historian of the LDS Church. During his service in that capacity for the next ten years, his Historical Department became staffed with scholars with academic training and were given an extensive research and writing agenda. Arrington and his assistant church historians, Davis Bitton and James B. Allen, actively encouraged fuller access to the rich holdings of the church's archives. The scholarly production of these ten years was astonishing.[41] They produced two one-volume histories of the church, commissioned a multivolume history of the church, began a documents series, initiated projects that opened research on new topics, began scholarly biographical projects of church leaders and others, and offered fellowships to others to Salt Lake City to research their own topics in the rich holdings of the church's archives. It was truly a renaissance in Mormon studies.[42]

But given the religious underpinnings of the earlier historiography, it was apparent that not everyone would be pleased with the work of the Historical Department. Some church leaders occasionally voiced concern with its products; others thought the historians were moving too fast and too far ahead for church membership to keep up with. A lively discussion about the nature of Mormon historiography ensued; this produced its own literature.[43] At the heart of much of the concern of church leaders were the issues of using secular language to describe sacred events and that the religious center of the Mormon experience was not coming through these new histories clearly enough.[44] The Historical Department scholars, including Arrington, were transferred in 1982 to Brigham Young University and renamed Joseph Fielding Smith Institute for Latter-day Saint History, where many felt their scholarship would find a more congenial home. Since Arrington's death in 1999, some of the Smith Institute scholars have retired, moved into academic departments, or returned to the Historical Department in Salt Lake City to assist in the preparation of the multivolume Papers of Joseph Smith project.

The issues, of course, did not go away. In the 1980s several LDS scholars were excommunicated from the church, in part for their historical writings but also for lifestyle choices or for public criticisms of church leaders.[45] One of those disciplined was D. Michael Quinn, who worked with Arrington's Historical Department. After completing his Ph.D. at Yale University in 1976, writing his dissertation on the history of the Mormon hierarchy, he returned to Utah to accept a position in Brigham Young University's history department. He produced a number of important, deeply researched studies, but in each there seemed to be a subversion of the traditional Mormon story. While he has denied he was following any one model in his work, one could argue that his work was gradually "Foucaulting" Mormon history. Like Michel Foucault's, Quinn's major works examined (1) power/authority; (2) folk beliefs and magic; (3) issues of gender and sexuality; and (4) violence.[46] While students of Mormon history must read his historical studies, they can be interpreted as subversive attempts to "deconstruct" the traditional interpretation of the Mormon past.

While these excommunicates are surely a loss to the Mormon community, many have continued to produce Mormon historical scholarship. Of course, not all Mormon historical scholarship was produced by Arrington's Historical Department. But since the 1960s Mormon scholarship has gone from a small stream to a river. Given our space limitations, here we can only suggest some of the areas where Mormon history has seen important advances.

The Emerging Social Science Literature

The topic of Mormon social science literature is large and growing, but there are several excellent guides to this material.[47] What follows is just a sampling of some of the key areas that relate most directly to Mormon historical study.

The study of the lives of Mormons is slowly coming of age. The first Mormon biographies were missionary accounts in pamphlets and periodicals. The first biography was the history of the Smith family, prepared by Lucy Mack Smith, Joseph's mother. She painted in broad strokes and sought to document the role of the Smith and Mack families in the beginnings of the church. Really a memoir, her *History of Joseph Smith the Prophet and His Progenitors for Many Generations* contained useful and honest insights into the economic struggles and deep religiosity of the family out of which Joseph Smith came.[48] In more recent years, major biographies of Mormons have been published that are well researched and have placed their subjects into their larger cultural context.[49] Most of the best work has focused on the first generation of Latter-day Saints, but this is also changing, and the choices have moved slowly away from the elites to more common Mormons.[50]

Historical studies of Mormon women and the family, including the practice of plural marriage, have begun to appear. Mormon women's history still has a long way to go to fully tell this important part of the Mormon experience, but there are good models available for others to follow.[51] Family studies, examining such topics as child-rearing practices, marriage, and divorce are also available.[52] Plural marriage, practiced by Mormons in the nineteenth century, has also attracted the attention of scholars, especially as attitudes have begun to shift from defensive to the need for understanding this peculiar marriage form. Scholars from Kimball Young to Kathryn Daynes have worked to better understand this often bittersweet chapter in Mormon history.[53] The origins of its practice lay with Joseph Smith, although the exact details remain unknown.[54] The official ending of the practice, which extended from 1890 to 1904, has also generated important scholarship.[55] Those who have continued to practice plural marriage, through various fundamentalist churches, have also been the subjects of important studies.[56]

Mormon missiology, ranging from missionary accounts to the history of specific missions to studies of convert retention, have produced a large but uneven historical literature. But, without much chance of exaggeration, it could be said that Mormon history is mission history. In the nineteenth century, most of the published material was a record of faithful service, spiritual experiences, and defenses of the faith. More scholarly studies began to appear in the last century, but until most recently it could not be said that the study of Mormon missiology was coming of age.[57]

Converts in the nineteenth century gathered to the headquarters of the church. For most of the period they were then assigned to help establish Mormon communities throughout the Great Basin. Based on the early instructions of Joseph Smith, these towns or villages were laid out in specific patterns and functioned as sacred space intended for the making of saints. Some of the best of recent Mormon historical writing has addressed this topic.[58] Connected with these villages, and growing out of the religious doctrines of Mormonism, were various economic programs that sought to establish unity, frugality, equality, and economic independence for the communities of

Latter-day Saints.[59] Dealing with federal prosecutions in the 1880s and 1890s, and facing accommodation with American society in the early years of the twentieth century, the Mormon village gradually gave way; in its place, the Mormon ward (parish) assumed more and more importance for the creation and maintenance of active Latter-day Saints.[60]

Topics of race and ethnicity have become more important, especially after 1950 as the church reached its first million members and was increasingly becoming international in its reach for converts. Church leaders had begun to put an end to the gathering of converts to church headquarters by the 1890s, encouraging converts to remain in their homelands, and, slowly through two world wars and a depression, foreign missions gradually grew. It was under church president David O. McKay that the first stake (diocese) was created outside North America—in Manchester, England, in 1960—and his extensive global travels brought the world more and more into the Mormon sphere of interest. Important studies that trace racial attitudes and missionary growth have pushed Mormon historiography in new directions.[61]

Whether Mormons themselves could be considered an ethnic group is itself a fascinating topic. Surely their communal villages in the nineteenth century, their health code (the Word of Wisdom), and their separation from the larger society could be studied from this perspective. Dean May's essay on the Mormons in the *Harvard Encyclopedia of American Ethnic Groups* encourages such a consideration.[62] But the issues of accommodation and Americanization, beginning in the early years of the twentieth century, have become an important part of this discussion.[63]

There have been over 150 organized break-offs from the church since 1830. Most did not survive their founders, but most have lessons to teach. Thus, scholarly trajectories through the literature of dissent and disaffiliation can teach historians about the centrifugal tendencies in Mormon history, forces that have both attracted and repelled members and occasionally leaders.[64]

Not necessarily connected with this topic, a subject that has generated its own literature is that of anti-Mormonism. The subject is a large one, as the church has attracted critics from its earliest years. Really beyond our interest here, it is a topic worth exploring, because it can shed light on the tensions and challenges of the Mormon experience throughout its history, and because a number of Mormon historians have written their histories, in part, as critiques of the church and the issues that concerned them the most.[65]

Visitors and Outside Observers

Since its earliest days, people came to or through Mormon communities, and many left in print their impressions, both positive and negative. In the nineteenth century most were just passing through, perhaps as a part of the American version of the "grand tour," but occasionally they looked beneath the surface and left valuable commentary. Rev. Diedrich Willers's 1831 letter was among the earliest, but there were many other visitors and commentators, among them Nancy Towne, Josiah Quincy, Charles McKay, Charles Dickens, John Gunnison, and Richard Burton. Mormon historiography is surely enriched because of these observations.[66]

More serious scholarship came in the twentieth century. A German scholar of Oriental history and cultures, Eduard Meyer, in a 1912 study of the origins of Mormonism, offered important insights, suggesting that Mormonism was a new religion comparable to Islam.[67]

Thomas O'Dea, a Catholic sociologist who participated in the Ford Foundation–sponsored Harvard University Comparative Study of the Cultures of the Four Corners, an area of the American Southwest, produced several important studies on the Mormon aspects of this project, and several scholar-participants like Robert Bellah later offered additional perspectives on the Mormon experience.[68] Thomas F. O'Dea's 1957 book *The Mormons* is one of the best studies of the Mormons. Like Meyer, O'Dea thought Mormonism could be studied as a new religion in the making, and he was particularly interested in how the church had managed to adapt and accommodate itself to its American setting without losing its core values and identity, and why the Mormondom had not stagnated in secularism like so many other American religions. For O'Dea, the Mormons' ability to combine the sacred with the secular in their daily lives throughout their history was one answer.[69]

But perhaps the best-known "outsider" today is Jan Shipps, a Methodist scholar who has devoted over four decades to the study of Mormonism. Like O'Dea, Shipps abandoned the traditional categories of church and sect in the course of her study. The more she studied the Mormons, the more she struggled with the basic problems of taxonomy. Historians of American religion had been influenced by Robert Baird's 1844 *Religions in America*, which had classified American religions into two groups, evangelical and nonevangelical. Mormons and Catholics were placed in the latter category, and for over one hundred years, scholars of American religion like Philip Schaff, Shirley Jackson Case, and William Warren Sweet had used Baird's approach to write their books and to demonstrate their preference for frontier Baptist-Methodist religious groups that seemed best to reflect the American way. Such attitudes have continued, and Sydney Ahlstrom's discussion of Mormonism seemed to end in frustration: was Mormonism "a sect, a mystery cult, a new religion, a church, a people, a nation, or an American subculture"? He concluded that "at different times and places it is all of these!"[70]

Jan Shipps sought to move the discussion beyond the Baird paradigm and the frustrations of scholars like Ahlstrom. In her major work, *Mormonism: The Story of a New Religious Tradition,* she avoided discussing its truth claims but insisted on taking the church as a serious new religion. By adopting a behaviorist stance, and drawing on the models in the discipline of religious studies, she tried to understand Mormonism from the inside. She took seriously what the Mormons thought and did, and then gave these views a nonpejorative analysis. Her volume is rich in insight because she adopted a view that was friendly and open to understanding the Mormon experience. And she was willing to look beyond the Protestant Reformation to see Mormonism as outside the usual traditions of treating modern Christianity.[71]

Books and Sacred Texts

Mormons are people of the Book; actually, they are people of Books. They hold the Bible to be the Word of God—as far as it is translated correctly—but they also have three additional sacred texts in their canon of scripture.[72] The Book of Mormon has given them their nickname, but it has functioned as a complement to, not a replacement for, the Bible, with accounts of the appearance of Christ in the New World following his death and resurrection in ancient Palestine.[73] Its importance in Mormon culture cannot be overemphasized; in 2005 the 100 millionth copy was printed. In addition, the *Doctrine and Covenants* contains revelations, epistles, and directives given to the church by Joseph Smith and his successors, thus giving textural evidence to the Mormon belief in continual revelation. Finally, there is *The Pearl of Great Price* (1851), a volume that gathered various revelatory items Joseph Smith had given to the church before 1844, including selections from the writings of Enoch, Abraham, and Moses, and a brief summary of Joseph Smith's early history. In addition to these "standard works," Mormons have published wherever they have settled or traveled. Thus, the student of Mormon historiography must follow this typographical trail. Again, there are a number of useful guides to assist the researcher in getting a handle on what is a mountain of printed items.[74]

Some Concluding Thoughts

Mormon historical writing has traveled a long road since the 1830s. For most of Mormon history the religious perspective of the founding generation has run through its histories and biographies. By the mid-twentieth century, there was a growing polarity, much of it caused by the challenges of secular models applied to sacred stories and the tensions of modernism. These issues came to a head in the 1970s and 1980s, and they were exacerbated by the historical forgeries of Mark Hofmann, which seemed to challenge the historical and foundational claims of the church.[75] All these tensions seemed to polarize Mormon historiography, to privilege "faithful" scholarship, and to marginalize more critical views. And this polarization has come just as Mormon studies have begun to enter into religion departments across the nation.[76]

There has never been a better time for studying Mormon history, and we can hope that the best scholarship is yet to come; the existing canon certainly has established a broad foundation upon which to build for the twenty-first century.

Notes

1. "Prophet, seer, and revelator" is a title used for the Mormon leader since Joseph Smith's lifetime. The words first appeared in a revelation given April 6, 1830, the day the church was organized. *Doctrine and Covenants of the Church of Jesus Christ of Latter-day Saints, Containing Revelations Given to Joseph Smith, the Prophet, with Some Additions to His Successors in the Presidency of the Church*, (Salt Lake City: Church of Jesus Christ of Latter-day Saints, 1981), sec. 21:1. Joseph Smith was sustained by this title in a conference vote of church members on March 27, 1836. See B. H. Roberts, *History of the Church of Jesus Christ of Latter-day Saints, Period I: History of Joseph Smith the Prophet* (Salt Lake City: Deseret News, 1902–12), 2:417.

2. There are two useful one-volume histories of the Latter-day Saints: a chronological narrative, James B. Allen and Glen M. Leonard, *The Story of the Latter-day Saints*, rev. ed. (Salt Lake City: Deseret Book, 1992); and an interpretative study organized by topics: Leonard J. Arrington and Davis Bitton, *The Mormon Experience: A History of the Latter-day Saints* (New York: Alfred A. Knopf, 1979). Most recently, see Terryl L. Givens, *People of Paradox: A History of Mormon Culture* (New York: Oxford University Press, 2006). A useful reference guide to all aspects of Mormonism is Daniel H. Ludlow et al., eds., *The Encyclopedia of Mormonism*, 5 vols. (New York: Macmillan, 1992). Two studies of contemporary Mormonism are Terryl L. Givens, *The Latter-day Saint Experience in America*, American Religious Experience series (Westport, CT: Greenwood, 2004); and Claudia L. Bushman, *Contemporary Mormonism, Latter-day Saints in Modern America* (Westport, CT: Praeger, 2006). A useful collection of scholarly essays is Eric A. Eliason, ed., *Mormons and Mormonism: An Introduction to an American World Religion* (Urbana: University of Illinois Press, 2001).

3. The fullest account of the history of Mormon historical writing is Ronald W. Walker, David J. Whittaker, and James B. Allen, *Mormon History* (Urbana: University of Illinois Press, 2001). An early attempt to sketch out the development of Mor-

mon historiography was Leonard J. Arrington, "The Search for Truth and Meaning in Mormon History," *Dialogue: A Journal of Mormon Thought* 3 (Summer 1968): 56–66. Also very useful is Davis Bitton and Leonard J. Arrington, *Mormons and Their Historians,* Publications in Mormon Studies 2 (Salt Lake City: University of Utah Press, 1988).

4. The Book of Mormon was first published in March 1830. Joseph Smith said he translated it from metal plates entrusted to him by an angel, identified as Moroni, who was the son of Mormon, the main abridger/compiler of the ancient record (hence the title of the volume). The Book of Mormon contains an account of several groups and families that were led by God to the New World in ancient times, down to about 400 CE. The volume contains history, genealogy, commentary, and accounts of the teaching of prophets sent to instruct these early inhabitants of the Americas as well as an account of the personal ministry of Jesus Christ in the New World following his Old World ministry. Contrary to popular belief, the volume makes no claim to be an account of all the peoples living in the Americas. See Richard Lyman Bushman, "The Book of Mormon in Early Mormon History," in *New Views of Mormon History: Essays in Honor of Leonard J. Arrington,* ed. Davis Bitton and Maureen Ursenbach Beecher (Salt Lake City: University of Utah Press, 1987), 3–18.

5. Joseph Smith's accounts of his life are in *The Personal Writings of Joseph Smith,* 2nd ed., ed. Dean C. Jessee (Salt Lake City: Deseret, 2002); and *The Papers of Joseph Smith,* vol. 1, *Autobiographical and Historical Writing,* ed. Dean C. Jessee (Salt Lake City: Deseret, 1989).

6. For the directives, see *Doctrine and Covenants,* sec. 47:1–4; 69:2–3, 8; 85:1–2. See also Dean C. Jessee, "Joseph Smith and the Beginnings of Mormon Record Keeping," in *The Prophet Joseph: Essays on the Life and Mission of Joseph Smith,* ed. Larry C. Porter and Susan Easton Black (Salt Lake City: Deseret, 1988), 138–60; Howard C. Searle, "Early Mormon Historiography: Writing the History of the Mormons, 1830–1858" (Ph.D. diss., UCLA, 1979), 69–143.

7. *Doctrine and Covenants,* sec. 123:1–17. Originally published in *Times and Seasons* (Nauvoo, IL) 1, no. 9 (1840): 133–34.

8. The most important of these early histories are John P. Greene, *Facts relative to the Expulsion of the Mormons or Latter Day Saints, from the State of Missouri* (Cincinnati: R. P. Brooks, 1839); and John Corrill, *A Brief History of the Church of Christ of Latter Day Saints* (St. Louis: n.p., 1839). For a useful printing of the petitions for redress, see Clark V. Johnson, ed., *Mormon Redress Petitions: Documents of the 1833–1838 Missouri Conflict,* Religious Studies Monograph 16 (Provo: Religious Studies Center, Brigham Young University, 1992).

9. See Richard Lyman Bushman, *Joseph Smith, Rough Stone Rolling: A Cultural Biography of Mormonism's Founder* (New York: Alfred A. Knopf, 2005), 389–90, 401–2. For further discussions relating to the "History of Joseph Smith," see Dean C. Jessee,

"The Writing of Joseph Smith's History," *Brigham Young University Studies* 11 (Summer 1971): 439–73; and Searle, "Early Mormon Historiography," 200–336.

10. George H. Callcott, *History in the United States, 1800–1860: Its Practice and Purpose* (Baltimore: Johns Hopkins University Press, 1970), 109–19.

11. Useful places to identify the manuscript sources are Davis Bitton, *Guide to Mormon Diaries and Autobiographies* (Provo: Brigham Young University Press, 1977); and David J. Whittaker, ed., *Mormon Americana: A Guide to Sources and Collections in the United States* (Provo: BYU Studies Monograph Series, 1995).

12. On Jenson, see chapter 4 of Bitton and Arrington, *Mormons and Their Historians*, 41–55; see also Andrew Jenson, *Autobiography of Andrew Jenson* (Salt Lake City: Deseret News, 1838).

13. *Historical Record: A Monthly Periodical Devoted Exclusively to Historical, Biographical, Chronological and Statistical Matters*, 9 vols. (Salt Lake City: Andrew Jenson, 1882–90); *Latter-day Saints' Biographical Encyclopedia*, 4 vols. (Salt Lake City: Andrew Jenson History, 1901–36); *Encyclopedic History of the Church of Jesus Christ of Latter-day Saints* (Salt Lake City: Deseret News, 1941). See also his *Church Chronology*, 2nd ed. (Salt Lake City: Deseret News, 1914).

14. Jenson also compiled 133 volumes of stake (diocese) histories, 178 volumes of mission histories, and other useful compilations. See the summary in Bitton and Arrington, *Mormons and Their Historians*, 50.

15. Charles P. Adams and Gustive O. Larson, "A Study of the LDS Church Historian's Office, 1830–1900," *Utah Historical Quarterly* 40 (Fall 1972): 370–89. More recently, see T. Edgar Lyon, "Church Historians I Have Known," *Dialogue* 11 (Winter 1972): 370–89; and Leonard J. Arrington, *Adventures of a Church Historian* (Urbana: University of Illinois Press, 1998).

16. T. B. H. Stenhouse, *The Rocky Mountain Saints: A Full and Complete History of the Mormons . . .* (New York: D. Appleton, 1873). On T. B. H. Stenhouse and his wife, Fanny, who wrote exposés of plural marriage, see Ronald W. Walker, "The Stenhouses and the Making of a Mormon Image," *Journal of Mormon History* 1 (1974): 51–72. For a history of the Godbeite controversy, see Ronald W. Walker, *Wayward Saints: The Godbeites and Brigham Young* (Urbana: University of Illinois Press, 1998).

17. Edward W. Tullidge, *The History of Salt Lake City and Its Founders* (Salt Lake City: by the author, 1886). Tullidge's other major historical publications include *Tullidge's Quarterly Magazine* 1–3 (1881–84); *The Women of Mormondom* (New York: by the author, 1877); *Life of Brigham Young; or, Utah and Her Founders* (New York: Tuillidge and Crandall, 1876); *Life of the Prophet Joseph Smith* (New York: Tullidge and Crandall, 1878). For a study of Tullidge as a historian, see Ronald W. Walker, "Edward Tullidge: Historian of the Mormon Commonwealth," *Journal of Mormon History* 3 (1976): 55–72.

18. On Bancroft, see his *Literary Industries*, vol. 39 of *Works of Hubert Howe Ban-*

croft (San Francisco: History Company, 1890), which describes the material the author collected on Utah and the Mormons. See also S. George Ellsworth, "Hubert Howe Bancroft and the History of Utah," *Utah Historical Quarterly* 22 (April 1954): 99–124; and Charles S. Peterson, "Hubert Howe Bancroft: First Western Regionalist," in *Writing Western History: Essays on Major Western Historians,* ed. Richard W. Etulain (Albuquerque: University of New Mexico Press, 1991), 43–70.

19. Orson F. Whitney, *History of Utah,* 4 vols. (Salt Lake City: George Q. Cannon and Sons, 1892–1904). For biographical information on Whitney, see *Through Memory's Halls: The Life Story of Orson F. Whitney as Told by Himself* (Independence, MO: Zion's, 1930). Also see Bitton and Arrington, *Mormons and Their Historians,* 56–68.

20. Brigham Henry Roberts, *Comprehensive History of the Church: Century I,* 6 vols. (Salt Lake City: Deseret News, 1930) On Roberts, see *The Autobiography of B. H. Roberts,* ed. Gary James Bergera (Salt Lake City: Signature, 1990); Truman G. Madsen, *B. H. Roberts: Defender of the Faith* (Salt Lake City: Bookcraft, 1980); and Bitton and Arrington, *Mormons and Their Historians,* 69–86.

21. See John Parley Dunford, "Students Leave Zion: An Impetus in Twentieth Century Utah" (master's thesis, Utah State University, 1965); John L. Fowles, "A Study Concerning the Mission of Week-day Religious Educational Program of the Church of Jesus Christ of Latter-day Saints from 1890–1990: A Response to Secular Education" (Ph.D. diss., University of Missouri, Columbia, 1990); and Tom Simpson, "Mormons Study Abroad: Latter-day Saints in American Higher Education, 1870–1940" (Ph.D. diss., University of Virginia, 2006).

22. Dean D. McBrien, "The Influence of the Frontier on Joseph Smith" (Ph.D. diss., George Washington University, 1929); Joel E. Ricks, "Forms and Methods of Early Mormon Settlement in Utah and the Surrounding Region, 1847–1877" (Ph.D. diss., University of Chicago, 1930); and Milton R. Hunter, "Brigham Young, the Colonizer" (Ph.D. diss., University of California, Berkeley, 1936). Two more recent studies present opposing views: supporting it, Alexander Evanoff, "The Turner Thesis and Mormon Beginnings in New York and Utah," *Utah Historical Quarterly* 33 (Spring 1965): 157–73; and opposing it, Davis Bitton, "A Re-evaluation of the Turner Thesis and Mormon Beginnings . . . ," *Utah Historical Quarterly* 34 (Fall 1966): 326–33.

23. Levi Edgar Young, *The Founding of Utah,* 2nd ed. (New York: Charles Scribner's Sons, 1924); Andrew Love Neff, "The Mormon Migration to Utah" (Ph.D. diss., University of California, Berkeley, 1918); Andrew Love Neff, *History of Utah, 1847–1869,* ed. Leland H. Creer (Salt Lake City: Deseret News, 1940); and Leland H. Creer, *The Founding of an Empire: The Exploration and Colonization of Utah, 1776–1856* (Salt Lake City: Bookcraft, 1947).

24. LeRoy R. Hafen and Ann W. Hafen, eds., *Handcarts to Zion: The Story of a Unique Western Migration, 1856–1860,* Far West and Rockies Historical series 14 (Glendale, CA: Arthur H. Clark, 1960); and *The Utah Expedition, 1857–58: A Documentary*

Account, Far West and Rockies Historical series 8 (Glendale, CA: Arthur H. Clark, 1958). See also Hafen and Hafen, *The Joyous Journey of LeRoy R. and Ann W. Hafen: An Autobiography* (Glendale, CA: Arthur H. Clark, 1973).

25. See Wallace Stegner, *The Uneasy Chair: A Biography of Bernard DeVoto* (New York: Doubleday, 1974); Leland Fetzer, "Bernard DeVoto and the Mormon Tradition," *Dialogue* 6 (Autumn–Winter 1971): 23–38; and, in the same issue, "Bernard DeVoto and the Mormons: Three Letters," 39–47.

26. Bernard DeVoto, "Utah," *American Mercury* 7 (March 1926): 319; "A Reevaluation," *Rocky Mountain Review* 10 (Autumn 1945): 7; *The Year of Decision: 1846* (Boston: Little Brown, 1943); *Across the Wide Missouri* (Boston: Houghton Mifflin, 1947); and *The Course of Empire* (Boston: Houghton Mifflin, 1952).

27. See Charles S. Peterson, "Dale Morgan, Writer's Project, and Mormon History as a Regional Study," *Dialogue* 24 (Summer 1991): 47–63; and Richard L. Saunders, "'The Strange Mixture of Emotion and Intellect': A Social History of Dale L. Morgan, 1933–42," *Dialogue* 28 (Winter 1995): 39–58.

28. See Richard L. Saunders, *Eloquence from a Silent World: A Descriptive Bibliography of the Published Writings of Dale L. Morgan* (Salt Lake City: Caramon, 1990).

29. See *Utah Historical Quarterly* 8 (April, July, October 1940): 65–239.

30. These chapters are available in John Philip Walker, ed., *Dale Morgan on Early Mormonism: Correspondence and a New History* (Salt Lake City: Signature, 1986).

31. The best sources are Juanita Brooks, *Quicksand and Cactus: A Memoir of the Southern Mormon Frontier* (Salt Lake City: Howe Brothers, 1982); Brooks, "Jest a Copyin' Word f'r Word," *Utah Historical Quarterly* 37 (Fall 1969): 375–95; and, most fully, Levi S. Peterson, *Juanita Brooks, Mormon Woman Historian* (Salt Lake City: University of Utah Press, 1988).

32. Juanita Brooks, *The Mountain Meadows Massacre* (Stanford: Stanford University Press, 1950). A second edition was published by the University of Oklahoma Press in 1962.

33. Sources on Brodie's life are Shirley E. Stephenson, "Fawn McKay Brodie: An Oral History Interview" (conducted in November 1975 for the Oral History Program of California State University, Fullerton), with edited excerpts in *Dialogue* 14 (Summer 1981): 99–116; and Newell G. Bringhurst, *Fawn McKay Brodie: A Biographer's Life* (Norman: University of Oklahoma Press, 1999).

34. Fawn M. Brodie, *No Man Knows My History: The Life of Joseph Smith, the Mormon Prophet* (New York: Alfred A. Knopf, 1945); Dale L. Morgan to Fawn M. Brodie, January 7, 1946, as found in Walker, *Dale Morgan on Early Mormonism,* 118.

35. Useful evaluations of the application of psychological models to Joseph Smith are T. L. Brink, "Joseph Smith: The Verdict of Depth Psychology," *Journal of Mormon History* 3 (1976): 73–83; and especially Charles L. Cohen, "No Man Knows My

Psychology: Fawn Brodie, Joseph Smith, and Psychoanalysis," *BYU Studies* 44, no. 1
(2005): 55 –78; and Richard Lyman Bushman, "The Inner Joseph Smith," *Journal of
Mormon History* 32, no. 1 (2006): 65–81. The most recent attempt to build on Brodie's
view is Dan Vogel, *Joseph Smith: The Shaping of a Prophet* (Salt Lake City: Signature,
2004), which was also heavily influenced by Robert D. Anderson, *Inside the Mind of
Joseph Smith: Psychobiography and the Book of Mormon* (Salt Lake City: Signature,
1999).

36. Critiques and reevaluations of Brodie's biography have been gathered in Newell
G. Bringhurst, ed., *Reconsidering "No Man Knows My History": Fawn M. Brodie and
Joseph Smith in Retrospect* (Logan: Utah State University Press, 1996).

37. See Edward A. Geary, "Mormondom's Lost Generation: The Novelists of the
1940s," *BYU Studies* 18 (Fall 1977): 89–98. See also Newell G. Bringhurst, "Fawn M.
Brodie, 'Mormondom's Lost Generation,' and *No Man Knows My History*," *Journal of
Mormon History* 16 (1990): 11–23; Gary Topping, *Utah and Her Historians and the Reconstruction of Western History* (Norman: University of Oklahoma Press, 2003).

38. See Moses Rischin, "The New Mormon History," *American West* 5 (March
1969): 49.

39. Leonard J. Arrington, *Great Basin Kingdom: An Economic History of the Latter-
day Saints, 1830–1900* (Cambridge: Harvard University Press, 1958). S. George Ellsworth remains an underappreciated Utah and Mormon historian. His University
of California, Berkeley, dissertation of 1951, "A History of Mormon Missions in the
United States and Canada, 1830–1860," is the best history of early Mormon missiology. His overview of Utah historiography remains a useful guide: "Utah History:
Retrospect and Prospect," *Utah Historical Quarterly* 40 (Fall 1972): 342–67. See also
Thomas G. Alexander, "Toward a New Mormon History: An Examination of the Literature of the Latter-day Saints in the Far West," in *Historians and the American West,*
ed. Michael P Malone (Lincoln: University of Nebraska Press, 1983), 344–68.

40. For a complete bibliography, see David J. Whittaker, "Leonard James Arrington
(1917-1999): A Bibliography," in *Reflections of a Mormon Historian: Leonard J. Arring-
ton on the New Mormon History,* ed. Reid L. Neilsen and Ronald W. Walker (Norman,
OK: Arthur H. Clark, 2006), 317–51. Evaluations of Arrington's work/approach are in
Thomas G. Alexander, ed., *Great Basin Kingdom Revisited: Contemporary Perspectives*
(Logan: Utah State University Press, 1991).

41. See Davis Bitton, "Ten Years in Camelot: A Personal Memoir," *Dialogue* 16 (Autumn 1983): 9–33; Leonard J. Arrington, "The Founding of the LDS Historical Department, 1972," *Journal of Mormon History* 18 (Fall 1992): 41–56.

42. The one-volume histories were James B. Allen and Glen M. Leonard, *The Story
of the Latter-day Saints* (1976; rev. ed., Salt Lake City: Deseret Book, 1992), organized
chronologically and addressed primarily to educated members; and Leonard J. Arrington and Davis Bitton, *The Mormon Experience: A History of the Latter-day Saints*

(New York: Alfred A. Knopf, 1979), organized topically and addressed primarily to educated non-Mormons. Volumes so far published in the projected multivolume history include Richard Lyman Bushman, *Joseph Smith and the Beginnings of Mormonism* (Urbana: University of Illinois Press, 1984); Milton V. Backman Jr., *The Heavens Resound: A History of the Latter-day Saints in Ohio* (Salt Lake City: Deseret Book, 1983); Glen M. Leonard, *Nauvoo: A Place of Peace, a People of Promise* (Salt Lake City: Deseret Book/Provo: Brigham Young University Press, 2002); Eugene E. Campbell, *Establishing Zion: The Mormon Church in the American West, 1847–1869* (Salt Lake City: Signature, 1988); Thomas G. Alexander, *Mormonism in Transition: A History of the Latter-day Saints, 1890–1930* (Urbana: University of Illinois Press, 1986); R. Lanier Britsch, *Unto the Islands of the Sea: A History of the Latter-day Saints in the Pacific* (Salt Lake City: Deseret Book, 1986). The fullest bibliography, containing references to over sixteen thousand items (books, articles, chapters, theses, and dissertations) is James B. Allen, Ronald W. Walker, and David J. Whittaker, *Studies in Mormon History, 1830–1997: An Indexed Bibliography* (Urbana: University of Illinois Press, 2000). This bibliography is available online: http://mormonhistory.byu.edu. A recent volume of sixteen essays, covering both historical periods and key topics, is Newell G. Bringhurst and Lavina Fielding Anderson, eds., *Excavating Mormon Pasts: The New Historiography of the Last Half Century* (Salt Lake City: Kofford, 2004).

43. See, for example, Richard Lyman Bushman, *Believing History: Latter-day Essays*, ed. Reid L. Neilson and Jed Woodworth (New York: Columbia University Press, 2004); D. Michael Quinn, ed., *The New Mormon History: Revisionist Essays on the Past* (Salt Lake City: Signature, 1992); and George D. Smith, ed., *Faithful History: Essays on Writing Mormon History* (Salt Lake City: Signature, 1992).

44. See Boyd K. Packer, "The Mantle Is Far, Far Greater than the Intellect," *BYU Studies* 21 (Summer 1981): 259–78.

45. One perspective is provided in Lavina Fielding Anderson, "The LDS Intellectual Community and Church Leadership: A Contemporary Chronology," *Dialogue* 26 (Spring 1993): 7–64.

46. See D. Michael Quinn's works: *The Mormon Hierarchy: Origins of Power* (Salt Lake City: Signature and Smith Research Associates, 1994); *The Mormon Hierarchy: The Extensions of Power* (Salt Lake City: Signature and Smith Research Associates, 1997); *Early Mormonism and the Magic World View*, rev. ed. (Salt Lake City: Signature, 1998); and *Same-Sex Dynamics among Nineteenth-Century Americans: A Mormon Example* (Urbana: University of Illinois Press, 1996).

47. See the essay by Armand Mauss, "Flowers, Weeds, and Thistles: The State of Social Science Literature on the Mormons," in Walker, Whittaker, and Allen, *Mormon History*, 153–97.

48. See Lavina Fielding Anderson, ed., *Lucy's Book: A Critical Edition of Lucy Mack Smith's Family Memoir* (Salt Lake City: Signature, 2001). For recent scholarship on the

Smith and Mack families, see Richard Lloyd Anderson, *Joseph Smith's New England Heritage*, rev. ed. (Provo: Brigham Young University Press, 2003); and Kyle R. Walker, ed., *United by Faith: The Joseph Smith Sr. and Luck Mack Smith Family* (American Fork, UT: Covenant Communications, 2006).

49. See Ronald W. Walker, "The Challenge and Craft of Mormon Biography," *BYU Studies* 22 (Spring 1982): 179–92; and Newell G. Bringhurst, "Telling Latter-day Saints Lives: The Craft and Continuing Challenge of Mormon Biography," *Journal of Mormon History* 27, no. 1 (2000): 1–41.

50. See, for example, recent biographies of Mormon Church leaders: Bushman, *Joseph Smith;* Leonard J. Arrington, *Brigham Young: American Moses* (New York: Knopf, 1985); D. Michael Quinn, *Elder Statesman: A Biography of J. Reuben Clark* (Salt Lake City: Signature, 2002); and Gregory Prince and Wm. Robert Wright, *David O. McKay and the Rise of Modern Mormonism* (Salt Lake City: University of Utah Press, 2005).

51. For bibliographical guides to Mormon women, see Carol Cornwall Madsen and David J. Whittaker, "History's Sequel: A Source Essay on Women in Mormon History," *Journal of Mormon History* 6 (1979): 123–45; Claudia L. Bushman, ed., *Mormon Sisters: Women in Early Utah,* 2nd ed. (Logan: Utah State University Press, 1997); Maureen Ursenbach Beecher and Lavina Fielding Anderson, eds., *Sisters in Spirit: Mormon Women in Historical and Cultural Perspective* (Urbana: University of Illinois Press, 1987). For perspectives on contemporary issues, see Maxine Hanks, ed., *Women and Authority: Re-emerging Mormon Feminism* (Salt Lake City: Signature, 1992).

52. Most of these studies can be found listed in Allen, Walker, and Whittaker, *Studies in Mormon History.*

53. Two bibliographies will lead the serious student to the main sources: Davis Bitton, "Mormon Polygamy: A Review Article," *Journal of Mormon History* 4 (1977): 101–18; and Patricia Lyn Scott, "Mormon Polygamy: A Bibliography, 1977–92," *Journal of Mormon History* 19 (Spring 1993): 133–55. See Kimball Young, *Isn't One Wife Enough?* (New York: Henry Holt, 1954), although the best recent study is by Kathryn M. Daynes, *More Wives than One: Transformation of the Mormon Marriage System, 1840–1910* (Urbana: University of Illinois Press, 2001).

54. Most scholars think Joseph Smith had taken at least thirty-one "wives" before his death in 1844. See Danel W. Bachman, "A Study of the Mormon Practice of Plural Marriage Before the Death of Joseph Smith" (master's thesis, Purdue University, 1975); Bachman, "New Light on an Old Hypothesis: The Ohio Origins of the Revelation on Plural Marriage," *Journal of Mormon History* 5 (1978): 19–32.

55. Allen, Walker, and Whittaker, *Studies in Mormon History,* will lead researchers to the relevant materials.

56. See Janet Bennion, *Women of Principle: Female Networking in Contemporary Mormon Polygamy* (New York: Oxford University Press, 1998); Brian C. Hales, *Modern*

Polygamy and Mormon Fundamentalism: The Generations After the Manifesto (Salt Lake City: Kofford, 2006).

57. David J. Whittaker, "Mormon Missiology: An Introduction and Guide to the Sources," in *The Disciple as Witness: Essays on Latter-day Saint History and Doctrine in Honor of Richard Lloyd Anderson,* ed. Stephen D. Ricks, Donald W. Parry, and Andrew H. Hedges (Provo: Foundation for Ancient Research and Mormon Studies, Brigham Young University, 2000), 459–538.

58. On the original ideals, see Steven L. Olsen, "The Mormon Ideology of Place: Cosmic Symbolism of the City of Zion, 1830–1846" (Ph.D. diss., University of Chicago, 1985); Richard Lyman Bushman, "Making Space for the Mormons," Leonard J. Arrington Mormon History Lecture, October 22, 1996, in *The Collected Leonard J. Arrington Mormon History Lectures* (Logan: Special Collections and Archives, University Libraries, Utah State University, 2005), 31–53, 248–51. Guides to the settlement literature are Wayne L. Wahlquist, "A Review of Mormon Settlement Literature," *Utah Historical Quarterly* 45 (Winter 1977): 4–21; and Dean L. May, *Three Frontiers: Family, Land, and Society in the American West, 1850–1900* (Cambridge: Cambridge University Press, 1994).

59. Essential overviews are Arrington, *Great Basin Kingdom;* and Leonard J. Arrington, Dean L. May, and Feramorz Y. Fox, *Building the City of God: Community and Cooperation among the Mormons,* 2nd ed. (Urbana: University of Illinois Press, 1992).

60. The best overview of this period is Thomas G. Alexander, *Mormonism in Transition: A History of the Latter-day Saints, 1890–1930* (Urbana: University of Illinois Press, 1986).

61. See David J. Whittaker, "Mormons and Native Americans: A Historical and Bibliographical Introduction," *Dialogue* 18 (Winter 1985): 33–64; Lester E. Bush Jr., "Mormonism's Negro Doctrine: An Historical Overview," *Dialogue* 8 (Spring 1973): 11–68; Lester E. Bush Jr. and Armand L. Mauss, eds., *Neither White nor Black: Mormon Scholars Confront the Race Issue in a Universal Church* (Midvale, UT: Signature, 1984); Armand L. Mauss, *All Abraham's Children: Changing Mormon Conceptions of Race and Lineage* (Urbana: University of Illinois Press, 2003).

62. Dean L. May, "Mormons," in *Harvard Encyclopedia of American Ethnic Groups,* ed. Stephen Thernstrom (Cambridge: Harvard University Press, 1980), 720–31. On the history of Mormon food and health beliefs and practices, see Lester E. Bush Jr., *Health and Medicine among the Latter-day Saints: Science, Sense, and Scripture* (New York: Crossroad, 1993).

63. Important studies include Donald W. Meinig, "The Mormon Cultural Region: Strategies and Patterns in the Geography of the American West, 1847–1964," *Annals of the Association of American Geographers* 55 (June 1965): 191–220; Klaus J. Hansen, *Mormonism and the American Experience* (Chicago: University of Chicago

Press, 1981); Armand L. Mauss, *The Beehive and the Angel: The Mormon Struggle with Assimilation* (Urbana: University of Illinois Press, 1994); and Kathleen Flake, *The Politics of American Religious Identity: The Seating of Senator Reed Smoot, Mormon Apostle* (Chapel Hill: University of North Carolina Press, 2004).

64. A good place to begin is with Steven L. Shields, *Latter-day Saint Churches: An Annotated Bibliography* (New York: Garland, 1987); and Shields, *Divergent Paths of the Restoration: A History of the Latter-day Saint Movement,* 4th ed. (Los Angeles: Restoration Research, 1990). A collection of scholarly essays is Roger D. Launius and Linda Thatcher, eds., *Differing Visions: Dissenters in Mormon History* (Urbana: University of Illinois Press, 1994).

65. The "Index to Historical Writings," in Allen, Walker, and Whittaker, *Studies in Mormon History,* will lead researchers to the published material on anti-Mormonism: see 483–86, 908–914. Especially valuable are Terryl L. Givens, *The Viper on the Hearth: Mormons, Myth, and the Construction of Heresy* (New York: Oxford University Press, 1997); and Gary L. Bunker and Davis Bitton, *The Mormon Graphic Image, 1834–1914: Cartoons, Caricatures, and Illustrations,* Publications in the American West 16 (Salt Lake City: University of Utah Press, 1983).

66. See the following for guides to this genre: Edwina Jo Snow, "Singular Saints: The Image of the Mormons in Book-Length Travel Accounts, 1847–1857" (master's thesis, George Washington University, 1972); and Michael W. Homer, ed., *On the Way to Somewhere Else: European Sojourners in the Mormon West, 1834–1930,* Kingdom in the West, the Mormons and the American Frontier series (Spokane: Arthur H. Clark, 2006). An excellent selection of travel accounts is William Mulder and A. R. Mortensen, eds., *Among the Mormons: Historic Accounts by Contemporary Observers* (New York: Knopf, 1958).

67. See Eduard Meyer, *Ursprung und Geschichte der Mormon en . . .* (1912). The work was translated into English by Heinz F. Rahde and Eugene Seaich as *The Origin and History of the Mormons, with Reflections on the Beginnings of Islam and Christianity* (Salt Lake City: University of Utah Press, 1961).

68. Such cross-fertilization has been a valuable part of the growing Mormon rapprochement with the larger scholarly world. See, for example, the essays in Truman G. Madsen, ed., *Reflections on Mormonism: Judaeo-Christian Parallels* (Provo: Religious Studies Center, Brigham Young University, 1978). See especially Robert N. Bellah, "American Society and the Mormon Church," in *Reflections on Mormonism,* 1–12. Bellah's essay "The Mormons," prepared for the Harvard Values Study Project in 1952, while never published, is available in the BYU Library.

69. An account of the Harvard project is Evon Vogt and Ethel M. Albert, *People of Rimrock: A Study of Values in Five Cultures* (Cambridge: Harvard University Press, 1966). Thomas F. O'Dea had studied the Mormon village of Ramah, New Mexico.

His main studies include "Mormon Values: The Significance of a Religious Outlook for Social Action," 2 vols. (Ph.D. diss., Harvard University, 1953); "Mormonism and the Avoidance of Sectarian Stagnation: A Study of Church, Sect, and Incipient Nationality," *American Journal of Sociology* 60 (November 1954): 285–93; "Mormonism and the American Experience of Time," *Western Humanities Review* 8 (Summer 1954): 181–90; and *The Mormons* (Chicago: University of Chicago Press, 1957). See also Cardell K. Jacobson, John P. Hoffmann, and Tim B. Heaton, eds., *Revisiting Thomas F. O'Dea's "The Mormons": Contemporary Perspectives* (Salt Lake City: University of Utah Press, 2008).

70. Robert Baird, *Religion in America; or, An Account of the Origin, Progress and Relation to the State, and Present Condition of the Evangelical Churches in the United States, with Notices of the Unevangelical Denominations* (New York: Harper and Brothers, 1844); Sydney E. Ahlstrom, *A Religious History of the American People* (New Haven: Yale University Press, 1972), 500. See also Thomas G. Alexander, "The Place of Joseph Smith in the Development of American Religion: A Historiographical Inquiry," *Journal of Mormon History* 5 (1978): 3–17.

71. Jan Shipps, *Mormonism: The Story of a New Religious Tradition* (Urbana: University of Illinois Press, 1985). See also Shipps, *Sojourner in the Promised Land: Forty Years among the Mormons* (Urbana: University of Illinois, Press, 2000). See also the thoughtful review essay by Philip L. Barlow, "Jan Shipps and the Mainstreaming of Mormon Studies," *Church History* 73 (June 2004): 412–26.

72. See Philip L. Barlow, *Mormons and the Bible: The Place of the Latter-day Saints in American Religion*, Religion in America series (New York: Oxford University Press, 1991). Joseph Smith made corrections and additions to some of the Bible's text (mostly in the books of Genesis and the Four Gospels). For the details, see Robert J. Matthews, *"A Plainer Translation": Joseph Smith's Translation of the Bible: A History and Commentary* (Provo: Brigham Young University Press, 1975).

73. Terryl L. Givens, *By the Hand of Mormon: The American Scripture That Launched a New World Religion* (New York: Oxford University Press, 2002).

74. *The Pearl of Great Price: A Selection from the Revelations, Translations, and Narrations of Joseph Smith* (Salt Lake City: Church of Jesus Christ of Latter-day Saints, 1981); Chad J. Flake and Larry W. Draper, eds., *A Mormon Bibliography, 1830–1930: Books, Pamphlets, Periodicals, and Broadsides relating to the First Century of Mormonism*, 2nd ed., 2 vols. (Provo: Religious Studies Center, Brigham Young University, 2004). See also Peter Crawley, *A Descriptive Bibliography of the Mormon Church, 1830–1857*, 2 vols. (Provo: Religious Studies Center, Brigham Young University, 1998-); and "Mormon Imprints as Sources for Research: A History and Evaluation," in Walker, Whittaker, and Allen, *Mormon History*, 199–238.

75. For the best accounts, see Linda Sillitoe and Allan D. Roberts, *Salamander: The*

Story of the Mormon Forgeries and Murders, 2nd ed. (Salt Lake City: Signature, 1989); and Richard E. Turley Jr., *Victims: The LDS Church and the Mark Hofmann Case* (Urbana: University of Illinois Press, 1992).

76. See John-Charles Duffy, "Faithful Scholarship: The Mainstreaming of Mormon Studies and the Politics of Insider Discourse" (master's thesis, University of North Carolina, Chapel Hill, 2006); and M. Gerald Bradford, "The Study of Mormonism: A Growing Interest in Academia," *FARMS Review* (issued by the Neal A. Maxwell Institute for Religious Scholarship, Brigham Young University) 19, no.1 (2007): 119–74.

8

Interpreting American Pentecostal Origins

Retrospect and Prospect

Randall J. Stephens

Pentecostalism is a large, relatively new religious movement that claims hundreds of millions of followers around the globe. Believers speak in unknown tongues, practice healing, and claim a number of gifts of the Spirit.[1] Chief denominations include the primarily white Assemblies of God; the largely African American Church of God in Christ; the Pentecostal Assemblies of the World; the Church of God, Cleveland, Tennessee; and the International Pentecostal Holiness Church. Additionally, millions of followers have joined unaffiliated congregations, a clear sign of devotees' fierce independence and nontraditional sympathies. Though contemporary adherents are much like other conservative and moderate evangelicals, one hundred years ago converts distanced themselves from the American mainstream. The earliest outside observers were invariably negative in their appraisals of the new movement.

Not long after Pentecostalism first took root in early twentieth-century America, one bitter opponent lamented, "There is not a town of three thousand population in the United States where the movement is not represented." Stalwarts antagonized mainline Christians, harangued "half-hearted" believers, and claimed that Jesus would swiftly return to wipe out Pentecostalism's many foes. It is no wonder that another early observer shot back with an acerbic rebuttal. Writing in the scholarly journal *Social Forces* in 1937, a professor from Alabama's Tuskegee Institute derided "holy roller" religion as an "escape from reality." Practitioners warped their minds with hypnotic frenzies and epileptic fits. He concluded: "Psychologically, the communicants of sanctification fall into two general classes: neurotics, and [the] mentally retarded." Their churches harbored "childminded types."[2]

Such cultured despisers predicted that the unconventional, regressive faith would soon disappear. They were completely wrong. The movement grew by leaps and bounds as the century progressed. By 1936 Pentecostalism claimed at least 350,000 followers in the United States. It had become a powerful stream within American and global Protestantism. In 1958 *Life* magazine took note and published a photo essay on what it called the "third force in Christendom." Pentecostal and Holiness churches, wrote the main author of the piece, consisted of " 'fringe sects'—those marked, in the extreme, by shouting revivalists, puritanical preachers of doomsday, faith healers, jazzy gospel singers." *Life*'s relatively kind treatment contrasted sharply with earlier, caustic critiques. Indeed, the new faith could no longer be dismissed or wished away. Followers came from all walks of life, they hailed from big cities as well as rural areas, and they were now joining the middle class as never before. *Life*'s wide-eyed reporters announced that in the 1940s and 1950s membership in the third force jumped as much as 600 percent.[3]

That growth rate continued apace in the succeeding decades. Pentecostalism is now arguably the most important mass religious movement of the modern era. American Pentecostalism claimed at least 11 million adherents by 2000. It is today the second largest subgroup of global Christianity. Of the 81 percent of Americans who call themselves Christians, 14 percent identify themselves as Pentecostals.[4]

Pentecostalism's inauspicious beginnings at the turn of the twentieth century make its growth and influence all the more surprising. First-generation followers were anonymous radicals. Now, by contrast, those associated with the faith are known by millions. Music legends like Elvis Presley, Jerry Lee Lewis, B. B. King, Johnny Cash, Tammy Wynette, and Dolly Parton grew up in the tradition or attended Pentecostal churches. Many of them credited the free-form worship and energetic music of their childhood churches for inspiring later innovations.[5] Former attorney general John Ashcroft and Ronald Reagan's secretary of the Interior James G. Watt were long-standing members of the Assemblies of God. Since the 1920s charismatic and Pentecostal preachers and faith healers—including Aimee Semple McPherson, Oral Roberts, Kathryn Kuhlman, Jimmy Swaggart, Jim Bakker, John Hagee, and Benny Hinn—have profoundly influenced American spirituality. Their use of the latest technology to tell an ancient story made them media trailblazers.

Historians have been interested in the institutional growth and the rising profile of Pentecostalism over the century. Yet most scholarly interest in the subject is relatively recent. Roughly forty years ago, few outside the faith knew much about it. Researchers now understand a great deal concerning this once neglected yet important tradition. As with most fields, though, obstacles to a fuller picture remain. First-generation followers cared little about archiving their history. Their unwavering evangelism and apocalyptic outlook tended to push aside such "worldly" concerns. Although some early leaders wondered why more preachers had not kept diaries or written of their faith in newspapers or books, a few disciples considered the piling up of any earthly treasures a sure sign of vanity and sinfulness. One key evangelist associated with the 1906 Azusa revival in Los Angeles burned five hundred of his personal letters. Those mementos, worried Frank Bartleman, would puff him up.[6] Fortunately for scholars today, few early converts went to such extremes. Records in denominational, college, and state archives are plentiful.

Even so, either because the study of Pentecostal history is a relatively new field or because scholars' personal interests do not incline them to it, much about the movement remains unstudied. Biographies on some of the most significant founders have yet to be written. Historians have barely scratched the surface in the study of large African American denominations like the Church of God in Christ. Similarly, few have studied the various forms of ethnic Pentecostalism.[7] And, in a most glaring omission, only a handful of historians have examined Pentecostalism after the period of the 1930s. Accordingly, this essay details a rich historiography of the early movement, but reveals that much about the history and historiography of Pentecostalism remains shrouded in mystery.[8]

Early Appraisals

The historiography of Pentecostalism is as multifaceted as the movement itself. Initial historical works came from within the movement. Believing historians wrote within a "providentialist" framework, tracking the work of God rather than human and natural causation. These historians, as premier scholar of Pentecostalism Grant Wacker notes, were apologetic and largely ahistorical. They depicted the revival of the Spirit as dropping from heaven like a Holy Ghost comet. That approach is evident in the titles of such early works as *The Apostolic Faith Restored* (1916) and *Suddenly from Heaven: A History of the Assemblies of God* (1961).[9]

Before 1970 few historians outside of Pentecostalism expressed interest in it. Many agreed with Will Herberg, a scholar of American religion who in his book *Protestant-Catholic-Jew*, originally published in 1955, described Pentecostals as poor, apolitical, inconsequential "outsiders." Enthusiasts, he wrote, gathered in "very minor denominations, hardly affecting the total picture" of American religion. Academics' unfamiliarity with the world of ecstatic religion accounted for that oversight. Scholars also thought the conservative religion of Pentecostalism, like fundamentalism, was backward, crude, and not worthy of serious attention. Historians with a strictly materialist or functionalist understanding of religion had reason to doubt Pentecostalism's significance. Thus, E. P. Thompson famously dismissed early Methodism in his classic *The Making of the English Working Class* (1963) as "a ritualized form of psychic masturbation." In the late 1960s, the historian William G. McLoughlin argued that Pentecostalism did not constitute a dynamic new force in American religion. According to McLoughlin, Pentecostalism, like other reactionary religious movements, would vanish with time. Indeed, before the 1970s, scholars limited their study to "articulate" religious bodies and to groups that were pertinent to scholars' own academic interests. Accordingly, historian of American religion Robert Orsi has recently commented that religious studies departments have all too often been "departments of the study of desirable religion."[10]

Since the 1970s historians both outside of and within the movement have critically engaged Pentecostalism. The rapid expansion of Pentecostalism in the United States and abroad drew scholars' interest. At the same time scholarship on Pentecostalism grew along with the increase in university- and seminary-trained Pentecostal historians. The establishment of the Society for Pentecostal Studies in the early 1970s is indicative of that new historical enterprise.[11]

As historians analyzed Pentecostalism, they have developed several explanations for its origins, growth, and denominational strength. Some scholars focus on the historical-theological roots of the tradition and emphasize the primacy of doctrine. They note the importance of Pentecostalism's historical and theological precursors and emphasize the movement's religious appeal. A few historians look at Pentecostalism's seemingly progressive, interracial character to assess its origins and growth. In its initial stages, Pentecostalism was multiethnic and often challenged racial norms. Scholars looking at that aspect view the movement as a radical protest against segregation and as a dynamic force of social change. With the ascendance of the new social history in the early 1970s, some began to analyze the demographics of Pentecostalism, assessing the movement's adherents according to social status and class.

Before the rise of historical inquiries, sociological studies employed class analysis and theories of deprivation to describe Pentecostalism's appeal. Hence, theology was not of primary importance. They reflected H. Richard Niebuhr's class analysis of religion and posited that theology mirrored cultural and political conditions.[12] The prevailing view was that Pentecostalism flourished because it compensated for adherents' loss of social and political control. As such, in the 1940s, sociologists John Holt and Liston Pope argued that the movement gathered disciples among society's dispossessed, rural poor. For Holt and Pope, Pentecostalism's response to crises was a natural by-product of social disorganization. Holt thought that "migration and con-comitant urbanization of an intensely rural, and religiously fundamental-ist population" led to the creation of Holiness sects that hoped to "recapture their sense of security."[13] David Edwin Harrell's historical study of Pentecos-talism follows that pattern. Harrell finds that class rather than theological presuppositions conditioned the racial and social views of pentecostals.[14]

Robert Mapes Anderson also summarizes Pentecostal success in terms of socioeconomic factors. In *Vision of the Disinherited,* the first wide-ranging scholarly treatment, Anderson observes that extreme social strain among the nation's poor and dispossessed gave rise to Pentecostalism. Following Eric Hobsbawm, Richard Hofstadter, and E. P. Thompson, Anderson locates so-cial tension such as class conflict and class stratification in industrialization. The shift from an agrarian to an industrial society fed estrangement, and those most at odds with this change suffered "status anxiety" and turned to Pentecostalism. Anderson compiles biographical data on forty-five leaders of early Pentecostalism and perceives that "the group as a whole lay in a sort of limbo between working and middle-class. Neither quite one nor the other, they were marginal men and women."[15]

To explain how Pentecostals coped with failure and frustration, Anderson looks at two major features of the movement: millennialism and tongues speech. Pentecostals' belief in the imminent apocalyptic return of Jesus, he contends, brought order to chaotic lives and alleviated social strain. Similarly, speaking in tongues provided psychic escape through religious ecstasy. The premise was simple enough. In fact, Anderson's critique bears striking re-semblance to one of the earliest studies of Holiness and perfectionism, Mer-ill Elmer Gaddis's 1929 University of Chicago dissertation, "Christian Perfec-tionism in America." Perfectionist sects, wrote Gaddis, attracted beleaguered outsiders during periods of national economic and social crises.[16]

Anderson, like Gaddis half a century before, concluded that Pentecostal-ism represented a kind of dysfunctional reaction to life's pressures. Because of Pentecostals' negative appraisal of society and their pessimistic outlook, they were an apolitical "conservative bulwark of the status quo." Hence, they channeled their social protest "into the harmless backwaters of religious ide-ology."[17] For Anderson, the radical social impulse inherent in the vision of the disinherited was squandered away in escapism and conservative con-formity.

Anderson's study is one of the most thorough monographs on Pentecos-tal origins. The breadth of his book and the amount of data he analyzes makes it a monument in the field. Nonetheless, Grant Wacker and others take issue with Anderson's basic arguments. Wacker contends that Anderson

assumes Pentecostal faith is irrelevant if it does not foment social and economic protest. He also criticizes Anderson for judging religious rewards to be
less satisfying than material ones. By contrast, Wacker argues that theology
and doctrine, as much as social class, explain the emergence and growing influence of the movement.[18]

Pentecostals as Innovators

Wacker counters that the positive functions of faith were critical to the origin and spread of Pentecostalism. He notes that the movement provided
individuals with certitude about the reality of the supernatural. Stalwarts
coped with economic uncertainties, social ostracism, and racism by order-
ing their lives with a primitive faith. Seeing the world as morally degener-
ate, adherents championed scriptural inerrancy, opposed scientific evolution
and biblical criticism, and issued numerous cultural prohibitions. Pentecostalism, maintains Wacker, was appealing because its doctrines were situated
in a traditional mythic system that protected believers from the encroach-
ments of modernity.[19]

Wacker explores these and other themes in his authoritative 2001 survey of
the early movement, *Heaven Below: Early Pentecostals and American Culture.*
Two powerful forces drove disciples, Wacker claims: primitivism and pragmatism. On the one hand, they turned to the early church and hoped to restore an unadorned New Testament Christianity. On the other hand, followers were shrewd and pragmatic when it came to living out their faith from day
to day. Devotees "proved remarkably willing to work within the social and
cultural expectations of the day," he argues. Indeed, they adopted the newest
technologies and techniques to spread their apostolic message. Roger G. Robins, a former student of Wacker, has picked up on this theme in his insightful
biography of first-generation leader of the Church of God (Cleveland), A. J.
Tomlinson. Robins calls Tomlinson a "plainfolk modernist." "Tomlinson and
the world he inhabited," asserts Robins, "expressed a vibrant strain of modernism, though one voiced in the idioms of plainfolk culture."[20]

That emphasis on the progressive, innovative character of the charismatic
movement and Pentecostalism represents a promising area of study. An example drawn from midcentury America is illustrative. Groundbreaking rocker
Elvis Presley is the most well known American linked to a tongues-speaking
church. The Tupelo, Mississippi, native learned much from the exuberant
faith. He attended Memphis's First Assembly of God in the late 1940s and
early 1950s. In that two-thousand-member church Elvis listened with rapt
attention to Pastor James Hamill's powerful sermons and stomped his feet

and sang along with dynamic gospel groups the Blackwood Brothers and the Stamps Quartet. All left a life-changing impression on the young southerner. In 1956 Presley told an Associated Press reporter: "We used to go to these religious singins all the time. There were these singers, perfectly fine singers, but nobody responded to 'em. Then there were these other singers—the leader wuz a preacher—and they cut up all over the place, jumpin' on the piano, movin' every which way. The audience liked 'em. I guess I learned from them singers." Lively services opened the teenager's mind to novel music and performance styles.[21] The adaptability and free-form nature of Holy Ghost religion made it liberating.

Scholars such as Grant Wacker, Roger G. Robins, Matthew Avery Sutton, Tona J. Hangen, Jerma Jackson, James R. Goff, David Edwin Harrell, and Shayne Lee focus on the original, even modern aspects of Pentecostalism.[22] The old-time religion, it turns out, was strikingly new. Early twentieth-century critics of fundamentalism and Pentecostalism like H. L. Mencken and W. J. Cash assured readers that believers were hookworm-belt oddities, living on the premodern fringe of civilization. However, all through the twentieth century Pentecostals and fundamentalists broke new ground in their use of mass culture, skillfully employing the mediums of print, radio, and television. The faithful used up-to-date advertising techniques and eagerly embraced a host of innovations to spread the "Good News." Fittingly, the Pentecostal TV empire Trinity Broadcasting Network has proclaimed the wonders of its "Devil Bustin' Satellite" without the faintest hint of irony. In her work on conservative Christianity and radio, Tona J. Hangen writes, "it does seem high time we acknowledge that without the institutions of modern mass culture religious fundamentalism could not have taken its present shape—and that mass culture, in turn, owes something to religion's aggressive advance in the twentieth century."[23]

Restorationism, Millennialism, and Conflict

At the same time, what Grant Wacker emphasized as the primitive, restorationist element of the movement remains a powerful explanatory device. Historians like Edith Blumhofer and D. William Faupel look at the restorationist and millennial roots of the movement. Wacker describes the old-time religion impulse as "a yearning to return to a time before time, to a space outside of space, to a mythical realm that Alexander Campbell [founder of the Disciples of Christ] called the 'ancient order of things.'" Campbell did not dream of a nostalgic, frontier revivalism; rather, he hoped to reestablish first-century Christianity. One hundred years after Campbell preached his message in the American interior, Pentecostals longed for much the same. They linked the spiritual gifts they received—speaking in tongues, prophesying, and healing—with those described in the book of Acts. Edith Blumhofer argues that restorationism and millennialism were critical to the early Assemblies of God. Pentecostals, according to Blumhofer, proclaimed that the new era of the Spirit, before Christ's Second Coming, would bring about a return to *primitive* Christianity. Assemblies of God members were caught up in a kind of historylessness and sought a return to apostolic, ecclesiastical foundations. Church leaders advocated strict congregational government and opposed creeds and the formulation of doctrine.[24]

The parallel millennial vision, according to James R. Goff, led to increased missionary activity. Charles Fox Parham, for example, concluded that speaking in foreign tongues enabled Pentecostals to missionize the world before Jesus came back. Goff indicates that this missionary impulse explains both the origins and rapid growth of Pentecostalism. The end was near. Enthusiasts hoped to save as many sinners as they could before Armageddon. Preaching Christ's imminent return, Pentecostals won converts among uneasy followers. Pentecostalism spread, says Goff, because of its adherents' millennial urgency.[25]

Yet it is unclear how much premillennialism, and its emphasis on a time of tribulation and the rapture of the saints, still influences Pentecostals, who are now much more affluent than they were in previous decades. The doctrine still holds sway in many quarters. In 2006 an extensive survey conducted by the Pew Forum revealed that 90 percent of American Pentecostals believed that the devout would be raptured before the end of the world. Only 53 percent of non-Pentecostal Christians thought the same. The survey does not, however, break down categories by region, race, or ethnicity. African American initiates seem less concerned with the vagaries of end-time doctrine than their white brethren. Indeed, premillennialism never gained as intense a following among black Holiness groups. C. H. Mason and C. P. Jones, founders of the Church of God in Christ, occasionally emphasized a vague sort of premillennialism. But for them it was never an all-consuming theory, as it was for so many early white adherents. Why the difference in emphasis? Correct praxis, it seems, not correct doctrine or detailed theories of the world's demise, remained most important to black followers.[26]

Other religious bodies of the late nineteenth and early twentieth centuries—including fundamentalists, Jehovah's Witnesses, and Adventists—stressed the Second Coming. Accordingly, some students of Pentecostalism highlight the late nineteenth-century religious context. Like Spiritualism or Christian Science, so goes the logic, Pentecostalism was a product of a specific era. Donald

Dayton suggests that the roots of Pentecostalism can be traced to four doctrines from the late nineteenth century: salvation, healing, baptism of the Holy Spirit, and the Second Coming of Christ.[27] Dayton looks at how these doctrines developed within the Holiness movement and were then taken up by Pentecostals. He stresses both the Wesleyan-Holiness element, which accented the perfectionist side of Spirit baptism, and the reformed aspect, which emphasized Spirit baptism as a spiritual empowerment of the believer. Similarly, Wacker has studied the wave of interest in the Holy Spirit among other late-century Protestants.[28] Like both Dayton and Wacker, Raymond J. Cunningham has examined Pentecostalism's emergence in the healing and faith cure movements of the period. By accentuating divine gifts, healing sects often fed directly into Pentecostalism.[29]

Vinson Synan's seminal *The Holiness-Pentecostal Tradition* is a general survey that also highlights the context of the era. Synan emphasizes that Pentecostalism was rooted in the Wesleyan-Holiness doctrine of sanctification or the "second blessing." Pentecostals, states Synan, made the second blessing synonymous with the Pentecost account in Acts. Thus, speaking in tongues became a sign of sanctification.[30]

Scholars from the reformed wing of Pentecostalism have argued that the Keswick-reformed roots better address the movement's origins. The term *Keswick* comes from a series of Holiness conferences held in Keswick, England, beginning in 1875. Leaders of the Keswick Convention, mostly evangelical Anglicans, adhered to the teachings of John Calvin. Accordingly, they taught that sin remained in believers until death. Scholars who stress the Keswick element contend that Pentecostals were not as influenced by Wesleyan perfectionism.[31] Keswickians upheld the finished work of conversion and did not believe in a second work of grace as did Wesleyans. Edith Blumhofer's 1977 Harvard dissertation counters Synan's Wesleyan thesis. The theological contributions of reformed and fundamentalist leaders, Blumhofer asserts, were vital.[32] Blumhofer argues that such churchmen and theologians provided Pentecostals with a solid understanding of Spirit baptism that little resembled the Wesleyan view. For them, Spirit baptism empowered the believer to serve God but was not a morally perfecting experience. Assemblies of God historian William Menzies has also challenged Synan's view. Menzies declares that second-blessing advocates were less influential than reformed, "finished work" Pentecostals. For most disciples, Menzies challenges, speaking in tongues was associated with spiritual power and with an anointing to serve rather than spiritual perfection.[33]

These interpretive debates illustrate an important point: from the beginning Pentecostal denominations experienced internal and external antagonisms that helped shape them. According to Wacker, "the secondary literature on Pentecostalism is almost as contentious as the controversies it describes." Both Wacker and Donald Dayton have written about these struggles and reveal how they shaped the movement. Examining the anti-Pentecostal forces within radical evangelicalism, Wacker shows how doctrinal differences precipitated conflict. Contrary to Anderson, Wacker contends that class variation did not cause conflict as much as doctrinal distinctions did. Holiness and Pentecostal factions early squared off in a pitched battle. W. B. Godbey, a widely read popular Holiness minister of the late nineteenth century, penned venomous attacks against the novel movement. Godbey shouted down Pentecostals as deceivers and agents of the devil. Others were even less restrained. In fact, apostles kicked up so much theological dust that even outsiders took note. In the 1920s wrangling between Pentecostal and Holiness factions caught the eye of journalist Duncan Aikman, who wrote about it in Mencken's *American Mercury.* Judging from the "mutual damnations" hurled back and forth, Aikman sneered, one would think that all "Holy Rollers" were hell bound.[34]

Some conflicts between Pentecostals and non-Pentecostals, though not as heated, remain to this day. The reason non-Pentecostal Holiness leaders so vehemently opposed Pentecostals, says Wacker, was because Pentecostals assumed that all truly sanctified Christians must speak in tongues.[35] Doctrine also gave rise to schisms within the movement. The Wesleyan factions—the Apostolic Faith Union and the Church of God—fought with the reformed wing—Assemblies of God—and reformed, Trinitarian Pentecostals waged war on Unitarian rivals.

Conflict remains a powerful theme. Some scholars focus on how Pentecostals reacted to and against the culture around them. Most agree that while Pentecostalism was largely apolitical, early Pentecostals' opposition to America's political and social culture was, in fact, politically charged.[36] Pentecostals were centered on soul winning and thought of politics and national events as dangerous diversions. But early followers were also both prohibitionists and pacifists. According to Mickey Crews, the predominately rural Church of God (Cleveland) often stood in opposition to prevailing contemporary attitudes toward wealth, recreation, and dress. Likewise, during the Jim Crow era, the Church of God was one of the more racially integrated churches in the South. Converts challenged society's power structures across the nation. Like third-party Populists, tongues-speaking fellowships offered women as well as blacks opportunities to serve in positions of leadership denied to them by more traditional organizations.[37]

A few historians view racial progressiveness and the conflict with Jim

Crow as critical to the movement's success. Church of God in Christ histo-rian Leonard Lovett observes that historians have not viewed black Pentecos-talism in its proper historical context and have failed to appreciate its African American roots. Lovett stresses the prominence of the black leader William Seymour and the importance of Azusa's interracialism. He also gives atten-tion to the Africanisms of the early revival. Similarly, Ian MacRobert stud-ies the black roots of Pentecostalism, emphasizing both the role of Seymour in the revival and the place of African concepts of "community, spiritual power, spirit possession . . . equality, black personhood," dignity, and a revo-lutionary spirit. MacRobert attributes schisms in the movement to white rac-ism. He argues that white leaders in the Apostolic Faith Union and the As-semblies of God turned their backs on their interracial heritage, segregating their churches according to race. That assessment, though overly simplistic, has gained wide acceptance. There were a number of factors that divided de-nominations along racial lines. (Some of these can be traced to the decisions of leaders. Others, however, owe more to the hardening of race ideology in early twentieth-century America, the migration of believers to other parts of the country, and theological divisions within denominations.) In a more recent work, Harvey Cox suggests that the interethnic, egalitarian character of Azusa Street is still the movement's sine qua non.[38]

Others are skeptical. Edith Blumhofer and Joe Creech have countered that a "myth of Azusa Street" still prevails. Early Pentecostalism, they suggest, was not a homogenous movement but developed from a variety of sources. Blum-hofer argues that "Azusa street could not hold the allegiance of its own en-thusiasts, who broke away to form numerous rival congregations nearby, none of which was known to replicate the racial mix of the mother congregation." Creech likewise maintains that Azusa has remained important in the histori-ography because it provides historians with a racially progressive narrative of Pentecostalism and because it serves to unify and homogenize a hetero-geneous movement.[39]

Pentecostalism's diverse heritage still draws the attention of historians who seek an explanation for the movement's origins. The rise of Spirit-centered churches at the turn of the century tells us how some Americans coped in various ways with the economic, social, and religious challenges of moder-nity. Like fundamentalists, Pentecostals built their faith on doctrinal certi-tude and religious zeal. But religious experience was far more important to tongues-speakers than it was to fundamentalists. Douglas Jacobsen has writ-ten at great length on the biblical, experiential faith of Pentecostals. Jacobsen notes that "the popular perception that Pentecostalism is about experience as opposed to theology—that Pentecostalism is an emotional rather than a cog-

184   Randall J. Stephens

nitive faith"—misses the mark. Though stalwarts still shun the formal theologies of mainline Protestants, "experience is only half the picture of the
Pentecostal faith." Theology, contends Jacobsen in his extensive *Thinking in
the Spirit: Theologies of the Early Pentecostal Movement,* has always circum-
scribed experience. Initiates faced their disordered world in various ways: returning to primitive Christianity, elevating the person of Jesus, and reinsti-
tuting New Testament spiritual gifts.[40] Convinced Christ would soon come
again, which so many read about on page after page of the Bible, their social
outlook was often otherworldly.

Certainly, at least until the 1960s, most Pentecostals did not engage politics
directly. Yet even early on, their actions nonetheless pointed to political and
social protests. In religious practice they stood in opposition to both racism
and the denigration of women.[41] It has become more difficult for historians to
dismiss Pentecostals as socially irrelevant ciphers. Their views on race, gender, and theology were complicated and deserve more critical analysis. However, American historians have paid little attention. Survey texts of the Gilded
Age and Progressive era seldom, if ever, mention the Holiness revival or the
awakening at Azusa Street. In fact, the only major American history survey
text to take Pentecostalism into account is *Unto a Good Land: A History of
the American People,* published by Eerdmans.[42]

Areas for Further Study

There are various areas of Pentecostal history that remain unstudied. Certain
institutional and biographical histories need to be written. A scholarly history of the predominately black 6-million-member Church of God in Christ
has yet to be undertaken. Similarly, few scholars have examined the thriving
non-Trinitarian "Oneness" Pentecostals.[43] There is also a paucity of biographies on some key leaders, including William J Seymour, Charles H. Mason
(Church of God in Christ), and a number of lesser-known men and women
who shaped the movement over the century, though James R. Goff and Grant
Wacker's *Portraits of a Generation: Early Pentecostal Leaders* and the copious
biographical material included in *New International Dictionary of Pentecostal
and Charismatic Movements* have shed much light on prominent figures.[44]

Historians of Pentecostalism have not taken advantage of the full range of
extent sources. Many still rely on institutional records and sources from the
movement's leadership. The documents of Pentecostalism's laity are largely
unstudied; personal records, diaries, and correspondences are virtually untouched.[45] Also overlooked are accounts by noninitiates. Pentecostalism still
needs work written, like American social history since the 1970s, from the

bottom up. Such undertakings might reveal how Pentecostalism differed among the lower levels of the movement. Did doctrinal controversies plague the laity as they did church leaders? Did the average men and women in the pews differ significantly from the clergy in social or economic status?[46] Did the typical believer accept gender and racial norms?

The role of women in the early movement in particular has received some attention, but much more work needs to be done.[47] Historians know that women often acted as worship leaders and evangelists, but as of yet few have critically assessed the role of women in the movement as a whole. Did women enjoy greater opportunities within Pentecostal fellowships than did women in mainline churches? How did the roles of women in patriarchal fundamentalist churches differ from those of women in tongues-speaking denominations?

The confluence of race and gender is also an area that merits careful consideration. A denomination like the Church of God in Christ did not ordain women, but still had the most powerful women's department of any black denomination in the United States. Did women wield the same kind of authority as those that Evelyn Brooks Higginbotham describes in the National Baptist Convention did? The Church of God in Christ, according to Cheryl Sanders and Anthea Butler, rejected the norms of white patriarchy and affirmed black female personhood by esteeming women leaders and educators. Sanders also suggests that it was not gender but spiritual gifts that qualified individuals for leadership in the Holiness and Pentecostal churches.[48] Comparative studies on other denominations would be useful.

Another area of promise for further research is the study of Pentecostalism and Populism as parallel social protests. Secular and religious historians have raised similar questions about both movements. Both arose during a period of economic and social instability in which America underwent drastic change. In this regard, both have been analyzed, too simplistically, as protests of the dispossessed and marginalized. Scholars also have been concerned with the racial and gender progressiveness of each.[49] Historians generally agree that the two groups' demographics were remarkably similar. Future studies might reveal why some were attracted to Holiness-Pentecostalism and others to the Farmers' Alliance and Populism. Was affiliation arbitrary? Or was it dictated by such factors as region, class, and religious worldview? Could the success of Pentecostalism in the South and Midwest after 1900 and 1906 be accounted for by the failures of Populism in those areas?

Historians have tended to treat American Pentecostalism as a cultural whole. Scholars seldom, therefore, consider how the movement varied from one region to another. In *Heaven Below* Wacker comments, "I pay little attention to regional, ethnic, and gender differences." Yet if the faith has thrived in certain sections of the United States, does regionalism not deserve more scrutiny? Today, 10 to 18 percent of the population in Arkansas, Oklahoma, Texas, Alabama, and West Virginia is Pentecostal.[50] What factors account for that strength? A few historians have focused on the cultural dynamics of the American South. Most find that converts to Holiness and Pentecostalism below the Mason-Dixon line were not typical southerners. Some initiates were part of a long tradition of southern dissent. Others were new arrivals from the North.[51] But for the most part, larger questions concerning regional variation remain unanswered.

To date, nearly all historians of Pentecostalism have concentrated on the early period, roughly 1900 to 1925. Why has that initial era dominated the historiography? In those years, believers established the first tongues-speaking denominations. Subsequent institutionalization helped formalize and tame certain features. Perhaps the resulting domestication is just not as interesting. The early period, for some historians, also held the promise of interracialism, gender equality, and a kind of democratic fellowship that faded in later years. But the persistence of this "golden age" consensus has cut short a fuller understanding of the movement.

What could be gained from an examination of the history from the 1930s forward? Studies of the Great Depression might reveal how the church helped initiates weather the economic storm. Journalist Dan Morgan's *Rising in the West: The True Story of an "Okie" Family from the Great Depression through the Reagan Years* chronicles the lives of California-bound Pentecostals during the Dust Bowl years. Historians, though, have yet to tell that and other stories of Pentecostalism and migration. Lisa McGirr's *Suburban Warriors: The Origins of the New American Right* links California's Holiness and Pentecostal newcomers to the burgeoning political Right. While her account is suggestive, it leaves much unsaid on the subject. One still wonders how important Pentecostals were to the post-1960s conservative ascendancy. Did the phenomenal growth of the faith in the postwar era coincide with greater participation in party politics? In the 1980s right-wing Christian television personality and politician Pat Robertson gained his largest following among Pentecostal and charismatic evangelicals. His hard-line stance on Communism and his fusion of patriotism and biblical literalism gathered tens of millions to his side.[52] How did this politicization of Pentecostals and charismatics occur?

Pentecostals' greatest contribution to American culture may have very little to do with politics. Their influence on music, religious worship styles, and the media have been profound.[53] In the future scholars might tell us much about the powerful influence the faithful exerted on America culture. To what extent was popular music, including rock and roll and country, shaped by Pentecostal music and performance styles? How have Pentecostal and charismatic Christians refashioned low and high church worship in the years since the 1970s? And why have those two groups had such a powerful role as multimedia innovators in the last thirty years?

In the coming years scholars may be asking these and other questions in their search for the origins and ongoing impact of Pentecostalism. Before the 1970s the history of Pentecostalism was not so much as a dot on the horizon of American historiography. The field has grown significantly in the last thirty years and will continue to expand into cultural, political, and social history in the twenty-first century. As of yet, however, the amount of scholarship is not equal to the movement's numeric strength. Pentecostalism's mass appeal should challenge historians to look deeper into the movement's recent as well as its distant past.

Notes

An earlier version of this essay appeared in Briane Turley, ed., *The American Religious Experience,* http://are.as.wvu.edu/.

1. Adherents, argues Grant Wacker, the leading historian of Pentecostalism, believe in a postconversion experience known as baptism in the Holy Spirit. Pentecostals, he says, hold that a person who has been baptized in the Holy Spirit will manifest one or more of the nine spiritual gifts described in 1 Corinthians 12 and 14. Grant Wacker, "Searching for Eden with a Satellite Dish: Primitivism Pragmatism and the Pentecostal Character," in *Religion and American Culture,* ed. David G. Hackett (New York: Routledge, 1995), 441. See also David Gonzalez, "A Sliver of a Storefront, a Faith on the Rise," nytimes.com, January 14, 2007 (accessed February 24, 2007).

2. C. W. Shumway, "A Study of 'The Gift of Tongues'" (bachelor's thesis, University of Southern California, 1914), 191; William A. Clark, "Sanctification in Negro Religion," *Social Forces* 15 (May 1937): 546, 549.

3. "The Third Force in Christendom," *Life,* June 6, 1958, 113, 116.

4. Wacker, "Searching for Eden with a Satellite Dish," 440.

5. Stephen R. Tucker, "Pentecostalism and Popular Culture in the South: A Study of Four Musicians," *Journal of Popular Culture* 16 (Winter 1982): 68–78; Jimmy Wayne Jones Jr., "Modern American Pentecostalism: The Significance of Race, Class, and Culture in Charismatic Growth, 1900–2000" (Ph.D. diss., University of Arkansas, 2002), 130–54; Vince Staten, *The Real Elvis: Good Old Boy* (Dayton, OH.: Media Ventures, 1978), 47–48; Van K. Brock, "Assemblies of God: Elvis and Pentecostalism," *Bulletin of the Center for the Study of Southern Culture and Religion* 3 (June 1979):

9–15; Johnny Cash, *Man in Black* (Grand Rapids, MI: Zondervan, 1975), 25; Tammy Wynette with Joan Dew, *Stand by Your Man* (New York: Simon and Schuster, 1979), 23–24; Charles Sawyer, *The Arrival of B. B. King* (Garden City, NY: Doubleday, 1980), 39–40; Myra Lewis with Murray Silver, *Great Balls of Fire: The Uncensored Story of Jerry Lee Lewis* (New York: William Murrow, 1982), 34–35, 308–11.

6. Rev. J. R. Flower, Springfield, Missouri, to M. M. Pinson, Oildale, California, January 4, 1950, Flower Pentecostal Heritage Center, Springfield, Missouri; Frank Bartleman, *Azusa Street* (1925; repr., South Plainfield, NJ: Bridge, 1980), 153.

7. For the most sophisticated study of Mexican American Pentecostalism, see Daniel Ramirez, "Migrating Faiths: A Social and Cultural History of Popular Religion in the United States–Mexico Borderlands" (Ph.D. diss., Duke University, 2005). See also Anthea D. Butler, *Women in the Church of God in Christ: Making a Sanctified World* (Chapel Hill: University of North Carolina Press, 2007).

8. For other historiographical summaries, see D. D. Bundy, "Bibliography and Historiography of Pentecostalism in the United States," in *New International Dictionary of Pentecostal and Charismatic Movements,* ed. Stanley M. Burgess (Grand Rapids, MI: Zondervan, 2002), 382–417; and Arlene M. Sanchez Walsh, "Whither Pentecostal Scholarship?" *Books and Culture* (May–June 2004): 34–36.

9. Grant Wacker, "Are the Golden Oldies Still Worth Playing? Reflections on History Writing among Early Pentecostals," *Pneuma* 8, no. 2 (1986): 86. For a discussion of the "providential" approach, see Augustus Cerillo Jr., "Interpretive Approaches to the History of American Pentecostal Origins," *Pneuma* 19, no. 1 (1997): 31–36.

10. Will Herberg, *Protestant-Catholic-Jew: An Essay in American Religious Sociology* (Chicago: University of Chicago Press, 1983), 123; E. P. Thompson, *The Making of the English Working Class* (New York: Penguin, 1963), 405; William G. McLoughlin, "Is There a Third Force in Christendom?" in *Religion in America,* ed. William G. McLoughlin and Robert N. Bellah (Boston: Beacon, 1968), 47, 52, 56. McLoughlin was responding to Henry P. Van Dusen's *Life* magazine article that acknowledged the growing importance of American sects: "The Third Force's Lesson for Others," *Life,* June 9, 1958, 122–23. Robert A. Orsi, *Between Heaven and Earth: The Religious Worlds People Make and the Scholars Who Study Them* (Princeton: Princeton University Press, 2005), 190. See also Randall J. Stephens, "Beyond the Niebuhrs: An Interview with Robert Orsi on Recent Trends in American Religious History," *Historically Speaking: The Bulletin of the Historical Society* 7, no. 6 (2006): 8–11.

11. Augustus Cerillo locates this change in Pentecostal denominations' growing historical consciousness, the rising social status of Pentecostals, and a greater interest in higher education. See "The Origins of American Pentecostalism," *Pneuma* 15, no. 1 (1993): 78.

12. H. Richard Niebuhr maintained that religion "is so interwoven with social circumstances that the formulation of theology is necessarily conditioned by these." *The Social Sources of Denominationalism* (Cleveland: World Publishing, 1957), 17, 75–76.

13. John B. Holt, "Holiness Religion: Cultural Shock and Social Reorganization," *American Sociological Review* 5, no. 5 (1940): 740–41; Liston Pope, *Millhands and Preachers: A Study of Gastonia* (New Haven: Yale University Press, 1942), 84–91, 126–40. For sociologists like Charles Y. Glock and Howard Ellinson, religion served as an escape mechanism for those unable to alter their social status. Charles Y. Glock, "The Role of Deprivation in the Origin and Evolution of Religious Groups," in *Religion and Social Conflict,* ed. Robert Lee and Martin E. Marty (New York: Oxford University Press, 1964), 27, 29; Howard Elinson, "The Implications of Pentecostal Religion for Intellectualism, Politics, and Race Relations," *American Journal of Sociology* 70 (1965): 403–15. For a counterview, see Harry G. Lefever, "Religion of the Poor: Escape or Creative Force?" *Journal for the Scientific Study of Religion* 16, no. 3 (1977): 525–34.

14. David E. Harrell Jr., *White Sects and Black Men in the Recent South* (Nashville: Vanderbilt University Press, 1971), xvi, 130–31. Racial integration most often occurred, says Harrell, in the poorest sects like the Church of God (Cleveland) and the Church of God of Prophecy, which were not vying for middle-class status.

15. Robert Mapes Anderson, *Vision of the Disinherited: The Making of American Pentecostalism* (New York: Oxford University Press, 1979), 113, 108, 136. In his study of the Church of God (Cleveland), Mickey Crews also emphasizes class origins. Crews argues that the Populist movement and the Church of God arose among farmers in similar socioeconomic circumstances. *The Church of God: A Social History* (Knoxville: University of Tennessee Press, 1990), 1–18. Yet others find the class element far more complex. Historian Daniel Woods observes that Pentecostals in western Virginia and southern West Virginia were usually members of the middle class and upper range of the working class. Converts were the "aspiring working class," Woods notes. "Living in the Presence of God: Enthusiasm, Authority, and Negotiation in the Practice of Pentecostal Holiness" (Ph.D. diss., University of Mississippi, 1997), 139–42, 143.

16. Anderson, *Vision of the Disinherited,* 80, 113, 96; Merill Elmer Gaddis, "Christian Perfectionism in America" (Ph.D. diss., University of Chicago, 1929), 441, 457–58.

17. Anderson, *Vision of the Disinherited,* 239. R. Laurence Moore also asserts that the otherworldliness of Pentecostals cut short social protests by diffusing class hostilities. R. Laurence Moore, *Religious Outsiders and the Making of Americans* (Oxford: Oxford University Press, 1986), 140–42.

18. Grant Wacker, "Taking Another Look at the *Vision of the Disinherited,*" *Religious Studies Review* 8, no. 1 (1982): 18, 19, 20.

19. Grant Wacker, "The Functions of Faith in Primitive Pentecostalism," *Harvard Theological Review* 77, no. 3 (1984): 355, 356, 363. On the theme of the positive role of faith and prayer, see Woods, "Living in the Presence of God"; D. William Faupel, "The Restoration Vision in Pentecostalism," *Christian Century,* October 17, 1990, 938. On the importance of restorationism to Pentecostal eschatology, see D. William Faupel,

The Everlasting Gospel: The Significance of Eschatology in the Development of Pentecostal Thought (Sheffield, UK: Sheffield Academic, 1996).

20. Grant Wacker, *Heaven Below: Early Pentecostals and American Culture* (Cambridge: Harvard University Press, 2001), 13, 14, 86, 99; Roger G. Robins, *A. J. Tomlinson: Plainfolk Modernist* (New York: Oxford University Press, 2004), 5.

21. Staten, *The Real Elvis,* 47–48; Brock, "Assemblies of God: Elvis and Pentecostalism," 9–15. On Elvis's relationship with the Blackwood Brothers, see James R. Goff Jr., *Close Harmony: A History of Southern Gospel* (Chapel Hill: University of North Carolina Press, 2002), 237–38. Saul Pett, "Why Do the Girls Love Elvis?" *Richmond Times-Dispatch,* July 22, 1956, L-7. Presley quote from "Elvis Says Jumping 'Arown' Comes Natural When He Sings" (newspaper clipping at the Flower Pentecostal Heritage Center, Springfield, Missouri). Peter Guralnick, *Last Train to Memphis: The Rise of Elvis Presley* (Boston: Little, Brown, 1994), 17, 67, 75.

22. For examples of this work, see Tona J. Hangen, *Redeeming the Dial: Radio, Religion, and Popular Culture in America* (Chapel Hill: University of North Carolina Press, 2002); Goff, *Close Harmony;* Jerma Jackson, "Sister Rosetta Tharpe and the Evolution of Gospel Music," in *Religion in the American South: Protestants and Others in History and Culture,* ed. Beth Barton Schweiger and Donald G. Mathews (Chapel Hill: University of North Carolina Press, 2004), 219–22, 230–32; Randall J. Stephens, *The Fire Spreads: Holiness and Pentecostalism in the American South* (Cambridge: Harvard University Press, 2008); Matthew Avery Sutton, *Aimee Semple McPherson and the Resurrection of Christian America* (Cambridge: Harvard University Press, 2007); and David Edwin Harrell Jr., *All Things Are Possible: The Healing and Charismatic Revivals in Modern America* (Bloomington: Indiana University Press, 1978). On the inventiveness of African American Pentecostal music, see Paul Oliver, *Songsters and Saints: Vocal Traditions on Race Records* (Cambridge: Cambridge University Press, 1984), 170–71, 188–89, 197–98; Paul Harvey, *Freedom's Coming: Religious Culture and the Shaping of the South from the Civil War through the Civil Rights Era* (Chapel Hill: University of North Carolina Press, 2005), 107–68; Shayne Lee, *T. D. Jakes: America's New Preacher* (New York: New York University Press, 2005).

23. Alistair Cooke, ed., *The Vintage Mencken* (New York: Vintage, 1990), 153–60; W. J. Cash, *The Mind of the South* (New York: Vintage, 1991), 289, 290; "TBN Newsletter," May 2000, tbn.org (accessed August 25, 2006); Hangen, *Redeeming the Dial,* 8.

24. Wacker, "Searching for Eden with a Satellite Dish," 442–44 (quote on 442); Wacker, "The Functions of Faith in Primitive Pentecostalism," 361, 364; Edith Blumhofer, *Restoring the Faith: The Assemblies of God, Pentecostalism, and American Culture* (Urbana: University of Illinois Press, 1993), 4–5, 84, 116; Faupel, *The Everlasting Gospel.* On American millennialism in general, see also Paul Boyer, *When Time Shall Be No More: Prophecy Belief in Modern American Culture* (Cambridge: Harvard University Press, 1992); Timothy P. Weber, *Living in the Shadow of the Second Coming:*

American Premillennialism, 1875–1925 (Chicago: University of Chicago Press, 1987). See also Amy Johnson Frykholm, *Rapture Culture: Left Behind in Evangelical America* (New York: Oxford University Press, 2004).

25. James R. Goff Jr., *Fields White unto Harvest: Charles F. Parham and the Missionary Origins of Pentecostalism* (Fayetteville: University of Arkansas Press, 1988), 15, 164.

26. *Spirit and Power: A 10–Country Survey of Pentecostals* (Washington, DC: Pew Forum on Religion and Public Life), 24, pewforum.org (accessed November 22, 2006); Mary Mason, *The History and Life Work of Elder C. H. Mason, Chief Apostle, and His Co-laborers* (n.p., 1924), 35, 94; Milton G. Sernett, "Black Religion and the Question of Evangelical Identity," in *The Variety of American Evangelicalism*, ed. Donald Dayton and Robert K. Johnston (Downers Grove, IL: InterVarsity, 1991), 135, 142. See also Donald Dayton, *The Theological Roots of Pentecostalism* (Metuchen, NJ: Scarecrow, 1987), 146.

27. Dayton, *Theological Roots of Pentecostalism*, 11, 173–74. Pentecostals often speak of a four-square gospel, using these doctrines to identify themselves.

28. Ibid., 92–106; Grant Wacker, "The Holy Spirit and the Spirit of the Age in American Protestantism, 1880–1910," *Journal of American History* 72 (June 1985): 45–62. Timothy Smith wrote about the Wesleyan perfectionist element of Pentecostalism in "How John Fletcher Became the Theologian of Wesleyan Perfectionism, 1770–1776," *Wesleyan Theological Journal* 15, no. 1 (1980): 67–86. On Spirit baptism as spiritual empowerment, see John Fea, "Power from on High in an Age of Ecclesiastical Impotence: The 'Enduement of the Holy Spirit' in American Fundamentalist Thought, 1880–1936," *Fides et Historia* 26, no. 6 (1994): 23–35.

29. Raymond J. Cunningham, "From Holiness to Healing: The Faith Cure in America, 1872–1892," *Church History* 43, no. 3 (1974): 507, 508.

30. Vinson Synan, *The Holiness-Pentecostal Tradition: Charismatic Movements in the Twentieth Century* (Grand Rapids, MI: Eerdmans, 1997), xi.

31. William W. Menzies, "The Non-Wesleyan Origins of the Pentecostal Movement," in *Aspects of Pentecostal Charismatic Origins*, ed. Vinson Synan (Plainfield, NJ: Logos International, 1975), 85–89.

32. Edith Waldvogel (Blumhofer), "The 'Overcoming Life': A Study in the Reformed Evangelical Origins of Pentecostalism," (Ph.D. diss., Harvard University, 1977). Blumhofer looks at such figures as Reuben A. Torrey, Albert B. Simpson, Dwight L. Moody, and a number of British Keswick leaders. Allen L. Clayton argues that the prominence of the reformed wing, which was Christocentric rather than pneumatocentric in orientation, gave rise to the Oneness, "Jesus only" Pentecostals. By emphasizing the central role of Christ, Oneness Pentecostals began to baptize in Jesus's name only. Allen L. Clayton, "The Significance of William H. Durham for Pentecostal Historiography," *Pneuma* 1, no. 2 (1979): 38–39.

33. Menzies, "The Non-Wesleyan Origins of the Pentecostal Movement," 93.

34. Grant Wacker, "Travail of a Broken Family: Evangelical Responses to Pente-costalism in America, 1906-1916," *Journal of Ecclesiastical History* 47, no. 2 (1996): 509; W. B. Godbey, *Tongue Movement, Satanic* (Zarephath, NJ: Pillar of Fire, 1918), 4-5; W. B. Godbey, *Spiritualism, Devil-Worship, and the Tongues Movement* (Cincinnati: God's Revivalist, n.d.), 26; Barry W. Hamilton, *William Baxter Godbey: Itinerant Apostle of the Holiness Movement* (Lewiston, NY: Edwin Mellen, 2000), 259-64; Duncan Aikman, "Holy Rollers," *American Mercury* 15 (October 1928): 183.

35. Wacker, "Travail of a Broken Family," 508, 526-27; Donald Dayton, "The Limits of Evangelicalism: The Pentecostal Tradition," in Dayton and Johnston, *The Variety of American Evangelicalism*, 49-51. Dayton gives insight into the recurrent battles between Holiness and Pentecostal Wesleyans laying claim to the Wesleyan heritage: "Wesleyan Tug-of-War on Pentecostal Link," *Christianity Today*, December 15, 1978, 43. On the enmity between Pentecostals and evangelicals, see Horace S. Ward Jr., "The Anti-Pentecostal Argument," in Synan, *Aspects of Pentecostal Charismatic Origins*, 102-7; and Wacker, "Travail of a Broken Family." Others look at the communal and societal opposition converts experienced: Vinson Synan, *Old Time Power: A Centennial History of the International Pentecostal Holiness Church* (Franklin Springs, GA: LifeSprings Resources, 1998), 140-45; and Crews, *Church of God*, 117-23, 74-78. Kurt O. Berends analyzes the communal antagonism Pentecostals spawned in "Social Variables and Community Response," in *Pentecostal Currents in American Protestantism*, ed. Edith Blumhofer, Russell P. Splitter, and Grant A. Wacker (Urbana: University of Illinois Press, 1999), 68-89.

36. Both R. Laurence Moore, *Religious Outsiders*, 142, and Wacker, "Are the Golden Oldies Still Worth Playing?" 155, have made this point. On the politicization of African American Pentecostals, see David D. Daniels III, "'Doing All the Good We Can': The Political Witness of African American Holiness and Pentecostal Churches in the Post-Civil Rights Era," in *New Day Begun: African American Churches and Civic Culture in Post–Civil Rights America*, ed. R. Drew Smith (Durham: Duke University Press, 2003), 164-65, 168-69, 171-73.

37. Crews, *Church of God*, 17-18, 93-107.

38. Leonard Lovett, "Black Origins of the Pentecostal Movement," in Synan, *Aspects of Pentecostal Charismatic Origins*, 127, 137-38. For a more nuanced reading of these developments, see Harvey, *Freedom's Coming*, 107-68. Iain MacRobert, *The Black Roots and White Racism of Early Pentecostalism in the USA* (New York: St. Martin's, 1988), 36; Harvey Cox, *Fire from Heaven: The Rise of Pentecostal Spirituality and the Reshaping of Religion in the Twenty-first Century* (Reading, MA: Addison-Wesley, 1995), 58-59. See also Jones, "Modern American Pentecostalism."

39. Edith Blumhofer, "For Pentecostals, a Move toward Racial Reconciliation," *Christian Century*, April 27, 1994, 445; Joe Creech, "Visions of Glory: The Place of

the Azusa Street Revival in Pentecostal History," *Church History* 65, no. 3 (1996): 408–10.

40. Douglas Jacobsen, *Thinking in the Spirit: Theologies of the Early Pentecostal Movement* (Bloomington: Indiana University Press, 2003), 2.

41. On women in the Holiness-Pentecostal tradition, see Cheryl J. Sanders, *Saints in Exile: The Holiness-Pentecostal Experience in African American Religion and Culture* (New York and Oxford: Oxford University Press, 1996), 32–34. According to Cheryl Townsend Gilkes, although the major black Pentecostal bodies denied women ordination, women nonetheless assumed powerful roles as exhorters, church mothers, missionaries, teachers, and deaconesses. "'Together and in Harness': Women's Traditions in the Sanctified Church," *Signs* 10, no. 4 (1985): 683. Anthea D. Butler, "Church Mothers and Migration in the Church of God in Christ," in Schweiger and Mathews, *Religion in the American South*, 195–218; Butler, *Women in the Church of God in Christ*. On the limits of female leadership, see David G. Roebuck, "Limiting Liberty: The Church of God and Women Ministers, 1886–1996" (Ph.D. diss., Vanderbilt University, 1997), 4.

42. David Edwin Harrell Jr., Edwin S. Gaustad, John B. Boles, and Sally Foreman Griffith, *Unto a Good Land: A History of the American People*, vol. 2, *From 1865* (Grand Rapids, MI: Eerdmans, 2005). For years, my area of specialization, southern history, was no exception to the rule of ignoring Pentecostalism. Historian Donald Mathews writes that before Edward Ayers's *Promise of the New South* (1993), "the major synthesizers of southern history," including U. B. Phillips, William Dunning, C. Vann Woodward, George Tindall, Wesley Frank Craven, and E. Merton Coulter, had "not been forced to explain the role of religion in southern life." Donald G. Mathews, "'We have left undone those things which we ought to have done': Southern Religious History in Retrospect and Prospect," *Church History* 67 (June 1998): 306. Other works that take no account of Holiness and Pentecostalism include Robert Wiebe, *The Search for Order, 1877–1920* (New York: Hill and Wang, 1995); Thomas J. Schlerth, *Victorian America: Transformations in Everyday Life, 1876–1915* (New York: HarperCollins, 1991); Leon Fink, ed., *Major Problems in the Gilded Age and the Progressive Era: Documents and Essays* (Boston: Houghton Mifflin, 2001); William A. Link, *The Paradox of Southern Progressivism, 1880–1930* (Chapel Hill: University of North Carolina Press, 1997); Alan Trachtenberg, *The Incorporation of America: Culture and Society in the Gilded Age* (New York: Hill and Wang, 1982); and Nell Irvin Painter, *Standing at Armageddon: The United States, 1877–1919* (New York: W. W. Norton, 1987). There is also no mention of Pentecostalism in all of the following: Arthur M. Schlesiger Jr., *The Almanac of American History* (Greenwich, CT: Brompton, 1993); Eric Foner and John A. Garraty, eds., *The Readers' Companion to American History* (Boston: Houghton Mifflin, 1991); and George Brown Tindall, *America: A Narrative History*, vol. 2 (New York: W. W. Norton, 1988).

43. See Jacobsen's chapter on Oneness in his *Thinking in the Spirit,* 194–259.

44. James R. Goff Jr. and Grant Wacker, eds., *Portraits of a Generation: Early Pentecostal Leaders* (Fayetteville: University of Arkansas Press, 2002); Burgess, *New International Dictionary of Pentecostal and Charismatic Movements.*

45. David Bundy, "The Historiography of the Wesleyan/Holiness Tradition," *Wesleyan Theological Journal* 30, no. 1 (1995): 70.

46. Mickey Crews suggests that in the Church of God there was a difference: "Although the overwhelming majority of Church of God members and ministers came from the lower socioeconomic classes, their principal spokesmen did not." Crews, *Church of God,* 6.

47. Few significant biographies exist on key women leaders of Holiness and Pentecostalism, and little has been written on less notable women. See, for example, Wayne E. Warner, *The Women Evangelist: The Life and Times of Charismatic Evangelist Maria B. Woodworth-Etter* (Metuchen, NJ: Scarecrow, 1986); Edith Blumhofer, *Aimee Semple McPherson: Everybody's Sister* (Grand Rapids, MI: Eerdmans, 1993); and Sutton, *Aimee Semple McPherson and the Resurrection of Christian America.* On the interplay of Holiness, gender, and sexuality, see Leslie Dawn Callahan, "Fleshly Manifestations: Charles Fox Parham's Quest for the Sanctified Body" (Ph.D. diss., Princeton University, 2002); and Clarence E. Hardy, *James Baldwin's God: Sex, Hope, and Crisis in Black Holiness Culture* (Knoxville: University of Tennessee Press, 2003). Scholarship on gender and fundamentalism may provide other clues as to how studies on Pentecostalism might look: Margaret Lamberts Bendroth, *Fundamentalism and Gender, 1875 to the Present* (New Haven: Yale University Press, 1993); and Betty A. DeBerg, *Ungodly Women: Gender and the First Wave of American Fundamentalism* (Minneapolis: Fortress, 1990).

48. Evelyn Brooks Higginbotham, *Righteous Discontent: The Women's Movement in the Black Baptist Church, 1880–1920* (Cambridge: Harvard University Press, 1993); Cheryl Sanders, "History of Women in the Pentecostal Movement," *Cyberjournal for Pentecostal/Charismatic Research* 2 (July 1997): 5, www.pctii.org\cybertab1.html (accessed April 1, 1999). See also Butler, "Church Mothers and Migration in the Church of God in Christ."

49. On Populism and women, see Julie Roy Jeffrey, "Women in the Southern Farmers Alliance: A Reconsideration of the Role and Status of Women in the Late Nineteenth-Century South," *Feminist Studies* 3 (Fall 1975): 72–91; Marion K. Barthelme, *Women in the Texas Populist Movement: Letters to the Southern Mercury* (Austin: Texas A&M University Press, 1997), 3–76; Michael Lewis Goldberg, *An Army of Women: Gender and Politics in Gilded Age Kansas* (Baltimore: Johns Hopkins University Press, 1997). On women in the Pentecostal-Holiness movements, see Gilkes, "'Together and in Harness.'" On Populism and race, see Herbert Shapiro, "The Populist and the Negro: A Reconsideration," in *The Making of Black America,* ed. August

Meier (New York: Atheneum, 1969), 32; and Gerald Gaither, *Blacks and the Populist Revolt: Ballots and Bigotry in the "New South"* (Tuscaloosa: University of Alabama Press, 1977). On Holiness-Pentecostal movements and race, see Iain MacRobert, *The Black Roots and White Racism of Early Pentecostalism in the U.S.A;* and Harrell, *White Sects and Black Men.* On the connections between Holiness and Populism, see Randall J. Stephens, "The Convergence of Populism, Religion, and the Holiness-Pentecostal Movements: A Review of the Historical Literature," *Fides et Historia* 32, no. 1 (2000): 51–64; and Joe Creech, *Righteous Indignation: Religion and the Populist Revolution* (Urbana: University of Illinois Press, 2006), 11–12, 18–20, 143–46, 177–80.

50. Wacker, *Heaven Below,* 16; Gonzalez, "A Sliver of a Storefront, a Faith on the Rise."

51. On the South, see Briane K. Turley, *A Wheel within a Wheel: Southern Methodism and the Georgia Holiness Association* (Macon: Mercer University Press, 1999); Robins, *A. J. Tomlinson;* J. Lawrence Brasher, *The Sanctified South: John Lakin Brasher and the Holiness Movement* (Urbana: University of Illinois Press, 1994); Gary Don McElhany, "The South Aflame: A History of the Assemblies of God in the Gulf Region" (Ph.D. diss., Mississippi State University, 1996); and Robert Stanley Ingersol, "Burden of Dissent: May Lee Cagle and the Southern Holiness Movement" (Ph.D. diss., Duke University, 1989).

52. Dan Morgan, *Rising in the West: The True Story of an "Okie" Family from the Great Depression through the Reagan Years* (New York: Alfred A. Knopf, 1992). Wallace Best's work serves as a guide for studies on black Pentecostalism and the Great Migration: *Passionately Human, No Less Divine: Religion and Culture in Black Chicago, 1915–1952* (Princeton: Princeton University Press, 2007). Lisa McGirr, *Suburban Warriors: The Origins of the New American Right* (Princeton: Princeton University Press, 2002), 31, 49, 254–61; David Edwin Harrell Jr., *Pat Robertson: A Personal, Political, and Religious Portrait* (San Francisco: Harper and Row, 1987), 131–37; Glenn H. Utter and James L. True, *Conservative Christians and Political Participation: A Reference Handbook* (Santa Barbara, CA: ABC CLIO, 2004), 167.

53. For a suggestive look at the influence of Pentecostals and charismatics on the larger Protestant world, see chapters in Blumhofer, Splitter, and Wacker, *Pentecostal Currents in American Protestantism.*

9

"We're All Evangelicals Now"

The Existential and Backward Historiography of Twentieth-Century Evangelicalism

Barry Hankins

The vast majority of the historiography of twentieth-century American evangelicalism has been produced since 1980, and that historiography has been done backward. Rather than several monographs written on particular aspects of evangelicalism followed by a synthesis that brings the parts together and makes sense of the whole, recent evangelical historiography began with the synthesis, then saw the details filled in later. Moreover, as illustrated in this essay, the vast majority of scholars who focus their attention on fundamentalism and evangelicalism are either evangelicals or former evangelicals. Both types seem to work existentially in an effort to understand the subculture that produced them.

The Marsden Paradigm

The historiographical synthesis was George Marsden's *Fundamentalism and American Culture: The Shaping of Twentieth-Century Evangelicalism, 1870–1925,* which first appeared in 1980. It was not only the most important book published on the history of evangelicalism but also one of the most important books ever published in the field of religion and America. Marsden defined evangelicalism and fundamentalism, setting the stage for the flood of books that appeared over the next quarter century. Published by Oxford University Press, Marsden's book moved the historical study of fundamentalism and evangelicalism firmly into the mainstream of historical scholarship.[1]

The groundwork for Marsden's book had been laid in 1970 by Ernest Sandeen's *The Roots of Fundamentalism: British and American Millenarianism.* Sandeen shifted the interpretation away from the view that fundamentalism was a last-gasp attempt to preserve a dying way of life. Instead, Sandeen took the ideas of fundamentalism seriously and attempted to account for the fact that the movement was flourishing in the final third of the twentieth century. For this reason, Sandeen's book was immensely valuable historiographically, but it also served as Marsden's foil. Sandeen argued that fundamentalism developed primarily from dispensational premillennialism as articulated by conservatives who adopted the Princetonian doctrine of inerrancy.[2] Marsden countered that Sandeen had found one root of fundamentalism and mistook it for the whole tree. Marsden argued to the satisfaction of nearly everyone that there were several roots of fundamentalism, among them nineteenth-century evangelicalism, Scottish Common Sense Realism, revivalism, Holiness impulses, pietism, Reformed confessionalism, Baptist traditionalism, dispensational premillennialism, and Baconian science. In the face of intellectual and cultural change, these elements coalesced as the militant defense of Protestant orthodoxy against theological modernism and the cultural changes modernism endorsed. Marsden's account helped explain the broad coalition of traditional conservatives that existed before fundamentalism became militant in the 1920s.

Before the flurry of dissertations could be completed, revised, and published to elaborate on Marsden's argument, he burnished his own work in the 1987 book *Reforming Fundamentalism: Fuller Seminary and the New Evangelicalism*.[3] This work is underappreciated because it can be mistaken as merely an institutional history of Fuller. In the book Marsden showed how a segment of the militant fundamentalism that emerged after the Scopes trial of 1925 gave way to neoevangelicalism in the 1940s and 1950s. Neoevangelicals were essentially nonseparatist, nonmilitant, more culturally engaged heirs of early twentieth-century fundamentalism. Marsden had prepared the way for this argument in the conclusion to *Fundamentalism and American Culture*, where he said that by 1960 only the most militant evangelicals still called themselves fundamentalists, and most of them were dispensationalists.

Although Marsden's interpretation of evangelicalism has hardly been revised, it was directly challenged, largely because the interpretation worked quite well for the Reformed wing of evangelicalism, but not as well for Holiness Arminian evangelicals. The 1980s saw a spirited debate, primarily between Donald Dayton and Marsden. Dayton emphasized the Holiness and Pentecostal wing of evangelicalism, arguing that Marsden's theological interpretation should give way to an understanding that sees the essence of evangelicalism as its social and political radicalism, not its theological particularities. In contrast to what he called Marsden's "presbyterian paradigm," Dayton posited a "pentecostal paradigm." In this view "evangelicalism is related to the rest of Christianity more as the Pentecostal or Charismatic movements [are]—that is as a specific and modern form of Christianity that disrupts the traditional and conservative churches—and less as the orthodoxy from which the mainstream churches have departed." Dayton's analysis draws on Marxist categories in which key identifying components of evangelicalism are not theological ideas but rather class awareness. The true evangelical spirit, for Dayton, has not been the desire to maintain orthodoxy but rather the resistance to "embourgeoisement" and a preference for the poor and disenfranchised. Dayton's arguments did not result in a book-length monograph but rather are contained in several articles. The Dayton-Marsden debate is summarized well in theologian Kenneth Collins's *The Evangelical Moment: The Promise of an American Religion.*[4]

At the same time Marsden was researching *Fundamentalism and American Culture,* Ferenc Szasz wrote a book that focused on the significance of the fundamentalist-modernist controversy for mainline denominations and for American culture as well. In *The Divided Mind of Protestant America, 1880– 1930,* Szasz argued that the primary result of the fundamentalist-modernist controversy was a two-party system within Protestantism that drastically reduced the usefulness of particular denominational identities that had been in existence since the Protestant Reformation of the sixteenth century. Moreover, Szasz argues that partly as a result of the fundamentalist-modernist controversy the entire nation moved further down the road toward secularization.[5]

This two-party system articulated by Szasz and before him by Martin Marty and others was challenged in a series of conferences at Messiah College in the mid-1990s that resulted in a book edited by William Vance Trollinger Jr. and Douglas Jacobsen titled *Reforming the Center: American Protestantism, 1900 to the Present.* Trollinger and Jacobsen sought to challenge the notion that the bulk of American Protestants fit into either evangelical/fundamentalist or liberal/modernist camps. More recently, Darryl Hart's *Deconstructing Evangelicalism: Conservative Protestantism in the Age of Billy Graham* argued that Protestants grouped under the evangelical rubric are so diverse that it might not be going too far to say evangelicalism does not actually exist.[6] Interpretations challenging the usefulness of evangelicalism as a category should not be ignored, but they have caused but a ripple in the torrent of scholarship that came in Marsden's wake.

Fundamentalism and American Culture called into being not only a historiographical movement but also a virtual field of study, most of which hinges on the evangelical/mainline dichotomy and also on the view that the rise of fundamentalism was crucial for the shaping of evangelicalism. In a 2007 issue of *Books and Culture* David Bebbington argued that it may be time to reevaluate this notion that fundamentalism was the primary repository of

American evangelicalism during the first half of the twentieth century. Instead, he suggested, there was substantial continuity between the vigorous nineteenth-century traditions and early twentieth-century evangelical movements, such as the Nazarenes and Salvation Army, that are not properly regarded as fundamentalist. Moreover, Bebbington noted that Methodism was substantially evangelical into the middle part of the century.[7] If Bebbington is correct, a new paradigm may evolve that ousts fundamentalism from its central role in the development of twentieth-century American evangelicalism. Fundamentalism may someday be viewed as a temporary and peripheral sideshow within an American and transatlantic evangelical tradition that spans the eighteenth through the twenty-first centuries.

Evangelicals, Gender, and Race

While Marsden's *Fundamentalism and American Culture* redefined evangelical historiography, the bookend on the other end of the shelf consists of recent works on evangelicals and gender, and to a lesser extent evangelicals and race. One of the best is sociologist James Ault Jr.'s *Spirit and Flesh: Life in a Fundamentalist Baptist Church.* The result of his becoming active in a fundamentalist church in Worcester, Massachusetts, Ault's study was much like sociologist Nancy Ammerman's *Bible Believers: Fundamentalists in the Modern World* and also Alan Peshkin's *God's Choice: The Total World of a Fundamentalist Christian School,* both of which appeared in the 1980s.[8]

Because of Ault's narrow focus on one congregation, *Spirit and Flesh* is not the most important work written on fundamentalism, but it may be the most insightful, fair-minded, and interesting. If a friend or acquaintance wanted to read a single book that would give one a feel for fundamentalism, Ault's *Spirit and Flesh* would be my recommendation. Ault's research resulted in the 1987 award-winning documentary film *Born Again.* It is not altogether clear why it took another seventeen years for the book to appear, but the gestation period allowed Ault to contextualize his study within the entire body of scholarship on evangelicalism and fundamentalism. Ault brings significant insight into how a single fundamentalist congregation in a New England urban setting functions as a community that resembles a small-town culture based on face-to-face relationships and oral tradition. Books that deal with rhetoric, discourse, and authority within communities based on oral tradition are essential complements to the historical work that seeks to comprehend fundamentalism and challenge widely held myths. Among the myths Ault challenges is the view that fundamentalists are incapable of compromise and that their antifeminist gender attitudes result in female subservience that leaves women with no power. Perhaps most fascinating is the way that Ault himself became a participant observer, singing in the choir and giving a prayer at a Bible study. Ault's experiences at Shawmut River Baptist Church became an existential turning point in his life, leading to his own return to the Christian faith, although not to fundamentalism.

Ault's focus on gender and family relationships at Shawmut River Baptist is part of an important area of evangelical and fundamentalist scholarship, much of it ethnographic. Brenda Brasher, for example, spent six months attending every women's event sponsored by two fundamentalist congregations in California. The result was her book *Godly Women: Fundamentalism and Female Power*. Her findings were almost identical to Ault's with regard to fundamentalist women. As Brasher writes, "[T]o Christian fundamentalist women, the restrictive religious identity they embrace improves their ability to direct the course of their lives and empowers them in their relationship with others." R. Marie Griffith's *God's Daughters: Evangelical Women and the Power of Submission* is a study of Women's Aglow, the largest women's interdenominational missions organization in the world. She found that the evangelical concept of submission operated in surprising ways in this charismatic organization. As Griffith puts it, her study focuses "on the practices by which female participants improvise, resist, and continually reshape their own roles and relations" and on "the interplay between the repressive or disciplinary aspects of women's devotionalism and the ecstatic, liberatory potential of particular practices."[9]

Christine Pohl and Nicoloa Hoggard Creegan's *Living on the Boundaries: Evangelical Women, Feminism, and the Theological Academy* is both ethnographic and existentially reflective. In addition to living and working permanently on the academic and ecclesiological boundary of evangelicalism and feminism, Pohl and Creegan surveyed nearly a hundred other women similarly situated in an effort to understand better how evangelicalism and feminism relate.[10]

By the time Pohl, Creegan, Brasher, and Griffith wrote their books there was a sturdy foundation of historical work on evangelicalism and gender. Janette Hassey's *No Time for Silence: Evangelical Women in Public Ministry around the Turn of the Century* was the first historical study of gender and evangelicalism to utilize Marsden's definitions. Hassey argued that a significant evangelical shift away from gender egalitarianism took place as fundamentalists between the world wars sought to separate from a culture that was allowing women more freedom. Similarly, Betty DeBerg argued in her book *Ungodly Women* that during the fundamentalist-modernist controversy, fundamentalists responded as much to modern social changes having to do with gender as they did to liberal theology. Inherent in the fundamentalist attack on the state of religion was an attack on the state of morality; and immorality, Deberg asserted, was often a code word for impropriety in gender and sexual relationships. In her 1993 book *Fundamentalism and Gender, 1875 to the Present*, Margaret Bendroth argued not only that fundamentalists rejected evangelical feminism but that they reversed the Victorian view that women were more moral than men and had a stronger aptitude for religion. Fundamentalists by the 1920s took the opposite view—that men were by nature better suited for preserving and extending orthodox religion. More recently, Sally Gallagher has argued in *Evangelical Identity and Gendered Family Life* that evangelicals in our own time do not merely react against nor accommodate to secular culture. "Rather," she writes, "evangelicals . . . draw on and retell the themes of their own multifaceted tradition in coming to understand and give meaning to their contemporary circumstances."[11]

Other studies of religion and gender worth mentioning are Virginia Brereton's *Stories of Women's Conversions, 1800 to the Present* and sociologist Mark Chaves's *Ordaining Women: Culture and Conflict in Religious Organizations*. Neither focuses exclusively on evangelicals, but the books help explain how gender plays out in conversion and ordination respectively, two very important issues for evangelicals and fundamentalists.[12]

Space limitations of this essay preclude a full discussion of the sociological work devoted to evangelicals, but special mention needs to be made of Christian Smith's 2000 book *Christian America? What Evangelicals Really Want*. Smith's work remains the best collection and interpretation of survey data on evangelicals. He and his team of researchers found that ambivalence runs deep in American evangelicalism, resulting in significant diversity that is either unknown to or willfully ignored by some media pundits and even many scholars. Evangelicals, Smith concludes, are neither angels nor demons in the larger culture. In addition to Smith, Bebbington's historical work on Great Britain and international evangelicalism has provided scholars with definitional clarity as to just who and what evangelicals are. In this respect he has been a pioneer in what is becoming the newest and most important phase of evangelical scholarship: global evangelicalism. For the study of evangelicalism as a transatlantic and global phenomenon, the place to start is the new History of Evangelicalism series by InterVarsity Press, which has contributions from Mark Noll, Bebbington, and others. Although his work is not part of that series, Douglas Sweeney, who spends most of his time on eighteenth- and nineteenth-century topics, has also written a useful brief introduction titled *The American Evangelical Story: A History of the Movement*.[13]

There has been very little scholarship focusing on evangelicals or fundamentalists and race, but sociologists Michael Emerson and Christian Smith have produced a valuable study titled *Divided by Faith: Evangelical Religion and the Problem of Race in America*. They interpret their statistical and interview data to mean that evangelical beliefs and practices contribute to a racialized society. This is not to say that evangelicals are more overtly racist than others but that their heightened sense of individualism and relationalism reduces racial problems to private matters with one-dimensional remedies. Essentially, whites who are evangelicals are more likely than other Americans to believe that blacks and whites need only change their attitudes for racial problems to disappear, just as individuals need only choose to accept Jesus in order to be saved. This view that individual choice has become the sine qua non of both evangelicalism and Americanism was echoed in the findings of sociologist Alan Wolfe. He argued in *The Transformation of American Religion: How We Actually Live Our Faith* that when it comes to individual choice, taking one's religion into one's own hands, and a variety of other distinctly American traits, evangelicals are not much different from others. As Wolfe writes, somewhat tongue in cheek, "We're all evangelicals now."[14]

Evangelical Biographies and Regional Studies

Scholarship on evangelicals, gender, and race represent the recent evolution of evangelical studies. Early evangelical historiography following Marsden's *Fundamentalism and American Culture* focused on biography and regional studies. Grant Wacker wrote an intellectual biography titled *Augustus H. Strong and the Dilemma of Historical Consciousness*. Wacker provided an important analysis of the role that rival epistemologies played in the fundamentalist-modernist controversy. He viewed Strong as "a tragic figure, forced to choose between incompatible yet, in his judgement, equally cogent conceptual worlds."[15] The book is a highly valuable inquiry into nascent fundamentalism.

Most of the fundamentalist subjects of biographies did not face Strong's epistemic dilemma, either because they completely rejected historicist epistemology or because they were not intellectuals and never reflected on epistemology at all. While for this reason they were not as interesting in the intellectual sense as a person like Strong, they were certainly more colorful. Even before Marsden, C. Allyn Russell covered several of these figures in his 1976 book *Voices of Fundamentalism: Seven Biographical Studies*. Russell included chapters on J. Frank Norris ("Violent Fundamentalist"), John Roach Straton ("Accusative Fundamentalist"), William Bell Riley ("Organizational Fundamentalist"), J. C. Massee ("Moderate Fundamentalist"), J. Gresham Machen

("Scholarly Fundamentalist"), William Jennings Bryan ("Statesman Fundamentalist"), and Clarence E. Macartney ("Preacher Fundamentalist").[16] There already existed several books on Bryan, but the others were ripe for the picking when it came to scholarly critical biographies, and students working on their Ph.D.s took notice.

Trollinger published the first of the new critical biographies on fundamentalist figures. His book *God's Empire: William Bell Riley and Midwestern Fundamentalism* filled a biographical hole and also helped start the regional analysis of fundamentalism. Barry Hankins followed the biographical/geographical trend in *God's Rascal: J. Frank Norris and the Beginnings of Southern Fundamentalism*, then the regional but not biographical trend with *Uneasy in Babylon: Southern Baptist Conservatives and American Culture*. The latter book views the Southern Baptist conservatives who took control of the Southern Baptist Convention (SBC) in the 1980s as American evangelicals influenced by Francis Schaeffer and Carl Henry, among others. At the time this essay was written Hankins had also authored a forthcoming biography of Francis Schaeffer. Darryl Hart followed the biographical trend but not the regional, at least not in his title. Rather, Hart honed in on a key intellectual figure in *Defending the Faith: J. Gresham Machen and the Crisis of Conservative Protestantism in Modern America*. Even without including a nod to regionalism in his title, Hart grappled with Machen's southern Presbyterian family roots as an important component of his life and work. Like Hart, Mark Taylor Dalhouse focused on a particular aspect of fundamentalism in his book *An Island in a Lake of Fire: Bob Jones University, Fundamentalism, and the Separatist Movement*. Closely related to the defense of the faith within fundamentalism has been fundamentalist separatism, both theological and cultural. Dalhouse argued that the Jones boys—Bob Sr., Jr., and III—made both types of separatism central features of their university.[17]

The biographical theme is represented in the Library of Religious Biography series published by Eerdmans. Lyle Dorsett's *Billy Sunday and the Redemption of Urban America*, Edith Blumhofer's *Aimee Semple McPherson: Everybody's Sister*, and Dana Robert's *Occupy until I Come: A. T. Pierson and the Evangelization of the World* all appeared in the series. Just as Hart and Dalhouse focused on defense of the faith and separatism in their biographies of Machen and the Joneses respectively, Robert organized her biography of Pierson around world evangelism, another key theme of fundamentalism. Dorsett's biography of Sunday was preceded by William McLoughlin's book *Billy Sunday Was His Real Name*, while previous biographies of McPherson included Robert Bahr, *Least of All Saints: The Story of Aimee Semple McPherson* and Thomas Lately's *Storming Heaven: The Lives and Turmoils of Minnie*

Kennedy and Aimee Semple McPherson. Matthew Sutton's *Aimee Semple McPherson and the Resurrection of Christian America* is likely to eclipse all other biographies of McPherson. Sutton seeks to contextualize her within American evangelicalism, Southern California, gender studies, and American popular culture. Another biography of a woman preacher from the early Holiness-Pentecostal tradition is Susie Stanley's *Feminist Pillar of Fire: The Life of Alma White.* White formed not only her own denomination, as did McPherson, but also a separatist community of Holiness believers.[18]

The regional theme stressed in some biographies was the centerpiece of William Glass's *Strangers in Zion: Fundamentalists in the South, 1900–1950.* Building on the work of Samuel Hill, Wayne Flynt, and David Edwin Harrell, Glass identified four types of southern fundamentalists: itinerant evangelists; interdenominational fundamentalists such as the Bob Joneses and Lewis Sperry Chafer; denominational fundamentalists in the southern Presbyterian, Southern Baptist, and Methodist Episcopal denominations; and separatist fundamentalists who broke away from those groups to form fledgling new fundamentalist denominations. Glass showed that fundamentalism in the South was a complex and multidimensional movement.[19]

A major part of the story of southern fundamentalism has been its diffusion beyond the region as southerners have relocated to other parts of the country, particularly to Southern California. Because of this fascinating demographic shift, historians of fundamentalism and evangelicalism eagerly await the publication of Darren Dochuk's award-winning dissertation, "From Bible Belt to Sunbelt: Plain Folk Religion, Grassroots Politics, and the Southernization of Southern California, 1939–1969." Completed under Marsden's direction, the study brings together regionalism, migration, urbanization, and suburbanization.[20]

Joining Glass, Hankins, Dalhouse, and Dochuk in probing the extent to which fundamentalism is or is not southern is Mary Beth Swetnam Mathews's recent book *Rethinking Zion: How the Print Media Placed Fundamentalism in the South.* Mathews explains how the South came to be perceived as fundamentalist, or at least as peculiarly amenable to fundamentalism, and she analyzes the forces that created the image of the South as the Bible Belt. As such, her book is not so much about fundamentalism or southern religion as it is about perceptions of religion in the South held by both southern and northern observers.[21]

Closely related to regionalism is the study of evangelicalism and fundamentalism in particular urban centers. Margaret Bendroth, who also helped pioneer the study of gender and evangelicalism, recently published *Fundamentalists in the City: Conflict and Division in Boston's Churches, 1885–1950.*

Dorsett's biography of Billy Sunday also deals with the urban component of early twentieth-century evangelicalism. Focusing on a smaller city and a single denomination, R. Stephen Warner, in his book *New Wine in Old Wineskins: Evangelicals and Liberals in a Small-Town Church,* tracked the transition from mainline to evangelical in a single Mendocino, California, congregation.[22]

Less self-consciously part of evangelical historiography but important nevertheless are David Harrell's two biographies, *Oral Roberts: An American Life* and *Pat Robertson: A Personal, Religious, and Political Portrait.* While most of the biographies on Christian Right figures published thus far have focused on high-profile activists such as Robertson, in 1994 L. Edward Hicks argued in his book *"Sometimes in the Wrong but Never in Doubt": George S. Benson and the Education of the New Religious Right* that an obscure Arkansas Church of Christ minister and educator helped lay the groundwork not only for the rise of the Christian Right but for the election of Ronald Reagan in 1980. Another contemporary Christian Right figure, Jerry Falwell, is yet to be covered in a scholarly historical biography, but anthropologist Susan Friend Harding's *The Book of Jerry Falwell: Fundamentalist Language and Politics* is a useful and fascinating study. Harding analyzes the way in which Falwell's people often interpret him much as Christians read scripture. Like a parable, he need not be factually correct in his pronouncements or always taken literally. This is because his particular words and actions serve as a myth or story that must be read in the context of his overall work. Harding's book, much like the biographies of Riley, Norris, and the Joneses, helps explain why fundamentalists who sometimes act and speak in ways that seem outrageous to outsiders can still be taken seriously by their followers. Riley became anti-Semitic in his late career, Norris shot and killed a man in his own office, the Joneses denounced secular culture while sponsoring an annual Shakespeare festival at their university, and Oral Roberts tried to blackmail his followers into upping their financial support by telling them if they failed to come through, God was going to kill him. Such ironies, inconsistencies, and behavioral lapses almost never result in fundamentalist leaders losing much of their following. Apparently, as the case of Jim and Tammy Faye Bakker illustrates, it takes not only an indictment but a conviction and lengthy prison stay to actually bring down a fundamentalist empire. All this points to the need for a book on the televangelist scandals of the 1980s that included Bakker and Jimmy Swaggart as culprits and Falwell as would-be rescuer of the Bakker empire.[23]

Many of the biographical figures started Bible schools or institutes, Riley, Norris, Jones, Roberts, and Robertson among them. Before those particular

schools, however, a Bible school movement already existed that was important for the rise of fundamentalism. The first book covering this phenomenon is Virginia Brereton's *Training God's Army: The American Bible School,
1880–1940*. Brereton demonstrated that the importance of Bible schools went
far beyond the numbers of students they enrolled. The schools were preservers and progenitors of an evangelical heritage, as they helped unify fundamentalism. They provided a marketing mechanism for the gospel, served as
vehicles for small and usually financially distressed conservative denominations, and, as Sandeen had argued, became the "headquarters of fundamentalism." As Joel Carpenter would show a few years later in *Revive Us Again*,
the Bible schools were an important component of the "evangelical united
front" that would pave the way for neoevangelicalism.[24]

As with the biographies and regional studies, Carpenter also expanded on
Marsden's work by explaining what happened to fundamentalism after the
Scopes trial of 1925. The question was: how did fundamentalism go from being culturally marginalized after Scopes to being highly significant politically
and culturally beginning in the 1980s? For much of the period in between,
the standard argument in many quarters of the academy was that fundamentalism and evangelicalism were dying out in the face of modern modes
of thought. Evangelicalism might continue as a private phenomenon, but it
would never again wield significant political and cultural influence publicly.
The rise of the Christian Right exploded that fallacy, and Carpenter's *Revive
Us Again: The Reawakening of Fundamentalism* showed how fundamentalism and evangelicalism remained viable by entering a post-Scopes period of
realignment and institution building that would sustain and revitalize the
movement. Most scholars knew that neoevangelicalism had emerged from
fundamentalism, but Carpenter told the story in detail. He traced the development of neoevangelical organizations such as Fuller Seminary, the National Association of Evangelicals, Youth for Christ, World Vision, various
radio ministries, and the like, and showed how these organizations worked
together as the "evangelical united front." Fundamentalists who became neoevangelicals were torn between their alienation from American culture and
their desire to be engaged culturally; they still are. As Carpenter argues in his
conclusion, when the disparity between the vitality of popular religion and
the decline of religious influence in American institutions became too great
to ignore, the result was the development of the Christian Right.[25]

Just as Marsden's *Fundamentalism and American Culture* identified new
opportunities for scholarship in the period before 1925, Carpenter's *Revive
Us Again* suggested avenues of scholarship for post-Scopes fundamentalism
and evangelicalism, particularly the ways that fundamentalists used modern

means to fight against modernism and spread the old-time religion. Tona Hangen zeroed in on evangelical broadcasting in *Redeeming the Dial: Radio, Religion, and Popular Culture in America,* while Douglas Carl Abrams focused a bit more broadly in *Selling the Old-Time Religion: American Fundamentalists and Mass Culture, 1920–1940.* Both books track how fundamentalists, while proclaiming militancy and separatism, also participated in mass culture.[26]

The Christian Right

The symbiotic relationship between current events and historical scholarship exists in many subfields of history, but the areas most affected by recent historical developments in America are African American studies, women's studies, and the study of evangelicals. Just as the civil rights and women's movements of the 1960s and 1970s called into being the study of African Americans and women to a degree never before seen, the rise of the Christian Right did the same for the study of evangelicals. In this regard, Marsden's *Fundamentalism and American Culture* was the most timely book ever published on religion in America. He had been working on it for about a decade, but it was published a year after the Moral Majority was founded and the same year Ronald Reagan was elected president, 1980. Suddenly, evangelicals were highly visible in the national media, and people wanted to know who they were and from whence they came.

Another similarity between the study of evangelicals, on the one hand, and African American and women's studies, on the other, is that all three areas of study resulted largely from an influx of scholars who were themselves products of the historical movements being studied. This is the existential component of all three subfields. The civil rights and women's movements opened doors for African American and women scholars to enter the academy and take the lead in those areas. Something similar has happened with the study of evangelicals, and this was especially so beginning in the 1980s in conjunction with the rise of the Christian Right. The Christian Right created a market for the study of evangelicals, and who better to study them than evangelical scholars? Some of the best books on the Christian Right have been written by sociologists and political scientists, who are more inclined than historians to take on contemporary topics. While historians scurried to the past to find the roots of the Christian Right, sociologists and political scientists tended to study what was happening on the ground in our own time. The most exhaustive of these books, covering the movement through 1996, was sociologist William Martin's *With God on Our Side: The Rise of the Christian*

Right in America. Martin was a longtime sociologist at Rice University who also wrote an exhaustive and balanced biography of Billy Graham, *A Prophet with Honor*. Both books are dated now, largely because the subjects have lived on for more than a decade after Martin wrote, but they are among the most fair-minded analyses available. *With God on Our Side* was the companion volume to the PBS television documentary series of the same title. The book is the best place to start in terms of secondary reading on the Christian Right through 1996.[27]

On the opposite end of the spectrum in regard to sympathy for one's subjects is Randall Balmer's 2006 book *Thy Kingdom Come: How the Religious Right Distorts the Faith and Threatens America, an Evangelical's Lament*. Balmer wrote his dissertation and first book on a colonial topic, but his niche in the study of evangelicalism has been highly readable, immensely interesting journalistic accounts of twentieth-century evangelicalism that are useful for scholars and lay readers alike. Like Martin's *With God on Our Side*, Balmer's earlier book *Mine Eyes Have Seen the Glory: A Journey into the Evangelical Subculture in America* was the companion volume for a PBS series. The book had twelve chapters, ranging in topic from Dallas Theological Seminary to "Episcopal Indians," with Curtis Frisby, the Phoenix prophet, thrown in for good measure. As he often does as editor at large for *Christianity Today* magazine, Balmer traveled to the various evangelical sites of which he later wrote fascinating accounts. He is what could be called a retailer of scholarship, selling to a popular audience as he also works out his own tortured relationship with evangelicalism. The result in *Mine Have Seen the Glory* is a winsome and insightful look into a variety of evangelical institutions.[28]

Balmer's more recent look at the Christian Right, however, is devoid of the winsome spirit he displayed in *Mine Eyes Have Seen the Glory*. In *Thy Kingdom Come*, it is clear that Balmer does not like the Christian Right and is frankly embarrassed to be associated with the same evangelical subculture that harbors the likes of Pat Robertson, James Dobson, and the late Jerry Falwell. The result is a book that has some helpful theological insights but is also highly contentious and often unfair. Balmer wrote in the prologue to *Mine Eyes Have Seen the Glory*, "My purpose in undertaking this project . . . was neither to vilify nor to vindicate American evangelicalism, and the reader will early on detect my own ambivalence toward the subculture and all it represents."[29] Perhaps it should be said that when a scholar lacks sufficient ambivalence toward a topic, the topic should be abandoned to someone else. Such is the case with *Thy Kingdom Come*. The ambivalence of *Mine Eyes Have Seen the Glory* is wholly absent.

Like Balmer, political scientist Clyde Wilcox grew up within the evangelical subculture. While he is no longer a part of evangelicalism, Wilcox retains the sort of healthy ambivalence that makes for good scholarship. His book *Onward Christian Soldiers? The Religious Right in American Politics* has stayed current by going through three editions, the most recent appearing in 2006. Wilcox's student and coauthor of the third edition is Carin Larson. They pull no punches in discussing the outrageous mass mailings and frightening rhetoric that emanate from many Christian Right organizations. They also consider, however, the degree to which Christian Right activists participate in the democratic process, exhibit democratic values that often conflict with their more extreme stated ideals, and possess the capacity to become more democratic the longer they participate in American politics.[30]

Another excellent study of the Christian Right is political scientist Michael Lienesch's *Redeeming America: Piety and Politics in the New Christian Right*, which appeared in 1993 and covers roughly the same time period as Martin's *With God on Our Side*. By the time *Redeeming America* was published, it was clear that the funeral orations for the Christian Right that had appeared in journalistic venues as well as in Steve Bruce's 1988 book *The Rise and Fall of the New Christian Right* had been premature. Lienesch and other scholars have recognized that what looked like the demise of the Christian Right was instead the maturing of the movement. That maturation included a turn to grassroots politics at the state and local levels that was less conspicuous to the national media and less bombastic in public pronouncements but perhaps more influential because of the diversity of Christian Right organizations working on the ground and behind the scenes. This shift away from the Christian Right's early fixation with national politics and presidential races looked like a decline to some, but, as Lienesch wrote, "[T]he Christian right has not disappeared; in some form or another, it will most certainly appear again. This book is preparation for the next time." While that statement sounds somewhat conflicted, leaving the reader wondering how a movement that has not disappeared will "certainly appear again," it is the first half of the sentence that was important for Lienesch. In other words, the Christian Right is here to stay; how should we understand it? Lienesch starts his interpretation with individual worldviews of the movement's leaders and works out in concentric circles to include the family, economy, politics, and world affairs. He follows sociologist Peter Berger in assuming "that religion and politics are aspects of a continuous social process of world-construction and world maintenance."[31]

By the late 1990s, Sara Diamond's title was much more apt than Bruce's premature eulogy. She wrote *Not by Politics Alone: The Enduring Influence of the Christian Right*. In an effort to explain the Christian Right's longevity, Diamond argued that the subcultural and less political institutions of the movement serve as centers of renewed strength that keep the Christian Right

going when legislative success wanes. While Diamond focused on the less political organizations of the Christian Right, Justin Watson examined the most
political Christian Right organization of the 1990s in his book *The Christian
Coalition: Dreams of Restoration, Demands for Recognition.* Watson's book
is a nuanced interpretation. He attempts to explain how the Christian Coalition's rhetoric calling for the restoration of a Christian America can be
squared with activism within the Republican Party, part of the mainstream
of American politics. Watson's answer is that coalition leaders, like many lob-
byists, have two languages—one they use with their own constituents and the
other for public consumption. The rhetoric of restoration serves to keep the
troops energized, while in reality coalition leaders understand that the art of
politics includes compromise and that no one ever gets everything he or she
wants. Watson concludes that while the coalition leaders dream of the restoration of Christian America, in reality they really expect and demand much
less. Primarily, they insist that the political community recognize their concerns and accept them as a legitimate part of public discourse.[32]

The evangelical Left has been far less visible and influential than the
Christian Right, and subsequently has received less scholarly attention. In
their book *Salt and Light: Evangelical Political Thought in Modern America,*
published in 1989, Murray Dempster and Augustus Cerillo Jr. attempted to
correct the imbalance of attention paid to the Christian Right by editing and
introducing a selection of texts that represents the entire spectrum of evangelical political thought. James Skillen has also covered the array of Christian
approaches to politics in *The Scattered Voice: Christians at Odds in the Public
Square.* With regard to a particular denomination, David Stricklin's *A Genealogy of Dissent: Southern Baptist Protest in the Twentieth Century* is an excellent study of the left wing of the SBC.[33] Whether these SBC progressives were
evangelical or not is an open and often contentious question among Southern
Baptists. Beyond these few studies, there is clearly a need for more work on
the history of the twentieth-century evangelical Left.

Evangelicals and Science

One of the major issues within Christian Right politics is the controversy
surrounding evolution and whether it should be taught in public schools.
This has been the case since the Scopes trial. The broader relationship of religion and science within which evolution and creation controversies reside
has been a major part of the twentieth-century story of evangelicals, and
there are a handful of superb books dealing with these issues. Putting the
Scopes trial at the heart of evangelicalism's troubled relationship with sci-

ence is Edward Larson's Pulitzer Prize–winning book *Summer for the Gods: The Scopes Trial and America's Continuing Debate over Science and Religion.* Before Larson's work, the standard history of the trial was Ray Ginger's *Six Days or Forever: Tennessee v. John Thomas Scopes,* but the public's memory of the event has been shaped mostly by the play and film *Inherit the Wind.* Larson deconstructs the mythic, anti-Bryan thesis of the film and brings new understanding to both sides of the controversy.[34]

Inasmuch as Larson debunked flat interpretations of fundamentalism that saw it one-dimensionally as antimodern and therefore antiscience, his work is in the same vein as David Livingstone's *Darwin's Forgotten Defenders: The Encounter between Evangelical Theology and Evolutionary Thought.* Livingstone, an Irish geographer and historian of science, critiqued the myth that from the appearance of Darwin's *Origin of Species* in 1859 forward evangelicals were unalterably opposed to evolution. Livingstone shows that for more than a generation after Darwin the best evangelical thinkers worked to reconcile the new science with the biblical stories of creation. Livingstone's and Larson's books are part of a small body of literature that argues convincingly that the warfare model for understanding the relationship between religion and science from Galileo through Darwin was promoted first by nineteenth-century secular educators such as John Draper and Andrew Dickson White. Livingstone shows that while Draper and White promoted this warfare model during the last third of the nineteenth century, evangelical thinkers worked to find harmony between the new science and the old religion. Larson's book then explained why evangelicals in the 1920s, hardened and alienated by the fundamentalist-modernist controversy, adopted the warfare model for themselves. By 1925 the ground of accommodation between evangelical Protestantism and evolutionary science had shrunk to almost nothing, making the Scopes trial possible if not inevitable.[35]

A recent prequel to Larson is Charles A. Israel's *Before Scopes: Evangelicals, Education, and Evolution in Tennessee, 1870–1925.* As well as being a study of evangelicals and science, Israel's book also fills another niche in the regional study of evangelicalism. Also of interest is a collection of six essays by emeritus intellectual historian Paul Conkin titled *When All the Gods Trembled: Darwinism, Scopes, and American Intellectuals.* Conkin views the crises of the 1920s as tragedies in that "honest people, no matter how reluctantly, had to give up one consoling certainty after another." Moreover, he laments the facile way in which many intellectuals explained away the convulsing changes taking place during the first three decades of the twentieth century.[36]

No historian has done more for the understanding of Christianity and science than Larson's mentor Ronald Numbers. On the question of the warfare model, he and David Lindberg edited the 1986 collection of essays *God and Nature: Historical Essays on the Encounter between Christianity and Science.* A few years later Numbers wrote the definitive work on the creation science movement, a movement that has animated much evangelical and fundamentalist political activism. Under the nifty title *The Creationists: The Evolution of Scientific Creationism,* Numbers shows how a fringe scientific endeavor that grew out of the Seventh-day Adventist denomination ended up the preferred view of origins for nearly all fundamentalists and many evangelicals. In chapter 16 he explains how "creation science floods the world," a pun on flood geology. Numbers was reared in a Seventh-day Adventist family and therefore learned creation science at his parents' knees. In his introduction he observes that many historians embrace the study of all manner of unusual beliefs chronologically and geographically removed from our own time—"fifteenth-century astrology, seventeenth-century alchemy, or nineteenth-century phrenology"—but when faced with creationism and fundamentalism they substitute condemnation for comprehension. For Numbers such a view was epitomized by a statement about fundamentalists and evangelicals he once heard at a conference. "[W]e've got to stop the bastards," a colleague told him. For achieving a remarkable sensitivity toward its subject, combined with exhaustive research, *The Creationists* won the Albert C. Outler Prize from the American Society of Church History.[37]

   In addition to Lindberg and Numbers's edited work mentioned above, Livingstone, Hart, and Noll edited a fine collection of essays called *Evangelicals and Science in Historical Perspective,* published in 1999 as part of Oxford University Press's Religion in America series. The essays were first given at a conference at the Institute for the Study of American Evangelicals at Wheaton College in the early 1990s and include contributions from many of the heavy hitters in evangelical historiography—Bebbington, Allen Guelzo, Hart, Livingstone, Marsden, Noll, and Numbers—as well as historians of science James Moore and Edward Davis and Canadian scholars Michael Gauvreau and Nancy Christie. The book as a whole was envisioned as a starting place for scholarship on evangelicals and science now that the confrontational warfare model has been thoroughly debunked.[38]

Premillennial Prophecy Belief

The interest evangelicals and fundamentalists have in the origin of humankind is rivaled only by their fascination for the other end of the historical spectrum. No study of evangelicals and fundamentalists would be complete, therefore, without addressing the role of dispensational premillennialism, or what is sometimes called simply prophecy belief. Sandeen's *The Roots of Fundamentalism* was the first significant historical work to take dispensational premillennialism seriously, even if, as said above, Sandeen overinterpreted its role in the development of fundamentalism. Still, prophecy belief was one of the central factors in the rise of fundamentalism and has received a fair share of attention from scholars. After Sandeen, Timothy Weber wrote the next important scholarly historical study, *Living in the Shadow of the Second Coming: American Premillennialism, 1875–1925*, which was then enlarged and republished by Zondervan's Academie Books division in 1983. In the enlarged version Weber traced the story of American premillennialism up to 1982, which included the prophecy views of Hal Lindsey and other popular prophecy teachers of the 1970s. In 2004 Weber published *On the Road to Armageddon: How Evangelicals Became Israel's Best Friend*. In this book Weber argues that for the first century of dispensational premillennialism its adherents sat in the bleachers and watched as events unfolded according to biblical prophecy. They interpreted the signs of the times. Since the founding of the nation-state of Israel, however, premillennialists have gone onto the playing field to become "important players in their own game plan." In an earlier work, Jewish scholar Yaakov Ariel also interpreted fundamentalist and evangelical support for Israel in his book *On Behalf of Israel: American Fundamentalist Attitudes toward Jews, Judaism, and Zionism*.[39]

Weber, like so many authors cited in this essay, is an evangelical scholar who studies evangelicals, but prophecy belief also attracted the attention of intellectual historian Paul Boyer, who is neither an evangelical nor a scholar of evangelicalism per se. Like his University of Wisconsin colleague Ronald Numbers, however, Boyer was reared in an evangelical denomination, and he grew up listening to his grandfather preach on dispensational themes at the Brethren in Christ Mission in Dayton, Ohio. In his outstanding 1992 book *When Time Shall Be No More: Prophecy Belief in Modern American Culture*, Boyer argued that cultural and intellectual historians have failed to appreciate the centrality of prophecy belief within American culture. Since World War II, Boyer continues, dispensational premillennialists have been significant in shaping public attitudes on issues such as the Soviet Union, the Common Market, the Middle East, computers, and the environment.[40]

Since Boyer wrote his book, dispensationalists have become ever more effective in shaping culture. This is especially so in the wake of Tim LaHaye and Jerry Jenkins's immensely popular Left Behind series of prophecy novels that appeared in twelve volumes beginning in 1995. The series has sold over 60 million copies, leading Weber to call Left Behind "the most effective disseminator of dispensationalist ideas ever." As Weber puts it, "[T]ens of millions of people who have never seen a prophetic chart or listened to a sermon on the Second Coming have read one or more novels in the Left Behind series." Already, three scholars have written books interpreting the Left Behind phenomenon. Glenn Shuck, in *Marks of the Beast: The Left Behind Novels and the Struggle for Evangelical Identity,* picks up on sociologist Christian Smith's book *American Evangelicalism: Embattled and Thriving.* Smith's book is important in that it shows how American evangelicals thrive on a certain level of tension between themselves and the wider culture. Shuck argues that prophecy belief serves as a "cultural thermostat" that helps evangelicals keep the tension at its proper level.[41]

Amy Johnson Frykholm shifted the attention from the Left Behind novels themselves to their readers in her book *Rapture Culture: Left Behind in Evangelical America.* Like Boyer and Numbers Frykholm grew up evangelical but no longer identifies with evangelicalism, and like Boyer and Numbers she brings sympathetic insight to her subjects. The book grew out of Frykholm's dissertation in literature at Duke University and consists of qualitative interviews with Left Behind readers. She examines how readers make sense of the books, how they formulate religious opinions in light of their reading, and how for many evangelicals the idea of the rapture motivates them to examine their own salvation and evangelize others. In this sense, Frykholm, like Boyer, argues for the cultural relevance of dispensational premillennialism as opposed to viewing evangelical eschatology as merely "the realm of isolated believers." Historian David T. Morgan would like to see dispensationalism become an isolated phenomenon. His book *The New Brothers Grimm and Their Left Behind Fairy Tales* is aimed at persuading a popular audience of the folly of dispensationalism. There is also one edited work on the Left Behind series that includes essays by Frykholm, the late evangelical theologian Stanley Grenz, the aforementioned Yaakov Ariel, historian Bruce Forbes, American studies scholar Jeanne Halgren Kilde, and New Testament scholar Mark Reasoner.[42]

Conclusion

In addition to the aforementioned need for a book on the Christian Right scandals of the 1980s, as well as a history of the evangelical Left, there remains much work to be done on American and global evangelicalism. Moreover, the time is ripe for a new synthesis that will explain why so many evangelicals today—for example, nearly all Christian Right figures—retain the militant feature of fundamentalism but have relinquished the separatist impulse. In his twenty-fifth anniversary edition of *Fundamentalism and American Cul-*

ture, Marsden suggested that Christian Right activists are "fundamental-istic evangelicals."[43] Fundamentalistic evangelicalism could be called non-separatistic fundamentalism just as accurately, and it may owe its existence to cultural developments in the 1960s, which is a decade of American religious history in need of further analysis. If and when such topics result in books, odds are that evangelicals and former evangelicals will be their authors.

Perhaps the reason evangelicals and former evangelicals gravitate to this area of study has to do with one of the most important books written by an evangelical for evangelicals, Mark Noll's *The Scandal of the Evangelical Mind.* Apparently, the anti-intellectual, intuitive, and populist habits of thinking that Noll tracks push some away from their evangelical roots while inspiring others to become evangelical scholars attempting to overcome the scandal. Douglas Frank wrote a book in the 1980s that might well have been called the scandal of the evangelical spirit. *Less Than Conquerors: How Evangelicals Entered the Twentieth Century* is the most overtly introspective and existen-tial work written on evangelicals by an evangelical. Whereas Noll traced the debilitating intellectual habits that twentieth-century evangelicals inherited from their nineteenth-century forebears, Frank probed the ways in which early twentieth-century evangelicals missed an opportunity for repentance and new birth during the wrenching fundamentalist-modernist controversy. Instead of moving in humble new directions, evangelicals and fundamental-ists traded their former cultural dominance for a pseudo-dominance of the after life in the form of dispensationalism and of the inner life in the form of victorious holiness. If sociologist Alan Wolfe is correct that evangelicals have met the culture and the culture has won, Frank may want to write a new book on how evangelicals entered the twenty-first century.[44]

Both Frank and Noll wrote as "wounded lovers," to use Noll's term, la-menting the state of their own beloved subculture but remaining within the community of faith as caring critics.[45] Others with similar evangelical expe-riences left evangelicalism spiritually but continued in their professional lives trying to understand their former selves. In either case, the evidence seems to indicate that scholars who stay as well as those who leave never quite shake the desire to better understand evangelicalism. In the sense that evangelical scholars have taken their religion, or their former religion, into their own hands, a quintessentially American habit, perhaps Wolfe is right—"We're all evangelicals now."

Notes

1. George Marsden, *Fundamentalism and American Culture: The Shaping of Twentieth-Century Evangelicalism, 1870–1925* (New York: Oxford University Press,

1980). I am indebted to Michael Hamilton for this notion that evangelical historiography has been done in reverse.

2. Ernest Sandeen, *The Roots of Fundamentalism: British and American Millenarianism* (Chicago: University of Chicago Press, 1970).

3. George Marsden, *Reforming Fundamentalism: Fuller Seminary and the New Evangelicalism* (Grand Rapids, MI: Eerdmans, 1987).

4. Kenneth Collins, *The Evangelical Moment: The Promise of an American Religion* (Grand Rapids, MI: Baker Academic, 2005), 64–70. For Dayton's embourgeoisement argument, see Donald Dayton, "The Embourgeoisement of a Vision: Lament of a Radical Evangelical," *Other Side* 23, no. 8 (1987): 19. The gist of the Marsden-Dayton debate can be found in *Christian Scholars Review* 23, no. 1 (1993). See also Donald Dayton and Robert K. Johnson, eds., *The Variety of American Evangelicalism* (Knoxville: University of Tennessee Press, 1991).

5. Ferenc Morton Szasz, *The Divided Mind of Protestant America, 1880–1930* (Tuscaloosa: University of Alabama Press, 1982).

6. William Vance Trollinger Jr. and Douglas Jacobsen, *Reforming the Center: American Protestantism, 1900 to the Present* (Grand Rapids, MI: Eerdmans, 1998); Darryl Hart, *Deconstructing Evangelicalism: Conservative Protestantism in the Age of Billy Graham* (Grand Rapids, MI: Baker Academic, 2004).

7. David Bebbington, "Not So Exceptional After All: American Evangelicals Reassessed," *Books and Culture*, May–June 2007, 18.

8. James Ault Jr., *Spirit and Flesh: Life in a Fundamentalist Baptist Church* (New York: Vintage, 2004); Nancy Ammerman, *Bible Believers: Fundamentalists in the Modern World* (New Brunswick: Rutgers University Press, 1987); Alan Peshkin, *God's Choice: The Total World of a Fundamentalist Christian School* (Chicago: University of Chicago Press, 1986).

9. Brenda Brasher, *Godly Women: Fundamentalism and Female Power* (New Brunswick: Rutgers University Press, 1998), 4; R. Marie Griffith, *God's Daughters: Evangelical Women and the Power of Submission* (Berkeley: University of California Press, 1997), 22. See also R. Marie Griffith, *Born Again Bodies: Flesh and Spirit in American Christianity* (Berkeley: University of California Press, 2004).

10. Christine Pohl and Nicoloa Hoggard Creegan, *Living on the Boundaries: Evangelical Women, Feminism, and the Theological Academy* (Downers Grove, IL: InterVarsity, 2005).

11. Janette Hassey, *No Time for Silence: Evangelical Women in Public Ministry around the Turn of the Century* (Grand Rapids, MI: Academie, 1986); Betty DeBerg, *Ungodly Women* (Minneapolis: Fortress, 1990), 122; Margaret Lamberts Bendroth, *Fundamentalism and Gender, 1875 to the Present* (New Haven: Yale University Press, 1993); Sally K. Gallagher, *Evangelical Identity and Gendered Family Life* (New Brunswick: Rutgers University Press, 2003), xi.

12. Virginia Brereton, *Stories of Women's Conversions, 1800 to the Present* (Bloomington: Indiana University Press, 1991); Mark Chaves, *Ordaining Women: Culture and Conflict in Religious Organizations* (Cambridge: Harvard University Press, 1997).

13. Christian Smith, *A Christian America? What Evangelicals Really Want* (Berkeley:University of California Press, 2000). See also James Davison Hunter, *American Evangelicalism: Conservative Religion and the Quandary of Modernity* (New Brunswick: Rutgers University Press, 1983); Mark Shibley, *Resurgent Evangelicalism in the United States: Mapping Cultural Change since 1970* (Columbia: University of South Carolina Press, 1996). In the InterVarsity series, see Mark Noll, *The Rise of Evangelicalism: The Age of Edwards, Whitefield, and the Wesleys* (Downers Grove, IL: InterVarsity, 2003); and David Bebbington, *The Dominance of Evangelicalism: The Age of Spurgeon and Moody* (Downers Grove, IL: InterVarsity, 2005). There are three more books planned in the InterVarsity series. Not a part of this series, Douglas A. Sweeney's helpful survey is *The American Evangelical Story: A History of the Movement* (Grand Rapids, MI: Baker Academic, 2005).

14. Michael Emerson and Christian Smith, *Divided by Faith: Evangelical Religion and the Problem of Race in America* (New York: Oxford University Press, 2000); Alan Wolfe, *The Transformation of American Religion: How We Actually Live Our Faith* (New York: Free Press, 2003), 36.

15. Grant Wacker, *Augustus H. Strong and the Dilemma of Historical Consciousness* (Macon: Mercer University Press, 1985), 12.

16. C. Allyn Russell, *Voices of Fundamentalism: Seven Biographical Studies* (Philadelphia: Westminster, 1976).

17. William Vance Trollinger Jr., *God's Empire: William Bell Riley and Midwestern Fundamentalism* (Madison: University of Wisconsin Press, 1990), 104–5; Barry Hankins, *God's Rascal: J. Frank Norris and the Beginnings of Southern Fundamentalism* (Lexington: University Press of Kentucky, 1996); Barry Hankins, *Uneasy in Babylon: Southern Baptist Conservatives and American Culture* (Tuscaloosa: University of Alabama Press, 2002); Barry Hankins, *Francis Schaeffer and the Shaping of Evangelical America* (Grand Rapids, MI: Eerdmans, 2008); D. G. Hart, *Defending the Faith: J. Gresham Machen and the Crisis of Conservative Protestantism in Modern America* (Baltimore: Johns Hopkins University Press, 1994); Mark Taylor Dalhouse, *An Island in a Lake of Fire: Bob Jones University, Fundamentalism, and the Separatist Movement* (Athens: University of Georgia Press, 1996).

18. Lyle Dorsett, *Billy Sunday and the Redemption of Urban America* (Grand Rapids, MI: Eerdmans, 1991); Edith Blumhofer, *Aimee Semple McPherson: Everybody's Sister* (Grand Rapids, MI: Eerdmans, 1993); Dana Robert, *Occupy until I Come: A. T. Pierson and the Evangelization of the World* (Grand Rapids, MI: Eerdmans, 2003); William G. McLoughlin, *Billy Sunday Was His Real Name* (Chicago: University of Chicago Press, 1955); Robert Bahr, *Least of All Saints: The Story of Aimee Semple*

McPherson (Englewood Cliffs, NJ: Prentice Hall, 1979); Thomas Lately, *Storming Heaven: The Lives and Turmoils of Minnie Kennedy and Aimee Semple McPherson* (New York: Morrow, 1970); Matthew Sutton, *Aimee Semple McPherson and the Resurrection of Christian America* (Cambridge: Harvard University Press, 2007); Susie Stanley, *Feminist Pillar of Fire: The Life of Alma White* (Cleveland: Pilgrim, 1993).

19. William Glass, *Strangers in Zion: Fundamentalists in the South, 1900–1950* (Macon: Mercer University Press, 2001); David Edwin Harrell, ed., *Varieties of Southern Evangelicalism* (Macon: Mercer University Press, 1981).

20. Darren Dochuk, "From Bible Belt to Sunbelt: Plain Folk Religion, Grassroots Politics, and the Southernization of Southern California, 1939–1969" (Ph.D. diss., University of Notre Dame, 2005). Dochuk's dissertation won the Society of American Historians' Alan Nevins Prize, which carries a guarantee of publication. The publisher is yet to be determined at the time of the writing of this essay. Another recent dissertation written under Marsden's tutelage and likely to be published soon is John G. Turner's "Selling Jesus to Modern America: Campus Crusade for Christ, Evangelical Culture, and Conservative Politics" (Ph.D. diss., University of Notre Dame, 2006). At the time this essay was written, Turner's study was under consideration by a university press.

21. Mary Beth Swetnam Mathews, *Rethinking Zion: How the Print Media Placed Fundamentalism in the South* (Knoxville: University of Tennessee Press, 2006).

22. Margaret Lamberts Bendroth, *Fundamentalists in the City: Conflict and Division in Boston's Churches, 1885–1950* (New York: Oxford University Press, 2005); R. Stephen Warner, *New Wine in Old Wineskins: Evangelicals and Liberals in a Small-Town Church* (Berkeley: University of California Press, 1988).

23. David Edwin Harrell Jr., *Oral Roberts: An American Life* (Bloomington: Indiana University Press, 1985); David Edwin Harrell Jr., *Pat Robertson: A Personal, Religious, and Political Portrait* (San Francisco: Harper and Row, 1987); L. Edward Hicks, *"Sometimes in the Wrong but Never in Doubt": George S. Benson and the Education of the New Religious Right* (Knoxville: University of Tennessee Press, 1994); Susan Friend Harding, *The Book of Jerry Falwell: Fundamentalist Language and Politics* (Princeton: Princeton University Press, 2000).

24. Virginia Brereton, *Training God's Army: The American Bible School, 1880–1940* (Bloomington: Indiana University Press, 1990); Sandeen, *The Roots of Fundamentalism;* Joel Carpenter, *Revive Us Again: The Reawakening of Fundamentalism* (New York: Oxford University Press, 1997).

25. Carpenter, *Revive Us Again,* 245.

26. Tona J. Hangen, *Redeeming the Dial: Radio, Religion, and Popular Culture in America* (Chapel Hill: University of North Carolina Press, 2002); Douglas Carl Abrams, *Selling the Old-Time Religion: American Fundamentalists and Mass Culture, 1920–1940* (Athens: University of Georgia Press, 2001).

27. William Martin, *With God on Our Side: The Rise of the Christian Right in America* (New York: Broadway, 1996); *A Prophet with Honor: The Billy Graham Story* (New York: W. Morrow, 1991).

28. Randall Balmer, *Thy Kingdom Come: How the Religious Right Distorts the Faith and Threatens America, an Evangelical's Lament* (New York: Basic, 2006); Randall Balmer, *Mine Eyes Have Seen the Glory: A Journey into the Evangelical Subculture in America*, 4th ed. (New York: Oxford University Press, 2006).

29. Balmer, *Mine Eyes Have Seen the Glory*, 29.

30. Clyde Wilcox and Carin Larson, *Onward Christian Soldiers? The Religious Right in American Politics*, 3rd ed. (Boulder: Westview, 2006).

31. Michael Lienesch, *Redeeming America: Piety and Politics in the New Christian Right* (Chapel Hill: University of North Carolina Press, 1993), 22. See Steve Bruce, *The Rise and Fall of the New Christian Right* (Oxford: Clarendon, 1988). Bruce did predict correctly that the Christian Right would switch from a strategy of claiming to be the Moral Majority to a posture of being a minority experiencing discrimination.

32. Sara Diamond, *Not by Politics Alone: The Enduring Influence of the Christian Right* (New York: Guilford, 1998); Justin Watson, *The Christian Coalition: Dreams of Restoration, Demands for Recognition* (New York: St. Martin's, 1997).

33. Murray Dempster and Augustus Cerillo Jr., eds., *Salt and Light: Evangelical Political Thought in Modern America* (Grand Rapids, MI: Baker Academic, 1989); James Skillen, *The Scattered Voice: Christians at Odds in the Public Square* (Edmonton, Alberta: Canadian Institute for Law, Theology, and Public Policy, 1996); David Stricklin, *A Genealogy of Dissent: Southern Baptist Protest in the Twentieth Century* (Lexington: University Press of Kentucky, 1999). Peter Heltzel is currently at work on a book titled "Lion on the Loose: Jesus, Evangelicals, and American Politics, 1996–2006," which covers the entire spectrum of evangelical political involvement.

34. Edward Larson, *Summer for the Gods: The Scopes Trial and America's Continuing Debate over Science and Religion* (New York: Basic, 1997); Ray Ginger, *Six Days or Forever: Tennessee v. John Thomas Scopes* (Boston: Beacon, 1958).

35. David N. Livingstone, *Darwin's Forgotten Defenders: The Encounter between Evangelical Theology and Evolutionary Thought* (Grand Rapids, MI: Eerdmans, 1987). For a critique of the warfare model and the view that it was promoted by secular scholars, see David C. Lindberg and Ronald Numbers, "Beyond War and Peace: A Reappraisal of the Encounter between Christianity and Science," *Church History* 55, no. 3 (1986). Lindberg and Numbers said there is "mounting evidence that [Andrew Dixon] White read the past through battle-scarred glasses, and that he and his imitators have distorted history to serve ideological ends of their own" (340). See also David Lindberg and Ronald Numbers, eds., *God and Nature: Historical Essays on the Encounter between Christianity and Science* (Berkeley: University of California Press, 1986).

36. Charles A. Israel, *Before Scopes: Evangelicals, Education, and Evolution in Tennessee, 1870–1925* (Athens: University of Georgia Press, 2004); Paul K. Conkin, *When All the Gods Trembled: Darwinism, Scopes, and American Intellectuals* (Lanham, MD: Rowman and Littlefield, 1998).

37. Ronald L. Numbers, *The Creationists: The Evolution of Scientific Creationism* (Berkeley: University of California Press, 1993), xvi–xvii. Numbers's new edition of this work, *The Creationists: From Scientific Creationism to Intelligent Design* (Cambridge: Harvard University Press, 2006), is expanded to cover the recent development of intelligent design.

38. David N. Livingstone, D. G. Hart, and Mark A. Noll, eds., *Evangelicals and Science in Historical Perspective* (New York: Oxford University Press, 1999).

39. See Timothy P. Weber's works *Living in the Shadow of the Second Coming: American Premillennialism, 1875–1925* (New York: Oxford University Press, 1979); *Living in the Shadow of the Second Coming: American Premillennialism, 1875–1982* (Grand Rapids, MI: Zondervan, Academie, 1983); and *On the Road to Armageddon: How Evangelicals Became Israel's Best Friend* (Grand Rapids, MI: Baker Academic, 2004), 15; Yaakov Ariel, *On Behalf of Israel: American Fundamentalist Attitudes toward Jews, Judaism, and Zionism* (Brooklyn: Carlson, 1991).

40. Paul Boyer, *When Time Shall Be No More: Prophecy Belief in Modern American Culture* (Cambridge: Harvard University Press, Belknap, 1992).

41. Weber, *On the Road to Armageddon,* 15; Glenn W. Shuck, *Marks of the Beast: The Left Behind Novels and the Struggle for Evangelical Identity* (New York: New York University Press, 2005); Christian Smith, *American Evangelicalism: Embattled and Thriving* (Chicago: University of Chicago Press, 1998).

42. Amy Johnson Frykholm, *Rapture Culture: Left Behind in Evangelical America* (New York: Oxford University Press, 2004), 4; David T. Morgan, *The New Brothers Grimm and Their Left Behind Fairy Tales* (Macon: Mercer University Press, 2006); Bruce David Forbes and Jeanne Halgren Kilde, eds., *Rapture, Revelation, and the End Times: Exploring the Left Behind Series* (New York: Palgrave, 2004).

43. George Marsden, *Fundamentalism and American Culture,* rev. ed. (New York: Oxford University Press, 2006), 235.

44. Mark Noll, *The Scandal of the Evangelical Mind* (Grand Rapids, MI: Eerdmans, 1994); Douglas Frank, *Less Than Conquerors: How Evangelicals Entered the Twentieth Century* (Grand Rapids, MI: Eerdmans, 1986); Wolfe, *Transformation of American Religion.*

45. Noll, *The Scandal of the Evangelical Mind,* ix.

Contributors

Margaret Bendroth, executive director of the American Congregational Association, is the author of *Fundamentalism and Gender, 1875 to the Present* and *Fundamentalists in the City: Conflict and Division in Boston's Churches, 1885–1950*.

Barry Hankins, professor of history, Baylor University, is the author of *God's Rascal: J. Frank Norris and the Beginnings of Southern Fundamentalism, Uneasy in Babylon: Southern Baptist Conservatives and American Culture*, and *Francis Schaeffer and the Shaping of Evangelical America*.

Keith Harper, professor of church history, Southeastern Baptist Theological Seminary, is the author of *The Quality of Mercy: Southern Baptists and Social Christianity, 1890–1920* and the editor of *Send the Light: Lottie Moon's Letters and Other Writings*.

Paul Harvey, professor of history at the University of Colorado, Colorado Springs, is the author of *Redeeming the South: Religious Cultures and Racial Identities among Southern Baptists, 1865–1925* and *Freedom's Coming: Religious Culture and the Shaping of the South from the Civil War through the Civil Rights Era*.

Amy Koehlinger, assistant professor of religion at Florida State University, is the author of *The New Nuns: Racial Justice and Religious Reform in the 1960s*, and she is currently working on "Rosaries and Rope Burns: Boxing and Manhood in American Catholicism, 1890–1970."

Sean Michael Lucas is chief academic officer and associate professor of church history at Covenant Theological Seminary. He is the author of *Robert Lewis Dabney: A Southern Presbyterian Life* and *On Being Presbyterian: Our Beliefs, Practices, and Stories*. He is currently working on a history of fundamentalism within the southern Presbyterian Church in the twentieth century.

Randall J. Stephens, assistant professor of history, Eastern Nazarene College, is the author of *The Fire Spreads: Holiness and Pentecostalism in the American South*. Randall also serves as editor of the *Journal of Southern Religion* and associate editor of *Historically Speaking*. He is currently coauthoring with Karl Giberson "The Anointed: American Evangelical Experts."

Jennifer L. Woodruff Tait, former Methodist librarian at Drew University and current adjunct professor of history, Asbury Theological Seminary, is working on a book that explores Methodist attitudes toward temperance. She is a frequent contributor to *Christian History and Biography*.

David J. Whittaker, senior librarian, curator of nineteenth-century western and Mormon manuscripts, L. Tom Perry Special Collections, Harold B. Lee Library; and associate professor of history, Brigham Young University, is the editor of *Mormon Americana: A Guide to Sources and Collections in the United States,* and coauthor with James B. Allen and Ronald W. Walker of *Mormon History*.